SPECIAL NOTE

Anyone receiving permission to produce DOG LADY, THE CUBAN SWIMMER, ROOSTERS and /or EVENING STAR is required to give credit to the Author as sole and exclusive Author of the Play(s) on the title page of all programs distributed in connection with performances of the Play(s) and in all instances in which the title(s) of the Play(s) appear(s) for purposes of advertising, publicizing or otherwise exploiting the Play(s) and/or a production thereof. The name of the Author must appear on a separate line, in which no other name appears, immediately beneath the title(s) and in a size of type equal to 50% of the size of the largest, most prominent letter used for the title(s) of the Play(s). No person, firm or entity may receive credit larger or more prominent than that accorded to the Author.

The following acknowledgment must appear on the title page in all programs distributed in connection with performances of the Play(s) for DOG LADY and/or THE CUBAN SWIMMER and ROOSTERS:

Originally produced in New York City by
INTAR Hispanic American Arts Center.

....

Printed by CreateSpace, Charleston, SC, United States of America

First Edition

iv

The Collected Plays of Milcha Sanchez-Scott

All plays written by
Milcha Sanchez-Scott

Edited by Jimmy Aleck and Glenn Williams

Contents

Introduction

The Collected Plays of Milcha Sanchez-Scott includes six produced theatrical works that center upon the Latino experience in America in general, and much more specifically, the Latina experience in America. All of the plays are set in either the American Southwest or Los Angeles, California. Collectively the plays chronicle the sometimes messy intersection of the distinctly Latino flavor of Catholicism inherent in the Latino culture, feminism, machismo, the more common deep yearning and striving for a better life in a better world, and total acceptance of the sometimes nuttiness of human nature. This is all presented with an adroit handling of humor, grace and magic – that is, the magic of magical realism. Ms. Sanchez-Scott has been described by critics as a deft observer of culture and human nature which she masterfully distills and crafts into these concise, colorful works of theater. Through the poetry in her plays that provides metaphors and images that leap cultural gaps, she is able to offer an interpretation of the Latino psychology to non-Latino audiences much in the same way that Robert Motherwell was able to elucidate the concept of abstract expressionism in art to mainstream America.

Milcha Sanchez-Scott is the daughter of a Colombian-Mexican agronomist father and a Dutch Indonesian-Chinese mother. She was born on the island of Bali in 1954. Educated in England into her early teens she graduated from the University of San Diego after her family emigrated to California. Although Ms. Sanchez-

Scott lives in Los Angeles, California, in her head all of her plays are set in New Mexico.

She holds a First Level Award for American playwrights from the Rockefeller Foundation for 1987. In 1983 Ms. Sanchez-Scott won the Vesta Award, given each year to a West Coast woman artist, and the Le Compte du Nuoy Foundation Award, which goes to "a young writer with a unique voice." In 1983-84 she was a member of INTAR Theater's Hispanic Playwrights-in-Residence Laboratory, directed by María Irene Fornes. During her New York residency she began work on a full-length play, *Roosters*, and three one-acts under the collective title *City of Angels.*

Milcha Sanchez-Scott's first play, **Latina**, was premiered by L.A. Theatre Works in 1980. The play explores the contrasts between the economic and legal plight of Latinas employed as maids, most of whom are illegal immigrants, and the young Latina protagonist's cognitive dissonance caused by the clash between her Latino culture and heritage, and her ambitions for a successful career in Hollywood. Set in Los Angeles in 1980, the play simply and humorously reveals the real life experiences of Ms. Sanchez-Scott working as a receptionist at a domestic agency in Beverly Hills. It reveals the emotional conflict caused by the clash of cultures, in this case even of various factions of Latino cultures, by employing the dichotomies of pathos and comedy, shame and pride, farce and satire, to make its point. It shows the playwright's skillful use of humor, drama, grace and magical realism in establishing her creative voice. While the play typifies the struggles of all Chicanos in search of their place in this society, the characters are depicted so meticulously that all audiences can relate to the themes of the play.

Latina was produced in 1980 by the New Works Division of Artists in Prison and the Pilot Theater in Los Angeles. It was notable for it's all female production/design staff including choreography by Lynn Dally, sets and costumes designed by Barbar Ling, costumes designed by Louise Haterby and sound engineered by Janet Dodson. Most recently it was produced at California State University-Los Angeles where it was directed by Stephen Rothman. It won seven Drama-Logue awards. *Latina* was included in *Necessary Theatre: Six Plays about the Chicano Experience*, by Jorge Huerta and published by Arte Publico Press in 1989.

The Cuban Swimmer and *Dog Lady* were written between 1980 and 1982 developed as a special project of the L.A. Theater Works in 1982. These one act plays were successfully produced together in both New York and London as a duo of playlets. The highly imaginative plays offer a humorous insight into the colorful and devout Latino family life involving aspects of the spirit of Santería – a blend of the religious beliefs of Roman Catholicism and *Yoruba* from coastal West Africa, peculiar to Cuban culture. The plays are filled with a sense of ritual and lyricism.

The Cuban Swimmer is set in the Pacific Ocean between San Pedro and Catalina Island. It centers on an instance in which a young Latina uses her athletic skills as an endurance swimmer in an attempt to escape from the underclass into the mainstream of middle-class life. The protagonist toward Catalina Island while her bickering family follows her in a beat-up boat. As her mother, father, brother and aunt argue amongst themselves and exhort the swimmer, she begins to weary and stray off her course until a spiritually tinged magical intervention reinvigorates and supercharges her. The Cuban Swimmer was included in *A Pocketful of Plays: Vintage Drama, Volume Two*, by David Madden and published by Wadsworth Cengage Advantage Books in 2006.

Dog Lady is set in a neighborhood situated in an East Los Angeles barrio, where a young Latina full of great aspirations for her future is training for a marathon sponsored by a local Catholic church. Dogged by a suitor, she is unable to achieve her best until the local *curandera*, or faith healer - a loopy old woman who lives with a pack of unruly dogs - endows her with magical powers which enable her to get a leg up on her fellow competitors in the marathon.

The Cuban Swimmer and Dog Lady were presented at INTAR, (Max Ferra, Artistic Director), in New York City from April 27 to May 27, 1984. Max Ferra directed the play. Sets were designed by Ming Cho Lee, costumes were designed by Connie Singer, lighting was designed by Anne E. Militello and sound was engineered by Paul Garrity. Mime/movement was choreographed by Pilar Garcia.

The cast for *The Cuban Swimmer included:* Jeannette Mirabal as MARGARITA, Carlos Cestero as EDUARDO, Manual Rivera as SIMÓN, Lillian Hurst as

AÍDA, Graciela LeCube as ABUELA, Carlos Carrasco as the voice of MEL MUNSON, Elizabeth Peña as the voice of MARY BETH WHITE, and Daniel Barrajanos and Arto Tuncboyaci as PERCUSSIONISTS.

The cast for *Dog Lady* included: Manual Rivera as RAPHAEL, Carlos Carrasco as ORLANDO, Jeannette Mirabal as ROSALINDA Luna, Graciela LeCube as MARÍA Pilar Luna, Lillian Hurst as LUISA Ruiz, Elizabeth Peña as *Jesse* Luna, Marcella White as MRS. AMADOR and, Daniel Barrajanos and Arto Tuncboyaci as PERCUSSIONISTS.

The Cuban Swimmer and *Dog Lady* were subsequently presented at the Gate Theatre in London, England from April 20-May 16, 1987. Christa van Raalte directed. The design was by Jane Green. The cast included Sheila Burrell, Joseph Long, Diana Brookes, Helen Keen, Katharina Tana and Christopher Simon.

The playlets were selected for inclusion in the "Plays in Process" series sponsored by the Theatre Communications Group (TCG). *Dog Lady* was published in *Best Short Plays of 1986.*

Roosters is set in an arid, agricultural valley in the American Southwest. This symbolic drama portrays the emotional turmoil within an underclass Latino family and unfolds while exploring overlapping themes of family, dysfunction, mistrust, disrespect, poverty, Hispanic culture, spirituality, stereotypes, an oedipal complex and violence. The characters are mythical and archetypal and are rendered, in turn, using humor, poignance, flights of poetic fantasy, soaring imagery and powerful drama. The characters range from the proud and deceitful father, just released from prison after serving out his sentence for a manslaughter charge, and the embodiment of *machismo*; the passive, long-suffering madonna-like mother; the promiscuous *macha* Aunt; a proud and rebellious son; a spiritually obsessed and intellectually precocious but socially slow daughter; a steady-handed farmworker, friend and cock fight enthusiast; and of course, fighting cocks. In this strange and amusing play Latino *machismo* is explored from a feminine point of view, yet the playwright invites the audience to draw its own conclusion.

Successfully presented Off-Broadway as a joint production by INTAR Theater and the New York Shakespeare Festival, *Roosters* marked the arrival of a singular and distinctively original new writer. *Roosters* was presented at INTAR in March 1987, (Max Ferra - artistic director, Dennis Ferguson-Acosta, - managing director and the New York Shakespeare Festival, - Joseph Papp, producer). It was directed by Jackson Phippin with sets by Loy Arcenas, lighting by John Gisondi, costumes by C. L. Hundley, sound by Janet Kalas, fight direction - Nels Hennum; dialect consultant - Tim Monich; stage manager - Michele Steckler. The cast included Joaquim De Almeida as GALLO (Spanish for rooster), Jonathan Del Arco as HECTOR, Sara Erde as ANGELA, Suzanne Costallos as JUANA, Ilka Tanya Payan as CHATA, Albert Farrar as ADAN.

The play was produced at the LA Theatre Center in the summer of 1988. José Luis Valenzuela directed the play and costumes were designed by Tina Navarro. Sets were designed by Timian Alsaker and lighting design was credited to both Timian Alsaker and Douglas D. Smith. Sound was by engineered by Mark Friedman and Jon

Gottlieb. It was choreographed by Wade Collings and the stage was managed by John Gallo. The cast included Pepe Serna as GALLO, Fausto Bara as HECTOR, Victoria Gallegos as ANGELA, Evelina Fernandez as JUANA, Lupe Ontiveros as CHATA, E. J. Castillo as ADAN, also with Frederic Anthony and Vernon David.

It was subsequently produced in Chicago directed by Mary McAuliffe, choreographed by Michelle Banks who along with Nilda Reillo played the dancing roosters, Additional cast members included Juan Ramirez as GALLO, Mark Fraire as HECTOR, Heather Graff as ANGELA, Laura Ceron as JUANA, Karol Kent as CHATA.

The New Mexico Repertory Theater produced *Roosters* in Santa Fe directed by Roxanne Rodgers.

Roosters was the second play produced by the Reno Little Theater's new series, La Gente: Latino Theater at RLT. The program was funded in part by Nevada Humanities, Nevada's nonprofit state affiliate of the National Endowment for the Humanities.

Additionally the play was produced in San Francisco, Texas and London.

Roosters was adapted into a screenplay for an American dramatic film by Ms. Sanchez-Scott. The film premiered at the Toronto International Film Festival in 1993 before being released in the United States in 1995. Robert M. Young directed the film. The cast included Edward James Olmos as Gallo Morales, Sarah Lassez as Angela Estelle Morales, Sonia Braga as Juana Morales, Maria Conchita Alonso as Chata, Danny Nucci as Hector Morales, and Valente Rodriguez as Adan.

Evening Star was commissioned and produced by New York's Theatre for a New Audience. Set amongst the less fortunate circumstances of a barrio this eloquently expressive play about broken families is sometimes lyrical and poetic, sometimes harsh and unstintingly realistic. It captures the vitality and turbulence of life—and love—in the barrio and the dynamic intermingling of the old and the new that characterizes it. The playwright's poetic sensitivity, theatrical flair and a lyrical command of language is expressed in the well developed, sympathetic treatment of her characters as much as in her artistic voice. The Village Voice called it, "… a wistful study of adolescent yearning …"

Evening Star was first presented by Theatre For A New Audience (Jeffrey Horowitz, artistic/producing director) at the Cubiculo Theater in New York on May 3, 1988. Paul Zimet directed the play; the sets and costumes were designed by G. W. Mercier; the lighting was designed by Mary Louise Geiger; the music was provided by Ellen Maddow; the production stage manager was Max Storch; managing director was Deirdre M. Moynehan; and the associate artistic director was Bill Reichblum.

The Old Matador is set in the American Southwest and chronicles the experiences of a hardworking, perhaps overworking, Hispanic family embroiled in internal conflict. It explores themes that range from new love to old love, high ideals and aspirations to failed dreams, love to scorn to love again, recriminations to redemption and, interpersonal obduracy to a calm and resigned denouement. The intervention of an angel through the devices of magical realism and subsequent transformation brings resolution to the conflict in a manner reminiscent of Ernest Hemingway's short story, "The Short Happy Life of Francis Macomber". The clear development of the characters reveals the deep and complex relationships between the family members – father, mother and a teenage daughter and son – with an overlay of Latino spirituality, Catholicism and hard scrabble work ethic.

The Old Matador was produced at the University of Texas, Pan American where it was directed by Milcha Sanchez-Scott. Tom Grabowski designed the sets and lighting, Micky Pelletier designed the costumes and Sonia Chapa was the choreographer. The cast included Luis Moreno as *Cookie*, Alberto Garza as ENRIQUE, Brenda Vallejo as MARGARITA, Edgar Ituarte as voice of NEWS ANNOUNCER, Voice of FRENCH SPORTS ANNOUNCER and EL BONITO, Henry Price as 1ST BOY, Orlando Mascorro as PACO and 2ND BOY, Didi Duron as JESSE, Rick Rosales as MANUEL, Araceli Lopez as EVELINA, Michael Moore as FATHER STEVEN, Fabian Cuellar as ANGEL, Miguel Treviño as Guitarist and Maria Luisa Rafols and Elizabeth Gonzales were Dancers.

Latina

1980

CHARACTERS in order of appearance:
NEW GIRL (Elsa María Cristina López de Moreno)
SARITA (Sara Gómez)
1ST MALE VOICE
2ND MALE VOICE
3RD MALE VOICE
EUGENIA (Doña Eugenia Carbajal)
DON FÉLIX Sánchez
LA CHATA (Chata)
LA CUBANA (Margarita)
CLARA
EVITA
SISTER AGNES
LOLA
MRS. HOMES
ALMA Gutiérrez (Almita)
MRS. LEVINE
SISTER
YOUNG SARITA
MS. HARRIS

Act 1

Scene 1

The stage is dark. Then we hear Peruvian flute music coming from distance. We see New Girl saying goodbye to a small group of PERUVIAN MOUNTAIN VILLAGE PEOPLE. The time is dusk. New Girl is carrying a satchel. She has a Peruvian shawl around her shoulders. Her hair is in braids. She has on a peasant skirt and a work shirt and sandals on her feet. The New Girl's mother steps out and puts a St. Christopher medal around New Girl 's neck. She embraces New Girl. New Girl tears herself away to leave. New Girl 's mother falls to her knees weeping. People around her help her up to wave at New Girl.

It becomes night as New Girl starts her journey through the tunnel of light. The music changes to heart beating escape tempo. At one point we see New Girl paying off a policeman. Another moment a woman steals her shawl. Then a man accosts her at knife point and tries to rape her, but she escapes. Next, she is giving money to a slick city coyote, dressed in American type work clothes, who takes her to the end of tunnel where it is night. There is only the moon and the sound and search light of an overhead helicopter. We see a large barbed wire fence. The coyote roughly holds New Girl by the wrist as the search-light almost hits them. They both hit the ground and crawl on hands and knees to the barbed wire fence. She crawls through. He helps her. She stands up the other side and looks back. There is triumph in the music with a moment of Peruvian flute. The coyote waves New Girl on.

The stage is dark. The music changes tempo to American city music after a moment. Car noises start coming in and lights come up on the front of FÉLIX SÁNCHEZ DOMESTIC AGENCY set.

Scene 2

Front of the Félix Sánchez Domestic Agency. There is a bus bench and a Wilshire Blvd. street sign. On the actual store front the words FÉLIX SÁNCHEZ DOMESTIC AGENCY are printed in big block letters over the door and window. In the window there are two dummies, one in a white uniform holding a pink baby dummy, the white dummy looks very maternal like a Madonna, the second dummy is in a short black uniform with a white frilly apron, holding a feather duster. She looks like a naughty French maid.

It is 7:50 on a Monday morning in October, the sounds of Wilshire Blvd. traffic in the background. A few moments after the curtain rises, Sarita, a young woman of twenty-three, walks briskly up to the agency door and tries it. It is locked. She jiggles the knob and knocks repeatedly ... no one answers.

SARITA: Christ! ... *(Looks at watch.)* Ah no, he's late! *(To audience.)* I don't like it when he's late. I just don't like it. I have to hang around here. Which is embarrassing. I have to go sit on the bus bench, which is also embarrassing ... everybody will think I am waiting for the bus, which means: (a) I can't drive, (b) I don't have a car, or (c) both of the above--in Los Angeles this is embarrassing. *(Turns around, looks at dummies, then back to audience.)* I could go back there and pretend to be a dummy. Yes ... but what if I got caught? That would really be embarrassing ... *(Pause.)* I am tired of always feeling embarrassed. Embarrassed! Embarrassed! *(She is embarrassed.)* I'm embarrassed to be standing here on the street. I'm embarrassed to be standing here on the street in front of that place. I'm embarrassed to be working in that place, and I'm really embarrassed to be here waiting for sleazy Sánchez to open up. And, I spent the better part of an hour deciding what to wear, because I don't want to be mistaken for a maid. I'm not a maid. You thought I was a maid ... I am not a maid or a housekeeper. Housekeeper is what polite people call their maids. *(Pause.)* I don't want to look Latina. *(Loud sound of car stopping, blare of radio with Disco sound and motor idling.)* That's embarrassing. *(Male whistle.)*

MALE VOICES: [1st.] *(off stage)* Oh, oh, oh, *(loud kissing sounds)* baby. [2nd.] Oh, señorita, I am in love. [3rd.] Hot *tamale!* Hey, little beaner. [2nd.] What a cute little maid! [3rd.] Hey, *señorita!* Hey little maid--you sure are pretty. You want to come to my *casa?*

(Sarita at first looks embarrassed, then bored. She has been through this before and knows how to stop it. She puts a stupid expression on her face, picks her nose and says ...)

SARITA: *(Like Goofy.)* Yuk, yuk.

(Loud sounds of car peeling off. From stage right, Eugenia walks on carrying a simulated leather hand-bag and paper

shopping bag with handles. She is old, but wiry and energetic. She stands watching Sarita.)

SARITA: *(Unaware of Eugenia.)* See, I hate that and I hate that dirty, stinking place! And I hate sleazy Sánchez, and I hate this stupid bus bench ... *(kicks bus bench)* and the illegal women who come here everyday looking for illegal jobs.... Well, I don't hate the women ... it's just that ... I am not one of them ... I don't want to be identified with them. It's all very mixed up and testy with me right now. Okay! I am not a maid, I am a counselor. Okay!... Oh God, listen to me ... I am a counselor, like it's some big deal.

EUGENIA: *Buenos días, niña Sarita. ¿Cómo amaneció? (Sarita sees Eugenia, realizes she has been watching her.)*

SARITA: *Buenos días, ... estoy bien.*

EUGENIA: *Ay, gracias a Dios. (She walks up to the bus bench.) ¿Qué te pasa mi hija?*

SARITA: *Nada. (Eugenia takes Sarita's face into her hands and feels for a fever.)*

EUGENIA: *¿Desayunastes?*

SARITA: Yes, I ate breakfast.

EUGENIA: *Te ves muy pálida y emocionada ... ¿Quieres qué te haga un Yu-Yu ?*

SARITA: No. No *Yu-Yu . No me pasa nada. Estoy bien, gracias, gracias.*

EUGENIA: *Andale pues. (To herself) Esta niña está grave. (Eugenia walks away to the alley singing "Luna qué se quiebre" ... In the alley she gets her broom and other cleaning equipment, a little tin can, which she takes to the faucet and fills with water.)*

SARITA: *(To audience.)* She says I look pale and emotional … That's Eugenia ... the old *Yu-Yu* vendor. She makes potions for everything, from everything ... herbs, frogs ... They call them *Yu-Yus*. She tells me she is 48 … more like 68. She says that so I'll send her on a job.

Actually, I don't think she cares about getting a job. Sleazy Sánchez gives her a few dollars to clean the office. She does a lousy job. But that's not why she comes. She loves this place ... the women, the gossip.

(With the clatter of trash can lids, Eugenia comes out of the alley with broom and tin can ... She starts sweeping and sprinkling water stage left. Light change. Lights should be like morning light. Sun coming up very bright. There is a ritualistic quality about this. Street sounds fade and there is soft music. We see Eugenia carry out her task as if she were a village woman in Juarez, 1915.)

SARITA: *(Smelling.)* Did I hear a rooster ... and the smell of *tortillas,* early morning charcoal. Oh, it's Eugenia. The way she sprinkles the water on the sidewalk ... like it was a dirt road in front of her little shack ... my grandmother used to do that in Mexico, my great-great-grandmother probably did it too. *(Lights bring us back to the present.)*
EUGENIA: *(Still sweeping.)* Sarita, *no se te olvide qué necesitamos jabón. ¡Ese jabón Lava, eh!*
SARITA: *(To audience.)* She wants me to get her Lava soap. She loves Lava soap. She uses Lava for everything ... the windows, the side-walk, everything. *(She pulls an imaginary microphone chord and puts on a very commercial spokeswoman's voice.)* Hi, this is Lorraine Lovely for Lava industrial soap. For years, Lava industrial soap was used by mechanics and machinists to remove grit and grime. Today, women all over America are discovering that Lava is a face soap--it not only removes pimples, it removes skin. Dead skin. Yes, that old skin that has been hanging around your face for years. Lava helps you lie about your age ... Today, we are here in front of the Félix Sánchez Domestic Agency talking to Mrs. Eugenia Carbajal, the oldest domestic worker in America.

6

Mrs. Carbajal, a satisfied Lava customer, is 115; she is still working. She tells the world she is 48 and Lava helps her lie. Tell our viewers Mrs. Carbajal ... do you use Lava on other parts of your body, eh? On your tushi? Eh, *en las nalguitas, eh? (Pinches butt. Eugenia registers mock shock and mock anger and chases Sarita towards bus bench with broom.)*

EUGENIA: *¡Muchacha grosera, sangrona!*

SARITA: *(On the run.)* Lava makes you cranky, too. *(Eugenia, unable to contain her laughter, starts laughing and cannot stop. Sarita is laughing also.)*

EUGENIA: *(Barely able to get the words out.) Lava por las nalgas ... (Eugenia starts coughing. Sarita pats her back. She starts coughing and laughing. She takes hanky from pocket and wipes her eyes.) Ay* Sarita, *¿Cómo me haces reír. Mi, hija, ¿cuando vas a salir en la television otra vez?*

SARITA: *(This is painful.) No sé. (Sarita walks over to bus bench and slumps down. Eugenia knows it is a painful subject, shakes her head and goes back to sweeping.) (To audience.)* She says I make her laugh. She wants to know when I am going to be on television again. I wish I knew. See, what I actually want to be ... I mean, what I really am is an actress. Now, why should that be embarrassing? Makes me feel like I am overreaching. I am only working here until I get ... oh, never mind. *(Pause.)* Have you ever noticed that when you meet an actor, instead of saying, "Hello, how are you?", they give you their credits ... I'll give you my credits. I was a *barrio* girl who got raped by a gang in *Police Story*, a young *barrio* mother who got shot by a gang in *Starsky and Hutch*, a *barrio* wife who got beat up by her husband who was in a gang in the *Rookies*. I was even a *barrio* lesbian who got knifed by an all girl gang called the *Mal-flores* ... that means Bad Flowers. It's been a regular *barrio* blitz on television lately. If this fad continues, I can look forward to being a *barrio* grandmother done-in by a gang of old Hispanics called *Los Viejitos Diablitos*, the old devils. *(Pause. Eugenia sweeps. Sarita looking at watch.)* Well, he's still late. I wonder what he'll be wearing--his Mickey Mouse pajamas or the ones with the sailboats. He's been wearing Mickey Mouse for the past seven days. Oh God, for our sake, I hope it's the sailboats.

(As Eugenia continues sweeping, flute music is heard as New Girl appears. She is tired and frightened. Very cautiously, she approaches Eugenia.)

NEW GIRL: Psssst, *seño. (Eugenia doesn't hear too well.) Psssst seño. (Eugenia looks up.) Señora, perdóneme, pero, ¿aquí es dónde tienen trabajos?*
EUGENIA: *¿De dónde vienes mi hija?*
NEW GIRL: *¿Aquí tienen trabajos en casas? ¿Aquí?*
EUGENIA: *Vienes de muy lejos, ¿verdad? ¿Cómo has llegado? ¿Tienes familia? Ven. (Grabs New Girl by the arm.) Ay, ésta es una de las señoritas qué te puede ayudar, horita te la presento. Es muy amiga mía.*
NEW GIRL: *No, no, mejor qué no. (Starts to run but Eugenia tries to stop her.)*
EUGENIA: *No tengas miedo. Aquí no llega la rnigra.*
NEW GIRL: *(Screams.) Ay, la migra no.*
EUGENIA: *(Struggling with New Girl.) Sarita, Sarita, ayúdame.*
SARITA: *(Bolts from bench.)* Now what?

(Sarita runs to Eugenia 's aid. There is a tussle. Eugenia who has been knocked down, gets up, while Sarita holds on to the New Girl.)

EUGENIA: *Aquí no viene la migra. Aquí le vamos a ayudar. Esta es la señorita Sarita. Yo soy* Doña *Eugenia Carbajal, le vamos a ayudar.*

SARITA: *(Still struggling with the New Girl.)* Will you stop with the introductions already. Who does she think we are, immigration? *(At the word "immigration," the New Girl panics again and bites Sarita.)* OHHHHHHHHH! *(Sarita drops New Girl.)* She bit me. *(Points at New Girl incredulously.)* I don't believe it. Eugenia, did you see that? She bit me like some kind of animal.

EUGENIA: *(To New Girl.) Mira no más lo qué hicistes. Y la señorita Sarita no más qué está aquí para ayudarte. No tienes vergüenza ... ¡Mal educada!*

SARITA: She bit my finger.

EUGENIA: Ahhh, *aver mi hija. ¿Duele mucho?*

NEW GIRL: *Ah, dispénseme. (Runs to her bag to get a hankie.) Perdóneme, es qué usted me dio mucho miedo.*

(New Girl gives hankie to Eugenia. Eugenia dips it into water can and then tries to apply it to Sarita's finger.)

SARITA: Not from there. That water's dirty. It has germs.

(Eugenia pays no attention to dirty water and applies compress to finger.)

SARITA: Ouch!

NEW GIRL: *Señorita, por favor, perdóneme. Es qué no sabía.*

EUGENIA: *(Looking at Sarita's finger and rubbing it.) Sana, sana, colita de rana. Ay niña, no es nada.*

SARITA: What do you mean, it's nothing? Human bites are very dangerous. I could catch something.

NEW GIRL: *Perdóneme. Ay, todo me ha salido mal.*

EUGENIA: *(Comforting New Girl.) No le hagas caso. Horita le vamos a encontrar un trabajito.*
SARITA: I am not getting her a job. Look ... *(Holds out finger.)* It's starting to swell. *(Offstage sounds of Don Félix singing, "Las Mañanitas." At hearing this, Sarita rushes for the bus bench to her purse. Eugenia frantically looks through pockets.) Ya es tiempo. Apúrate antes de qué llegue.*
EUGENIA: *Ay ¿dónde está mi peseta?*
SARITA: *(Excitedly takes quarter out of purse. To audience)* ... Hear that whistling? Sleazy Sánchez is coming. He only has two pairs of pajamas, the Mickey Mouse ones and the ones with the sailboats. She calls them los barquitos.

(Eugenia brings out her quarter Sarita brings out her quarter.)

EUGENIA: *(Agonizing.) ¡Ay! ¡Virgencita! ¿Qué será,* Mickey Mouse *o los barquitos?*

(Eugenia crosses herself and says a prayer.)

SARITA: *(Getting impatient.) Andale, mujer ... qué está a punto de llegar (Catching herself.)* Oh Christ, we go through this every day.
EUGENIA: *(Very sure.)* Mickey Mouse.
SARITA: *(Very sure.)* Sailboats, *los barquitos.*

(Sánchez comes around the comer from stage right carrying a pot of beans, a loaf of white bread, the L.A. Times and a ring of keys. He is wearing his Mickey Mouse pajamas. He puts key into lock. They all gather their things to go in. Eugenia must coax New Girl.)

EUGENIA: *Buenos días,* Don Félix, *¿Cómo amaneció?*
SÁNCHEZ: *(Grunts.) Sí, buenos días.*

(Sarita gives Eugenia a quarter. All go in except Sarita. She turns to audience.)

SARITA: I let her win.

(She goes in.)

Scene 3

Stage is dark. Store front turns to reveal Agency in three rooms: 1. front door and reception area, 2. interview room, 3. back room

DON FÉLIX: *(On phone.)* Carlos, Carlos, how many times I gotta tell you? 67, the line with the blue button is the Félix Sánchez Body Shop. The red button, 68, is the Félix Sánchez Domestic Wedding Chapel. Now, the new one, the one with no color is going to be the Félix Sánchez Teenager After School Discotheque. Carlos, it doesn't matter. Paint it any color you want. Now, what we got there? Over there, with you, in the downtown office? What we got there? How many girls? How many for maid jobs? Any English-speaking? One ... you think! She said, "Excuse me?" Carlos, I don't care if she is polite. I want to know if she speaks English. Well, talk to her. Ask her something. *Pues, preguntale algo. No le hace qué, pero preguntale algo, hombre. Ay,* I gotta think of everything. Ask her, ask her in English, idiot, ask her if she has any pets. If she likes dogs. You know, start a conversation. Okay, I'll hold.

(New Girl who has been standing in doorway with Eugenia, has summoned up all her courage, walks up to Don Félix.)

DON FÉLIX: *(Still holding phone.)* *Buenos días,* Félix Sánchez *a sus ordenes. ¿Cómo puedo servir a la señorita?*
NEW GIRL: Elsa María Cristina López de Moreno. *¿Aquí es dónde le consiguen trabajo?*
DON FÉLIX: *Sí señorita.* *(Puts his hand protectively on New Girl's shoulder.)* *¿Hablas ingles?*
NEW GIRL: *No.*
DON FÉLIX: *¿Has trabajado cómo criada?*
NEW GIRL: *Pues, en mi país he trabajado en muchas casas y en el campo.*
DON FÉLIX: *¿Pero Aquí en los Estados Unidos?*
NEW GIRL: *No, senor.*
DON FÉLIX: *(Pats her shoulder.)* *No le hace. Horita le buscamos un trabajito ... pase atrás con* Doña Eugenia.
(To Sarita.) No English, no references ... another $60 girl, if we're lucky. Ah, don't waste your time with her. Just work with the $100 and up girls. Wait a minute, wait a minute. Why don't you teach her to count to ten in English? Yeah, just to ten. That's all she'll need.
SARITA: What?
DON FÉLIX: See, honey, if she can count to ten in English, we can say she speaks enough English to answer the phone.
SARITA: Oh, that's brilliant. Does Berlitz know about this innovation?
DON FÉLIX: We all got to start somewhere, honey. *(Smiles brilliantly at New Girl and motions her on to back room.)* Pase, pase ...
SARITA: Oh, please!
DON FÉLIX: *(Returning to phone.)* Carlos, what did you find out? She doesn't like dogs, but she once had a cat. You asked her in English. Okay, she speaks English. So, send her up. Put her on the bus ... the 78 bus. Now, don't

forget about the phones. (*Hangs up phone.*) Sarita, I am going to ... (*Laughs, he thinks this is funny.*) to my private office. (*Picks up paper.*) You know where I mean.

SARITA: Yeah, yeah, you're going to the bathroom.

DON FÉLIX: Don't forget tonight. Grand opening. Félix Sánchez Teen Disco. Wear something sexy.

(*Don Félix goes to bathroom laughing, Sarita waits until he is out of ear shot, then picks up phone and dials.*)

SARITA: Oh, is, eh, Joan in? Well, this is Sara Gómez and I read ... well ... last Friday I read for the part of the nurse on *Eight is Enough* and, well, I wondered if Joan heard anything ... I'll hold.

(*María runs in out of breath. She has a heavy accent.*)

MARÍA: Ay, María Santísima. (*Flops on reception area sofa. Eugenia enters and starts dusting dummies.*) I am late.

SARITA: No, who cares?

MARÍA: Where is he?

SARITA: In his private office.

MARÍA: Ah, he'll be there for hours.

SARITA: (*Crossing her fingers and holding them up to María.*) Yes, I know, the director said I read really great. What? Too exotic? I know what that means. And you still think I have a chance for it? Well, listen, thanks for the vote of confidence, but I won't hold my breath. Goodbye.

(*Starts to slam receiver down, but with controlled effort, puts it down firmly.*)

MARÍA: Your agent? Do you get the part?

SARITA: They loved my reading ...

MARÍA: Of course, you are most terrific actress.

SARITA: But they think I may be too exotic for the part and they'll get back to me.

MARÍA: They'll get back to you, *¿y qué quiere decir eso?*

SARITA: I'll get back to you means ... you don't know what to say. You just say it when you don't know what else to say.

MARÍA: Ah, I'll get back to you ... Ah, Sarita there is still hope, be patient.

SARITA: Too exotic, María. They say I am too exotic.

MARÍA: You are?

SARITA: That means I am too dark, too unusual, they don't have people like me on their show.

MARÍA: What show?

SARITA: *Eight is Enough.* I am too dark and freaky for *Eight is Enough.* They don't have stupid Mexicans playing nurses on prime time, you know. I might scare the kids.

MARÍA: Oh, *sí. Eight is Enough,* that's the show with all the kids that live in the big white house, with the little white fence with all the flowers around the little fence and the kids always drinking milk in the kitchen, talking over their problems. Last week one of the girls made a dent in their papa's car. She afraid, she no want to tell him. All show she afraid. In the end, she tell him and you know what? He's not mad because insurance pay. *Ay, sí, muy bonito.* Ah, sure there's hope. I am positive. Sure, you'll be on that show. They're a good Catholic family, you'll see.

EUGENIA: *Sí, niña, hay qué tener esperanza.*

SARITA: Will you two just be quiet and look who's telling me to have hope.

MARÍA: Sarita! You're just upset about your agent.

EUGENIA: *Tengo mis hijos, mis nietos, todos sanos, gracias a Dios.*

(Eugenia leaves.)

MARÍA: That's right, Sarita, she has her children and her grandchildren.

SARITA: Oh, yeah, where are her precious children now, huh? They don't want her around. She doesn't fit in with their lives, so she hangs around here.

MARÍA: So sad, she fights to bring her children here, for a better life. She feeds them, educates them, and they turn against her. They take up new American ways and leave her and the old ways behind. Yet, she is proud of them.

SARITA: Oh, she's just a martyr and it makes me mad.

MARÍA: Mad ... Why?

SARITA: I, I ... don't know.

MARÍA: Because you really love her.

SARITA: Well ...

MARÍA: Then, why you take her home with you all the time?

SARITA: Not all the time, María. I don't know. She cleans up my apartment. Although, last time she used Lava on my walls, took all the paint off. What a mess, oh, I don't know, María. I understand her kids. I mean, all she does is tell old stories about Mexico.

MARÍA: And it reminds you about when you were little girl. How many people make fun, make less of you because you are Mexican.

SARITA: No! Yes. I just don't want to end up old, Mexican, unwanted. Why couldn't she change? Learn to speak English?

MARÍA: She doesn't want to, she likes to be Mexican.

SARITA: Well, I worked. real hard to change, to be different from my parents.

MARÍA: Ah, sure, you improve yourself, but you are *still* Latina.

SARITA: No, I'm not.

MARÍA: Okay, you're not ... you're Swedish, but Eugenia, she likes to be what she is. It's her life. *(Eugenia returns with wet rag and lipstick and cleans dummy's faces and applies lipstick.)* What happened to your finger?

EUGENIA: *Le mordió una muchacha.*

MARÍA: A girl bit you?

SARITA: Yeah ... the New Girl. She was so afraid. *(Looks at finger.)* Panicked like an animal.

EUGENIA: *¡Pobrecita! Vino de tan lejos. ¡Desde Perú y solita!*

SARITA: Oh, I don't believe that. She's lying. All the way from Peru by herself!

EUGENIA: *Sí, solita.*

SARITA: *(Looking at finger.)* She was so afraid.

MARÍA: She is very brave.

EUGENIA: *A lo mejor la mordida le va a traer suerte.*

ARITA: Eh? What?

MARÍA: Maybe the bite brings you good luck.

SARITA: Hey, if I get this television part I'll ... I'll treat you to ... Oh, what am I talking about? I won't get this. It's got no gangs. I only get parts with gangs in them.

EUGENIA: *(Takes quarter out of her pocket.)* *A ver, mi hija, una peseta qué vas a ganar esa parte.*

SARITA: Okay. It's a bet. Your quarter says I get the part, my quarter says I don't.

(They place in their bets.)

MARÍA: But, Sarita, that means you're betting against yourself.

(Phones start ringing. Lights go down as María picks up first call. We hear María and Sarita answering calls. Lights go up back room.)

MARÍA: Good morning. Félix Sánchez Domestic Agency, this is María speaking. How may I help you, Mrs. Rick ... ards? Oh, excuse me, Richards. Oh, yes, we having very nice maids. Oh yes, very ... *(While in back room New Girl sits in folding chair rather stiffly at first, eyeing the bathroom. She is afraid Don Félix might come out. She gingerly leaves the chair and looks down the hall. She goes back to the chair when she thinks she hears noise. She sees T.V. set and examines it carefully. She pushes a button and the volume and picture come on loudly. She jumps back and turns it off quickly. She is always on the alert, checking both doors. She very carefully goes to the food area and starts to wolf down some food. As María takes first call, she keeps eating. She is very hungry. Once again she checks both doors, then goes through closet and finds Eugenia's purse. She looks at the pictures in the wallet. She goes through agony trying to decide whether or not to take money. She takes one dollar from wallet, puts the rest of the money back into the wallet. She then reorganizes the closet and goes back to the chair.)* Honest, yes, experience, sure. First, I take the order, you tell me what you want then, I personally find the just right girl for you. Yes, I will. Then, will you pay the girl whatever salary we agree on? Yes, of course English speaking is more money. Oh, now, Mrs. Richards, we don't check if they are illegal. That is up to you, the employer. Oh yes, the agency has a fee which the employer pays. It's a three month guarantee. Well, if the first girl leaves, we find you another one, so we supply you with girls for three months. Yes, English-speaking and references: $80 to $100 a week. Your phone, yes, I'll find somebody very nice.
SARITA: Félix Sánchez Domestic Agency, Sarita speaking. Yes, sir. Yes, most of our girls come from Latin America. Yes, some speak English. Cheapest? $60 per week. How large a home do you have, sir? Oh, a trailer. No, she doesn't need her own room. How big is your

trailer? Two bedrooms? Children? Two pets? One cat. *(Phone rings again.)* Please hold. Félix Sánchez Domestic Agency, Sarita speaking. Oh, yes, Mrs. Camden *(Lights dim in back room. Lights up in front room.)* I am sorry to hear that. I said I am sorry to hear that. Hey, hey, don't yell at me, lady. I don't know where she is! Look, I'll find you a replacement. Oh, maybe a day or two. Don't yell at me lady. Hello? Hello? *(To María.)* Mrs. Camden. Lola didn't show up at work today. That's not like Lola.

MARÍA: You think maybe *la migra*?

SARITA: You better call her house.

MARÍA: No phone.

SARITA: Where do the kids stay?

MARÍA: With the neighbor lady and she got …

SARITA and MARÍA: No phone.

(Phone rings. María starts to answer, then freezes.)

MARÍA: *Ay,* Sarita, it's the Wedding Chapel line ... *(Practicing.)* Félix Sánchez Wedding Cha ... Oh, Sarita, please …

(Sarita concentrates a moment, then pushes the phone button and lifts receiver. As she does La Chata, La Cubana, Clara and Evita come in laughing and talking. They are promptly hushed by Eugenia and María as Sarita answers phone in low, low voice sounding like a sexy undertaker.)

SARITA: Félix Sánchez Wedding Chapel. How may I help you? … Oh yes, congratulations. No need for blood tests if you have been living together. Of course I can tell from your voice that you have the best intentions. The Reverend Sánchez can perform the ceremonies this

18

afternoon at 2:00. You have the address of our wedding chapel? Congratulations. I am sure it will be a lovely ceremony.

(Sarita hangs up. Ladies all laugh and clap.)

MARÍA: *Ay* Sarita, you do it so beautiful.
LA CHATA: *Ay, qué la* Sarita ... Sarita, don't forget your friend here ... *(Points to herself.)* needs a job with plenty of *lana.*
CLARA: Me too, Sarita.

(They all gather around Sarita 's desk. Lights dim in front area and go up in the back room.)

MARÍA: Sarita, this man with the cat, he's still on hold. See ...

(She points to flashing button. Sarita sits, lifts the phone. Don Félix comes out of bathroom. His hair is slicked back with pomade like patent leather. He is wearing a polyester, navy suit with white stitching, white shoes, a white satin tie. He closes the bathroom door which has a broken full length mirror behind it. He preens unaware of New Girl watching him. He puts a white plastic carnation in his lapel and makes dignified, reverend-like gestures in the mirror.)

DON FÉLIX: Friends, we are gathered here today to join this man to this woman ... no, it's ... Friends, we are gathered here today to join this woman to this man ... no ... Friends, we are gathered here to join this couple in holy matrimony today in the flower of their love ... *(He turns, sucks in his stomach, takes out cigar, lights it and continues to talk to himself in the mirror.)* Yes, ma'am, I am the Reverend Félix Silvestre Sánchez. Yes, I got a car place, I got a domestic agency, I got a wedding chapel and, starting tonight, I will be the owner of the Félix Sánchez Teen Discotheque ... I don't care what Sarita says, I am a man of success.

(La Chata walks into the back room, whistles in approval.)

LA CHATA: She also says you're wanted in Guatemala.
DON FÉLIX: *(Leaving for front room.)* That's not funny.

(Lights go up in the front room and dim in the back room. Clara is on her way to the back room.)

CLARA: *Buenos días,* Don Félix, *¿Cómo amaneció?*
DON FÉLIX: *Buenos días, Clara, ¿la familia?*
CLARA: *Bien, gracias a Dios.*
DON FÉLIX: *Hola,* Evita. I've been trying to reach you. *(He whistles in approval. Evita does pirouette, showing off her new clothes.)* Well, things are good for you, *chabelita!* You are still with Mr. Hodges, eh?
EVITA: *Ay, sí* ... yesterday he took me to the May Company and said, "Anything you want, Evita." *(The women "OOH" and "AH" and "Qué bueno.")* I got French blue jeans, the kind when you walk away they wish you was coming back.
DON FÉLIX: Oh, honey, those are my favorite.
EVITA: High, *pero,* real high heeled shoes. *Ay,* I got so many clothes, I don't have enough days to wear them ... and look ... this Boluva watch he gave me.
DON FÉLIX: Oh nice, very nice honey.

(He starts to leave. Evita follows him a few steps out of ear shot of the other women.)

EVITA: And he says he is going to buy me an LTD ... he says, he says ... *Ay,* it's a lie Don Félix. He used to say those things. He used to say he would be good to me. Help me with my momma. He used to say ... many things, like maybe he would marry me. *Ay,* Don Félix, I want another job ... make him jealous ... make more money.
DON FÉLIX: Oh, sure, honey, sure. That's why I been dying to reach you.
EVITA: He is *un desgraciado! ¡Un viejo pinchi!*
DON FÉLIX: Ah, sure, honey ... I got just the job for you, at my new disco, the Félix Sánchez Disco. The Félix Sánchez Disco, you heard about it, no?

(Phone rings and Sarita answers.)

EVITA: *Ay qué bruto, imbécil, ay,* he makes me so mad! What disco?
DON FÉLIX: I been trying to tell you, honey, you could teach the kids the new steps ...
EVITA: Ah, *sí,* perfect job ... make him really jealous. All those young boys who will dance with me ... *¡qué padre!*
SARITA: *(Holding out receiver to Don Félix.)* It's for you.
DON FÉLIX: *(To Evita.)* Eh ... later, honey. We'll talk later. Go practice, the opening is tonight.

(Don Félix rushes to take the phone from Sarita.)

SARITA: *(Holding the phone receiver without looking up from the desk.)* It's the I.R.S

(We see Don Félix pale before our eyes. He carries on phone conversation while La Cubana has been peeking through windows, careful not to be seen. She keeps this up for a few minutes. Finally, she puts on sunglasses and wraps the sweater that Evita left on the sofa around her head. This catches María's attention. La Cubana comes in again and peers through the window again.)

MARÍA: *¿Cubana, qué te pasa?*
LA CUBANA: My name is Margarita, *por favor*.
MARÍA: Margarita, *¿qué te pasa?*
LA CUBANA: Sssssssh! *(Looks carefully out of window then back to María.)* There's a car filled with men and they are following me.
MARÍA: *(Doesn't Look.)* Margarita, don't you want some coffee?
LA CUBANA: They were there yesterday and now today, waiting to get me.
MARÍA: *Andale, una taza de cafe.*

(Don Félix gets off the phone on Sarita 's desk and is quickly walking to his own desk. His mind is preoccupied. La Cubana rushes up to him and gets in his way.)

LA CUBANA: Ah, Don Félix, these men are outside. They're after me.
DON FÉLIX: Sure, sure, honey. *(She gets her big body in his way. They do a small dance trying to get out of each others way.)* Andale, Cubana, go sit in the back, honey.
LA CUBANA: Margarita. My name is Margarita!

(Don Félix pays no attention and goes to his desk. He makes a phone call. Evita and Eugenia go to the back room. La Cubana waits to talk to Sarita. María answers

*the phone and takes down an order. New Girl goes out of
the back room and into the front room to Sarita 's desk,
cutting in front of La Cubana.)*

NEW GIRL: *Seño, por favor ...*
LA CUBANA: *(To New Girl.) Un momento.* I am first.
*(New Girl backs up a step. She is not dissuaded. She
stands firm and looks at Sarita.) Ay,* Sarita ... *(Points to
her finger.) ¿Q
ué pasó con tú* finger?
SARITA: Nothing ... *(New Girl takes off the medallion her
mother gave her in the first scene and offers it to Sarita.)*
Oh, Christ ... Oh, put it back on. I don't want your St.
Christopher medal. María, you have your *diccionario?*
MARÍA: Sure. *(Holds up dictionary.) Ingles Sin Maestro.*
SARITA: Good. Take this application form and Miss Peru
here. Help her fill it out. It's in English.
MARÍA: Sure thing.
SARITA: And teach her to count to ten *(To herself)* ...
why not?
MARÍA: Okay dokey.

(New Girl just stands there.)

SARITA: María *le va a ayudar. (María takes New Girl by
the arm. They start to go to the back room.)*
MARÍA: *(To New Girl) Esperame un momento aquí.
(Hands New Girl dictionary to hold.)* Sarita, Don Félix's
appointment book ...

(She rushes around looking for it, then finds it.)

LA CUBANA: *(Hands on hips.) Andale,* Sarita, where is
my ladies' companion job? *(Fishes green card out of her*

bosom and waves it at Sarita.) I have my green card. You can't push me around like the rest.

(Phone rings and is quickly answered.)

SARITA: *Un momento,* Margarita. *(Picks up phone and La Cubana stalks off to the back room.)* Yes, Mrs. Camden, I am sorry. No, I told you Lola isn't here. I am trying to get ... hello, hello ... *(Puts phone down.)* Ohhh, that woman, and where is Lola?

(Don Félix gets off the phone.)

DON FÉLIX: María, the appointment book.
MARÍA: *Ahi voy. (Brings the appointment book to him.)* Don Félix, you have a wedding at 2:00 this afternoon.
DON FÉLIX: *(Looks at appointment book.)* Honey, honey, you gotta put down where. At their home, you put down their address.
MARÍA: *(Getting nervous.)* At the church.
DON FÉLIX: What church? Where is the address? Eh?
MARÍA: The wedding church. You built behind the body shop.
DON FÉLIX: The chapel! The chapel! The Félix Sánchez Wedding Chapel! You got it! So here ... *(Pointing at place in the book.)* After place, you put down at the W. C., that means Wedding Chapel.
MARÍA: The Chapel, *sí, sí,* W.C.

(María takes New Girl by the arm and they exit to back room.)

DON FÉLIX: Sarita, I gotta go.

(Preening to get her approval.)

SARITA: *(Without looking up from her desk.)* You look like a hair oil salesman.
DON FÉLIX: *(Visibly dejected.)* I'll be right back.
SARITA: Take your time. *(He leaves through the front door. Phone rings Sarita concentrates a moment.)* Félix Sánchez Wedding Chapel How may I help you? *(Lights start to dim.)* Oh, congratulations, I am sure.

(Front room dark. Back room lights up.)

LA CHATA: Think of it. Don Félix doing weddings?
EVITA: Well, maybe he'll do mine.
LA CHATA: You're getting married, *mi hija?*
EVITA: *(Opening compact and putting on mascara.)* Maybe.
CLARA: And what are you doing here? Don't you have a job with Mr. Hodges in the "motherless home"?
EVITA: So? *¿Ya ti, qué?*
CLARA: Hmmmmph!
EVITA: *Y eso.* Can't a person come here on her day off? Maybe Félix has a better job for me.
LA CHATA: *Ay, sí. (Dirty old lady chuckle.)* She wants to get ahead … girl should have ambition.
CLARA: A girl should live at home with her mama helping her, instead ...
LA CHATA: Clara, keep out of it.

(Evita not answering, continues putting on make-up.)

CLARA: Aren't you ashamed? I know your *mamá* since I come here twelve years ago in this very room. I met her twelve years ago. Of course, you wouldn't know, you was only six years old still in Mexico.

LA CHATA: *Ay, Dios,* I remember. I met you on that day too. My little Consuelo was only four. *Ay,* the three of us talking about our babies. Right here, in this very room. They was offering live-ins for $30 to $35 a week. Then it wasn't so hard for me, with my mother alive and my baby here, but for Clara and your mama, *ay,* times were rough, sending all their money for you kids back home.

CLARA: That's right, your mama and I was killing ourselves for $25 week.

LA CHATA: Don't exaggerate, it was $30, sometimes $25 if the people were nice.

CLARA: Hmmmmmph! We never had those nice people. Evita's mama and I, we were killing ourselves to send that money home, so you could have a crust of bread.

LA CHATA: Keep out of it, I tell you.

CLARA: Hmmmmmph! Now, look how she pays her mother back. *(Evita gathers her things and walks out of the back room.)* I hope you choke on your Mr. Hodges!

LA CHATA: *Ay, "vieja metichi,"* always putting your nose in people's business.

CLARA: Hmmmmmph! If her poor mother knew.

LA CHATA: I am telling you ... keep out of it. Always meddling, causing trouble. That's why people don't like you.

CLARA: Who doesn't like me?

LA CHATA: *La gente, pues* ... everybody.

CLARA: Name one person.

LA CHATA: Well, there was that woman, *ay,* what's the use. A person can't talk to you. *Ay,* I hope Sarita gets me more money.

CLARA: What woman?

LA CHATA: Never mind, never mind. Sarita says, if I got my papers ...

CLARA: You mean that woman who used to work in the tuna factory with you? The one whose hands smell of dead fish?

LA CHATA: Forget it. Sarita says President Carter made a law that if a person is here more than seven years, a person could get their papers.

CLARA: For her own good, I tell her to use Lava soap on her hands … for her own good. Is that the one who don't like me?

LA CHATA: *Te digo,* my lips are sealed.

CLARA: I don't care, anyway. Hmmmmmmmph! Aha! I know the one ... it was the woman who was here two months ago. The one with the red hair who tried to steal my Tuesday cleaning job in Encino.

LA CHATA: She didn't try to steal your job. That stupid job. Who would want it? Only you would take two buses to Encino on your day off 'and two buses back to go and clean in between the tile with a toothbrush! And what for? To get a check for $20? They don't even give you cash. And how are you supposed to cash the check with no I.D.? Tell her to give you the cash every week when you come to clean, *tonta!*

CLARA: You talk like it's so easy. "I am not used to paying my help in cash," she says, "I should be reporting your wages," she says, "My husband wouldn't approve." She makes like she's doing me the big favor, letting me scrub her floors. "You'll just have to wait," she says, but Ernestito's school don't wait.

LA CHATA: You shouldn't be sending him to that special school. You'll make a sissy outa him. A *maricón.* That's what he'll be ... the way you fuss over him.

CLARA: *¿Y tú qué sabes?* You big tuna packer. You're just like my *pendejo* husband. I try to make him see. Xavier, I say, Ernestito is special, he got this gift from God. But that idiot, Xavier, he say, "Well, tell him to give it back." All he knows is working in the car wash, but as long as *me duran los huesos*, I'll work so Ernestito can have his chance.

LA CHATA: Ahhh, he's gonna end up a priest.

CLARA: And your daughters gonna end up a ...

LA CHATA: *Oyes, tú* ... keep out of my daughters. Consuelo, she's ... she's got her own ways.

CLARA: Hmmmmph! She don't respect you.

LA CHATA: You keep this up, you'll be sorry. I'm warning you.

CLARA: *Comadre,* you know it's true. She don't have any use for you, you, her own mother.

LA CHATA: *Cállate la trompa.* I ain't gonna mix-up in my daughters life, you hear? That's the trouble with you. Always in other people's business. That's why they don't like you.

CLARA: Oh yes, well, who exactly doesn't like me, eh? Name that person.

LA CHATA: Never mind.

CLARA: Was it *la vieja* who ... ?

(María and New Girl sitting together in comer of back room. They are filling in the application form. Form is in English. María is doing the filling in and translating.)

MARÍA: *A ver,* "name " *quiere decir nombre.*

(María and New Girl both say name in unison, very slowly as María writes it down.)

MARÍA and NEW GIRL: Elsa María Cristina López de Moreno.

MARÍA: Address? *Su dirección.*

NEW GIRL: *(Shaking her head.) No tengo.*

MARÍA: No address? Oh, you use mine. Social security *numero.* Oh, no worry, we use Lola's. *Aquí lo tengo.*

(Gets number from wallet in purse and copies it onto the form). Do you speak English?

NEW GIRL: *(Shakes her head.) No, no* más, *aver,* beefsteak, Disneylandia.
MARÍA: *Ay, Dios, cómo le va a faltar. Le voy a ensenar los numeros. (María using her fingers to teach the numbers.)* One.
NEW GIRL: Gwone.
MARÍA: Two.
NEW GIRL: Tú.
MARÍA: Three.
NEW GIRL: Tree.

(Sound of phone ringing in the front room. Lights start to fade in back room. Lights up in the front room.)

MARÍA: Four.
NEW GIRL: Pour.

(Sarita at desk. She calls to María.)

SARITA: María, I'm on the phone. Get the other phone.
MARÍA: *Mira este libro, horita regreso. (Running to front room.)* Yes, Mrs. Camden, but ... but, Mrs. Camden. No, Lola is not here. *Ay,* Mrs. Camden, you must be calm. Sarita? Oh, sure.

(María hands phone to Sarita. Sarita shakes her head and won't speak to Mrs. Camden. This mortifies María and

leaves her helplessly tossing the phone receiver from one hand to the other as if it were hot. Silently pleading with Sarita. María gets back on the phone. Sarita trying to control laughter.)

MARÍA: Ah, Mrs. Camden, you'll never guess, Sarita, she's not here. She had to go ... Mrs. Camden? Mrs. Camden? *(María replaces receiver.)* She hung up. *Ay,* Sarita, you made me lie!

SARITA: I made you lie? We lie here everyday. That woman is trouble. Now we have to find Lola. Maybe where her husband works.

MARÍA: I'll ask St. Anthony.

SARITA: St. Anthony?

MARÍA: Sure, whenever I lose something, I pray to St. Anthony and pssst, right away, I find it. Remember last week when I lose my red pen that Aunt Cecilia gave me for my birthday? I prayed to St. Anthony and right away I found it.

SARITA: But María, you never lost your red pen. It was in your hair, where you put it. Don't be silly. You would have found it without St. Anthony.

MARÍA: Oh sure, silly, you call me the silly. All the time you call me the silly. You went to the big important school. You speak perfect English. You working here just for fun.

SARITA: Fun? You call this fun?

MARÍA: Sure to you is fun. You always laughing at us. When I make mistake in English, you laugh, you don't help me to say it better.

SARITA: *(Starting to laugh.)* Oh, come on, María.

MARÍA: No, you come on. You know what it means in my country when they say, *"Es una muchacha mal educada?"* *(María pauses looks at her.)* Do you? Do you know what it means?

SARITA: What is this, *Hollywood Squares*?

MARÍA: Do you know what it means?

SARITA: Yes, María, I know. It means a badly educated girl.

MARÍA: But not education from the books. It means you do not have manners, that you do not have respect for other people and their ways. *(This has a deep effect on Sarita. Eugenia walks in with mop and pail of water. She is wearing tennis shoes. Her skirt is rolled up revealing striped socks which are held up by means of ankle garters. She has a bandana on her head. On top of that an L.A. Dodgers baseball cap on sideways. The effect is comic. She starts mopping the floor behind Don Félix's desk.)* Doña Eugenia is better educated than you.

SARITA: *(Laughing.)* Oh no, not Eugenia. Oh, St. Anthony, save me, please.

MARÍA: *No eres una persona seria.*

SARITA: Oh, now you want me to be a serious person all the time. You don't want me to laugh?

MARÍA: When I say, *"No eres una persona seria,"* it means you are not sincere. That you do not value yourself and I don't care what you say, St. Anthony will find Lola.

(Crosses herself, folds her hands and bows her head in prayer.)

SARITA: Better him than immigration. *(Eugenia stops cleaning and holds mop in her hand like a staff; with the other hand she takes off the baseball cap and raises it, saying proudly)* Qué Dios la bendiga y qué no se encuentre con la migra. *(Sarita and Eugenia laugh.)*

MARÍA: Doña Eugenia!

EUGENIA: *Sí, mi hija.*

(Crosses herself and folds hands in prayer. They both say a prayer out loud and in unison.)

EUGENIA AND MARÍA: *En el nombre del padre, del hijo y del Espíritu Santo ... (Praying.)*
SARITA: Out loud?

Lights dim and we hear church music, a chorus of little girls singing, "Oh Mary We Bring You Blossoms Today." Far right corner of the stage by the file cabinet a vision appears: an elaborate Latin altar with a large crucifix and statue of the Virgin Mary covered with flowers. A little girl in a white communion dress is led to the altar by Sister Agnes.

SISTER AGNES: Say it out loud, Sarita, so God will hear.
LITTLE SARITA: Yes, Sister Agnes.
SISTER AGNES: Hail Mary ...
LITTLE SARITA: Hail Mary, full of grace, the Lord is with thee, blessed art thou amongst women and blessed is the fruit of thy womb, Jesus. God bless grandma, Mommy and Daddy and please protect Mr. Amador, who works hard in the fields and don't let immigration catch him ...
SISTER AGNES: No, Sarita, you can't pray for something that's against the law.
LITTLE SARITA: Oh, how about Mrs. Amador? Can I pray for all the Amador children?
SISTER AGNES: Yes, of course, you can.
LITTLE SARITA: God bless Mrs. Amador and Angie and Manuel and Trini and Louie and ...
MARÍA: Lola!

María's voice shatters the vision. The music stops. Sarita turns around. Lights go up on the front room and the

32

vision is lost. Lola has just come through the front door.
Eugenia and María stare at her.

LOLA: *Buenas.* What's wrong?

(María and Eugenia run up and embrace Lola.)

MARÍA: We thought. We were so worried. *¿Dónde estabas?*
SARITA: *(Looks up to heaven, then to audience.)* I'll never hear the end of this. *(Turns to Lola.)* Lola, what happened?
LOLA: Nothing. Everything, I'm up to here. *(Indicating her neck.) Aguantando y aguantando, ya no puedo.*
SARITA: Oh, that's terrific! And what about Mrs. Camden? She wants you back.
LOLA: *¡Nunca jamás!* No way José.
SARITA: Why didn't you call me? And why didn't you give her two weeks notice? At least you could have called.
LOLA: *Ay* Sarita, *no entiendes.* That job was driving me crazy I thought you would understand.
SARITA: What I don't understand is why you didn't give notice or at least call. It puts me in a bad position.
LOLA: *Pero,* I was the one working in the bad position. You don't think about me?

(Phone rings and María starts to answer, until she realizes that it's the Wedding Chapel line. She struggles but she can't bring herself to answer.)

MARÍA: Sarita, please, it's the Wedding.
SARITA: I have to do everything around here. *(She concentrates a moment, lowers her voice.)* Félix Sánchez Wedding Chapel, may I help you? Congratulations, Miss

Ramirez. *(Eugenia, María and Lola go to the back room while Sarita is on the phone.)* Yes, the Reverend Sánchez would be happy to perform the ceremony. Problems? *Ay,* no Miss Ramirez, we don't provide counseling service. No, ma'am, no I am not a marriage counselor. I really don't think it would help if I spoke to your boyfriend. *(Other phone rings.)* I mean that's between the two of you. Wait, wait, I can't talk to him. *(Puts hand over mouth piece and yells.)* María, María … *(Back to phone.)* Listen, can you hold a minute? *(Gets the other phone.)* Félix Sánchez Domestic Agency.

(La Cubana walks into the front room and goes to the windows and peeks out.)

LA CUBANA: Sarita, they're still there. Come and look, in the green Chevy. The same ones, Sarita, look!

(Sarita waves her away. Lights dim in the front room and lights up in the back room. Clara is knitting. New Girl is holding yarn. Evita is practicing disco steps. The radio is playing Tex-Mex Ranchera music. La Chata is singing along as María, Lola and Eugenia enter back room.)

EVITA: Chata, how can I practice my disco with that music?
LA CHATA: *Aquí está mi* Lola. *Me dan ganas de hacer una* party. We should have a party.
LOLA: With Alma's *tamales.*
LA CHATA: *Y unas cervecitas Carta Blanca, ayii, ayii.*
CLARA: *Ay, pensamos qué la migra* got you. Like Hortensia, last week.

(All women say, "Ah, no.")

LA CHATA: *(To Clara)* *¿Y por qué no me dijiste?*
Important things you don't tell me.
CLARA: *Porque te coges una rabia.* She gets so mad.
LA CHATA: *¿Y por qué no?* Makes me feel hunted, like
an animal.
EUGENIA: *¿Y los niños? ¿Con quien* están?
EVITA: The kids are staying with Armeda.
MARÍA: *Qué pena. Ay,* who would take care of my baby if
I got caught?
CLARA: *(Reflecting)* Ernestito, *ay* Chata, he would end
up in the car wash with Xavier. You're his godmother.
LA CHATA: *Ay, mira la chillona.* Don't worry. I'll send
him to interior decorating school.
CLARA: No, he wants to be a priest.
LA CHATA: What did I tell you?
EVITA: *Ay,* I would never see *mi amorcito, el* Mr.
Hodges.
MARÍA: *Y yo.* I could never go to the night school for to
be a nurse.
LA CHATA: I didn't know you wanted to be a nurse.
MARÍA: Sure thing. All my life, I dream to be a nurse.
CLARA: *Qué bien.*
NEW GIRL: *(Very upset.) Y yo qué llegue de tan lejos.*

(Runs to Eugenia and buries her head in her lap.)

LA CHATA: *(To Clara)* Look, you made her cry.
LOLA: *¿Quién es? ¿Qué le pasa?*
CLARA: *Es la* New Girl that bite Sarita.
LOLA: Good for her. That Sarita is a *gringa* in her heart.
EUGENIA: *(Stroking New Girl's head.) Ay, ay, pobre
inocente. Le abandonaron en la* supermarket *y le dio
mucho miedo.*
LA CHATA: Those damn coyotes. Leave her in *la*
parking lot of the Ralph's. "Here is where the rich people

live, you'll find a job here. "No English, nobody to help her in the middle of Beverly Hills. Lucky some gardener saw her walking in circles and told her where to go.

LOLA: *¡Desgraciados! ¡Hijos del diablo!* They don't care. It was the same when I came. The policeman on the road wants his *mordida.* What the police don't get, the bandits take. Better for them if it's a woman. Then they try to get paid in other ways or sometimes they just kill the people.

EUGENIA: *Sí, a veces matan a la gente.*

LA CUBANA: It should be a lesson to them to stop coming here like beggars. Get your green card, like I did, or stay in your own country.

(La Cubana enters the bathroom and closes the door behind her.)

LA CHATA: *(Loudly.) Oyeme,* Cubana, I am dying to teach you a lesson.

LOLA: *Ay,* don't be mean. I don't like her, *pero dicen qué* she has cancer, *pobrecita.*

CLARA: *Es muy mentirosa.* She lies. She just say about the cancer for attention. Like she say she's married, she's not.

LOLA: *(To Eugenia.)* No?

EUGENIA: *(Shakes her head no.) No, está mala aquí. (Puts finger to her head and makes crazy sign.)*

LA CHATA: No, she's only *loca* sometimes. She's from Cuba, those Cubans. *Se creen mucho,* like they are better than everybody.

EVITA: The ones from Colombia are the worst.

MARÍA: *No es cierto,* I am from Colombia.

EVITA: You're the only person from Colombia I ever like.

CLARA: *Los de Guatemala son los peores.*

LOLA: I am *de* Guatemala.

CLARA: *De veras,* you are? I thought you was like me, from El Salvador.

LOLA: Poor people are the same everywhere. They are the ones that suffer.

LA CHATA: *Ay, sí, es la vida.*

(Sounds of toilet flushing as La Cubana comes out of bathroom.)

LA CUBANA: Because you don't help yourself. You just have babies. You don't think how you will feed them. No, every year, plop, another baby and, plop, another baby. Then you come here and get on the Welfare. Help yourself, show some class, like me.

(She turns around and starts to walk out and there is a big piece of toilet paper stuck on the seat of her skirt. The women, seeing this all, point and howl with Laughter.)

LA CHATA: *Ay, Señorita* Margarita, help yourself to the toilet paper on your *nalgas.*

(The women are all Laughing as La Cubana removes the toilet paper from her buns. She is shame faced.)

LA CUBANA: *¡Cerdas!* Pigs! *(Exits from back room.)*

LOLA: *Qué loca.* Everybody knows you need papers to get on welfare.

LA CHATA: *Ay,* that made me feel good. We should have a party.

EVITA: *¿Celebrando qué?*

LA CHATA: What are you, a *gringa?* You don't need a reason for a party, see? *(She pulls a bottle of rum out of her bag.)* We got Cokes. We can make our own highballs.

We got food. We got friends, the radio for music. *(La Chata hits the side of her head as she spots tht New Girl staring at her with wide eyes.)* *Ay,* I am so stupid! We got a reason for a party. We got to celebrate the arrival of the New Girl. *(All the women agree and begin the party. They touch and embrace the New Girl and stand her up on a chair.)* After what she has been through, she should have a party. *(Lola and María start getting Cokes from the Coke machine. Some of the women clear the chairs. Someone turns up the radio.)* *Viva la* New Girl. *(New Girl stands on her chair in the center as lights dim.)*

(Mrs. Homes walks into agency. As she walks into reception area Alma Gutiérrez trails behind, painfully shy. Sarita is on the phone.)

MRS. HOMES: Well Alma, here we are. Why don't you sit over there, dear? *(Gestures to sofa.)*
SARITA: Yes, thank you very much, then we look forward to seeing you. *(Sees Mrs. Homes.)* Mrs. Homes, what ...
MRS. HOMES: I am returning Alma.

(She gestures, indicating Alma. Sarita Looks at Alma. Alma Looks up and then bows her head.)

SARITA: Let me get your file. Would you like some coffee?
MRS. HOMES: Oh, no, thank you, no, Sara dear.

(Sarita walks to flit cabinet, opens drawer, stage right, near edge of stage, while Mrs. Homes takes a hanky out of her purse and dusts the seat before sitting.)

SARITA: *(To audience with the same gesture of the hand and voice that Mrs. Homes used earlier.)* I am returning Alma. What does she think this is, the May Company?

MRS. HOMES: She is as sweet as can be, but not at all suited to our lifestyle. We take great pride in our surroundings. It has become obvious that Alma has never been around beautiful things. She has no respect for my blue and white Chinese porcelain, or any of our antiques and these things are irreplaceable, you know. Where do you people get these girls?

(Alma sits there in total disgrace.)

SARITA: *(To audience.)* The Greyhound bus station, Ralph's Market's parking lot, the RTD bus stop

MRS. HOMES: What was that, dear?

SARITA: (Getting file from drawer.) Nothing. Ah, here is your file.

MRS. HOMES: I mean, you should make sure their references are in order.

SARITA: (Looking at file.) According to Alma's references, she is very clean, takes a great deal of pride in her work and ...

SARITA: (Looking at file.) According to Alma's references, she is very clean, takes a great deal of pride in her work and ...

MRS. HOMES: Oh, she is very clean. I wouldn't allow a dirty girl in my home, but she just doesn't understand antiques and fine things. Now, I want someone who understands these things. Someone who know s how to polish silver properly, knows you wax English pine, not just Pledge it. Someone who will value and understand our fine things.

SARITA: Uh, for $65 a week it's going to be hard to find somebody like ...

MRS. HOMES: Oh, I'll be more than happy to go higher for a proper person. I'd go to, say, $100 a week. Of course that would be live-in with Mondays off. What about a black lady. *(Excited by the idea)* Or better still, an Oriental? How much would an Oriental run me?

SARITA: H ... How much?

MRS. HOMES: Some of our friends have Orientals. I hear and I can see they are efficient. Oh, yes, indeed, and very clean, energetic, too ... *(Sarita walks slowly to file cabinet area down stage right.)* no grass growing under their feet, but they are moody, surely too, I hear. No, I can't have that, now, you Mexicans ... *(At this Sarita turns her head with a start and looks directly at Mrs. Homes)* have the best dispositions. You people may not be the cleanest or the most energetic, but I'll say this for you ... you know your place. *(Sarita looks at Alma, Alma looks at Sarita and they both bow their heads.)* One thing, though, if you get Mexican girl, get me one with no relatives. You see, one day they can't come because their grandmother is sick, the next week it's the husband or the kids. *(Light goes on in the file cabinet area where the dummies appear.)* You people have no sense of responsibility. *(Dummies appear at first standing very still in the same pose appeared in the window. Sarita, startled, looks to see if anyone else sees them. Alma is sitting on the sofa looking dejected.)* Mr. Homes doesn't stay home when I am sick. Why, I remember our son had meningitis, poor thing ran such a fever . .

(Mrs. Home 's voice fades. Sarita realizes that the dummies are in her mind. She turns her back on them and tries to will them away.)

SARITA: Get back in the window. *(Turns around and they are still there. She turns her back on them again and says slowly ...)* Get back in the window!

(At this point, the dummies move. They are still and move like people who have been in one position too long.)

DUMMY IN BLACK: *(Stretches and reaches down in a long stretch to touch her toes.)* ¡Ay, Dios! *(Takes off her shoes and rubs her feet.)* Ay, cómo me duelen los pies.
DUMMY IN WHITE: *(Shifts the baby from one arm to the other and rocks it. With her free hand she rubs her back.)* Ay, sí, y a mí, la espalda.
DUMMY IN BLACK: *Ay,* it gets hot in there, this time of day! *Hola,* Sarita.
SARITA: Get back in the window.
DUMMY IN BLACK: Hey, Don Félix gave us the day off.
DUMMY IN WHITE: *Sí, pues,* he's got Orientals in the window
SARITA: Orientals in the window?
DUMMY IN BLACK: Sure, he's running a special. They even got a sign out there ... CLEAN AND EFFICIENT HELP.
DUMMY IN WHITE: With no grass under their feet. *Hijo,* but Orientals are mean. Did you see how the big one was looking at the baby?
DUMMY IN BLACK: *Oyes,* Sarita, how much money you got for those Orientals?
DUMMY IN WHITE: *Ay,* it isn't polite to talk about money. Don't you know your place?
DUMMY IN BLACK: (Looks up, looks down. Looks behind herself.) Sure, I know my place. Right here on this earth where God put me. You know your place?
DUMMY IN WHITE: Of course, I was just testing you.

DUMMY IN BLACK: Good. Does the baby know her place?

DUMMY IN WHITE: I will teach her. I will teach her not to be ashamed. I will show her the statues of Francisco de Zúñiga and she will see how it is to be a strong, proud Latina.

DUMMY IN BLACK: *¡Ayyyyy, qué vivan las Latinas!*

DUMMY IN WHITE: Shhhhh, you'll wake the baby.

DUMMY IN BLACK: Ah, I was just happy that some of us know our place. Listen, Sarita, if you can't stand up for yourself, stand up for Alma.

DUMMY IN WHITE: *(Wrapping rebozo around herself.)* Come on, we'll be late.

(Dummy in Black wraps rebozo around herself.)

SARITA: Where are you going?

DUMMY IN WHITE: Let's go to the park. The baby looks so yellow.

DUMMY IN BLACK: Ah, all babies look that way.

(Dummies disappear.)

SARITA: Wait!

(We hear Mrs. Homes' voice as lights go back on center stage.)

MRS. HOMES: And he was just yellow with the fever, but I still scrubbed and waxed the floors. The house was just spotless. You wouldn't have known any one was sick at all. Well, well, Sara ... Sara?

SARITA: Yes.

MRS. HOMES: Now that we've raised the salary, I am sure we'll have no problem in finding someone. You know, Sara, this wouldn't have happened except that my husband is always looking for bargains. But, some people just never learn that you get what you pay for. In the end, cheap is expensive. Let that be a lesson, dear. Well, Sara, you have the idea now and I'll be hearing from you. Let's see, anything else? *(Starts to walk off and trips on Alma 's paper shopping bag.)* Oh, here's your luggage, Alma. *(Alma rises as Mrs. Homes hands her the shopping bag.)* Oh, goodbye, Alma dear, and good luck.

ALMA: *Sí*, Mrs. Homes. *(Mrs. Homes exits. Alma is close to tears.)* ¡*Qué es lo qué hice?*

SARITA: *Nada, y porque ...* *(Alma starts to cry and runs out of the front room to the back room.)* Why is she so stupid? Why couldn't she know those things? Why, why did she look that way? Like a stupid, docile Mexican, like me, just like me. Oh, God. *(Clutches her chest.)* I can't breathe. I am so angry, I can't breathe, in, out, in, out, God, it hurts. Why didn't I say something? How could I allow her to say those things to us? To both of us?

(Lights dim. Back room lights on. Women gather around Alma. Alma is crying.)

LA CHATA: *(With drink in her hand. She is tipsy.)* *Andale, Almita, no llores. Ay,* what do you care? It's only a job. What do you care what that *vieja pinchi* said.

CLARA: Sssssssh! You big tuna packer, *cállate.* Sarita's gonna be mad.

LA CHATA: *Ay, tú. (Mimicking.)* Shhhh, it's a hospital. Sarita's gonna be mad. *Oyes tú,* I'm mad. Did that vieja Mrs. ... Mrs. ...

ALMA: *(Crying.)* Mrs. Homes.

LA CHATA: *Sí, esa.* Did she ever taste Alma's *ento ... ento ...*

ALMA*: (Still crying.) Entomatadas.*

LA CHATA: *Sí,* or her *mole,* eh? The best in all Mexico. *¡Viva Mexico!*

CLARA: Be quiet you!

LA CHATA: *Oyes tú, no me da la gana. (Sits down and sings "Estoy en un rincon de una cantina.")*

LOLA: *No llores, Almita. Cállate una rabia, pero no llores. Piensa en tú abuelita,* your grandmother, the one who followed your grandfather and fought with Pancho Villa. She wouldn't cry.

LA CHATA: *Ay,* what kinda party is this? Everybody saying, "Poor Alma, poor Alma." *Yo digo, ¡Viva Alma! ¡Viva Mexico! Viva la Revolción y viva mi viejo gordo y feo, qué le hace qué me dejó. (The women all laugh.) Andale, chabalonas.* Lets go on strike, or sing songs from the Revolution, *"Cama de Piedra," "Adelita."*

LA CUBANA: I don't know the words to those songs. You want to sing them because I don't know the words.

(Exit LA CUBANA.)

LA CHATA: *(Puts arm around Alma.) Andale, Almita, ponte a cantar.*

(They all sing "Cama de Piedra" with Alma reluctantly joining in. Then "Adelita" as Sarita comes back into the back room.)

LOLA: *(To Sarita while women sing softly.) Oyes,* Sarita, why didn't you defend Alma? You always take the *gringas'* side. First me, then Alma. Why don't you ever stand up for us.

SARITA: And why aren't you more responsible? Why do you put me these crazy positions? Why can't you stay in your jobs and do your work? Why do I have to get involved?

LOLA: If I tell you, you don't hear my side. In your eyes I am wrong, because I am the maid, because I am Latin, because you are ashamed. You want that I should be ashamed.

SARITA: That's ... that's not true.

LOLA: Then why don't you ever stand up for us? All you want to be is *gringa desteñida!*

(She turns her back on Sarita and throws herself into singing. "Adelita" singing gets louder.)

EVITA: *(Yelling and running to the T.V. set.) Ay,* Viviana.

(Phone rings as Evita turns T.V. set on. Viviana theme music blares, drowning out singing. Chata and Clara join Evita at. T.V., as María goes to back room phone, leaving Lola and Doña Eugenia to continue singing. New Girl tries to get Sarita's attention.)

MARÍA: *Ay* Sarita, it's the Wedding Chapel.

SARITA: María, you have to learn to answer it.

NEW GIRL*: Señorita Sarita, un trabajo, por favor.*

MARÍA: *Ay,* Sarita, please. I can't, *ay Jesús, no puedo.*

SARITA: No! I don't hear it, and I'm tired of doing all the work around here.

CHATA: *(Seeing T.V.) Ay, viva* Viviana ... *Qué sexy.*

CLARA: You big tuna packer, you're drunk.

CHATA: I'm not drunk!

(Other phone rings.)

CLARA: *Sí, sí,* you are, *bien borracha.*

LA CUBANA: *(Rushing into back room.)* Sarita, those men are still out there. You have to hide me.

EVITA: Shut up! I can't hear *Viviana.*

CLARA: Don't tell us to be quiet. We was here, your mother and me, much before you.

MARÍA: *(Frozen before phone.)* Sarita, please ...

SARITA: Stop! *(Looks towards heaven.)* Give me a break! *(Everybody freezes and the phones stop. Then Sarita walks to stage apron, as all women slowly and calmly gather around T.V., taking sandwiches out of bags and passing food among themselves. Sarita to audience.)* We need a break.

(As lights fade to dark, we hear commercials from T.V.. T.V. stays on all during intermission.)

Act 2

Scene 1

Lights go up slowly. Sarita sits alone in front room section of stage. As we hear Atahuelpa Yupanqui singing "Le Tengo Rabia al Silencio." Sarita translates phrases sporadically for the audience. Very slowly lights go up on back room. As lights go up we see various debris from lunch: paper plates, napkins, empty Coke bottles and paper cups. There also paper and plastic shopping bags, coats and sweaters, some shoes strewn about. The back room is in a general state of disarray, except the area around Clara's chair, which is very tidy. The women are sitting still listening to the song, in their various reflective moods except for Clara, who is knitting. She looks at them, shakes her head in disapproval and turns down the radio as the song ends.)

CLARA: Hmmmmmph! Wasting time!

LA CHATA: *(Pouring rum into her paper cup, from the bottle by her chair.)* That is why they call him El Poeta de las Pampas. *¡Qué hombre! Cómo sabe sufrir.*

ALMA: Mrs. Homes, no good?

MARÍA: *Sí,* the poet, like San Sebastián, he suffers. (The women, except Clara, all agree with nods of their heads, a few say, *"Ay sí's"* and *"Qué bien lo dice," "Qué bonito.")*

CLARA: *(Still knitting.)* Hmmmmmmph!

LA CHATA: *(Getting to her feet, with a large gesture to Clara.) ¿Y tú, qué sabes?* The trouble with you, Clara, is you have no soul.

CLARA: De soul, de soul don't pay my bills, only work.

ALMA: Almita, no good?

LA CHATA: Work, work, that's all you know. *Ay,* I feel it here. *(Strikes chest and starts to sing loudly.) Le tengo rabia al silencio por lo mucho qué perdí ...*

(Alma starts to cry, immediately comforted by Lola and María. They hug her and say things like, "Ya, ya no llores," "Andale, Almita." At this little commotion CHATA down again abruptly.)

ALMA: *Y yo perdí mi trabajo, ay, ¿qué hice mal?*

CLARA: *Ya ves, ya ves,* you and your singing make Almita cry.

LA CHATA: *Me? tú, vieja!* You and your long face *y* work, work, work.

CLARA: Hmmmph! *Por lo menos* I no talk of the suffering of a stupid poet. Almita don't need to hear of suffering. She need a job.

LA CHATA: *Ay tú,* Sarita will find her a job. Then she will suffer again silence, *así son los trabajos,* but if it makes Almita happy …

LOLA: *Ay,* Chata, didn't you listen to the song? Didn't the poet say that those that want to be happy should be silent? *(Turning to Alma.) Mira,* Almita, did Sarita defend you? No. So you gotta be strong and speak up to those people.

ALMA: *Sí,* Lola, *voy a tratar de aprender.*

CLARA: Hmmmmmmph! *Entonces te da la patada,* like this one *(Gesturing to Chata.)* always losing her job.

LA CHATA: *Y a ti, ¿qué?* I don't lose my jobs, I just leave them. Mira Almita, you do like me, eh? You work for a little bit, then take off. *Ay,* you have a good time. All this work, work. Life's too short.

MARÍA: *No te preocupes, Almita.* Go to the night school for the English. Do your work and God will help you.

EVITA: *(Going up to Alma.) Oye, Almita, yo te puedo ayudar* if you dress up, get a new hairstyle, maybe a little make up around your eyes *y* a little gloss on your mouth and then your eyebrows … *(Lola interrupting.)* No. Just speak up.

LA CHATA: *(Raising her paper cup.)* Have a good time.

MARÍA: Light a candle, *a la Virgencita.*

EVITA: Just pull your hair back.

LA CUBANA: *(Gets up from her distant chair and goes up to Alma.)* Psssst! Pssssst!

(Alma goes up to her. La Cubana puts her arm around her in conspiratorial fashion, looks around to make sure the others aren't listening. All of the women are straining to hear. Evita gets the closest.)

LA CUBANA: *(To Alma.)* Get your green card and don't trust anybody, eh!

WOMEN: *¿Qué dijo? ¿Qué dijo?*

EVITA: Get your green card and don't trust anybody. Big deal.

LA CUBANA: *Y tú, y tú, estás jealous porque* you don't have green card, green card, green card, green card? You don't have one. You want to know why?

EVITA: No, I don't want to know why.

LA CUBANA: They see you. You tell secrets and immigration knows this about you. They know, they see you telling the secrets and laughing at the people, yes, they know.

LA CHATA: *Esa cubana está bien chiflada.*

LOLA: *Ay, no seas mala. Encerrada todo el tiempo* in these people's homes can make you lonely and crazy.

EVITA: *Ay sí,* remember Josie, *la negrita, se volvió loca y* she was chasing *la patrona* all over the house trying to stab her *con un* fruit knife.

MARÍA: *¡No! ¿Sí?*

EVITA: *Sí, la pobre, la llevaron al* funny farm.

MARÍA: *(Crossing herself) ¡Ay, Dios mío de mi vida!*

LA CHATA: *Y* Violeta ...

LOLA: *Sí, pero* Violeta wasn't crazy. It was her nerves, those people she worked for were mean, *la maltrataron mucho.*

ALMA: *Sí, a veces así es la gente.*

CLARA: Hmmmmmph! I don't pay attention to them. I just do my job. *Mira, Almita, cómo mi trabajo en* Encino ...

LA CHATA: Encino, Encino, *es todo lo qué sabes.*

CLARA: *(Ignoring La Chata.)* The daughter complains anytime anything is missing, *los* sweaters, *los* jeans. The mother say to her, "ask the maid."

LOLA: *Sí, sí,* ask "the maid," tell "the maid."

EVITA: Mr. Hodges tell his friends I am the "housekeeper."

LA CHATA: *Ay sí,* housekeeper. *¿Por qué no domestic engineer?*

(Laughing uproariously. All women laugh.)

CLARA: Hmmmmph! *(Then determined to go on.)* She say, "Please tell your maid to stay out of my room." Hmmmmph! I don't pay attention, I just come and I clean. That's what they pay for. Then *la mamá* she say to the daughter, "From now on I want you to take care of your own things."

(Women all mumble their approval with, "Sí, así debe ser" and "tiene qué aprender.")

CLARA: *Sí, entonces la hija,* she say to *la mama,* "Look at you. You no take care of your things. Your maids do all your work."
LA CHATA: Daughters are mean to their mamas.
CLARA: *Y la mamá* she get mad. *Ay,* then they fight, oh, so loud. I don't pay attention. I just keep cleaning. And *el* husband when he come, he no like to talk but he say to her, "Some day your maid will learn to turn off the lights in the garage."

(The women react.)

LA CHATA: *Pinchi pendejo,* turn them off yourself!
EVITA: No, you say, "*Ay, amorcito,* I didn't want you to hurt your toes in the dark."

(Women all laugh.)

CLARA: Hmmmmph! I don't pay attention. If I am sick or my boy is sick and I don't come, they try to make me feel bad. *Comó sí fuera floja.* The next day, she just gives me that look.

LOLA: *Sí, una mirada qué mate.*

CLARA: Hmmmmmph! She don't talk to me. Then she starts, she say, "Everybody should be equal, *pero* the people who like to be equal, they have to be responsible and work hard at their job."

LA CHATA: *(Gives the raspberries.) Oyes, a tú patrona le gusta hablar.*

CLARA: *Sí,* she like to talk. *Eso de* everybody equal. She go to meet with the other women, they talk everybody equal *y de los* husbands *cómo los hombres le tratan mal.* They talk how the woman must equal to men. Then she come to me and say, "Clara, you and me equal." Hmmmmmph! I don't pay attention. *(Silence.)* She don't know nothing. I been taking three buses every day to clean houses for fifteen years and she …

LA CHATA: *Comadre,* you ain't equal to her. Any *pendejo* can see that.

CLARA: *Sí, pues,* but she likes to pretend. But I don't pay attention. I just do my job.

(There is a moment of silence when Clara sit down. María crosses herself, more silence.)

LA CHATA: *(To Clara.) Mira lo qué hace.* You put everybody in a bad mood. *Andale, muchachas.* What happened to our party? Evita, go put the radio on the Cuban station.

LOLA: *Ay,* it's so slow today. Aren't the jobs coming in?

(All the women agree.)

NEW GIRL: *¿Cuando nos van a conseguir trabajo?*

MARÍA: *Hay qué tener paciencia.* Sometimes it's slow, *pero yo les voy a hacer un* special prayer and you will see. All the ladies will be coming to get you.
EUGENIA: *Sí, sí, hay qué tener paciencia, mucha paciencia.*

(She picks up her bag, rummages through it.)

ALMA: *Ojalá qué sí.*
MARÍA: *¡Claro qué sí!*
EVITA: *(Seeing Doña Eugenia with her bag.) Ay, Almita,* María's prayers *son muy fuertes, pero* maybe Doña Eugenia can make a special *Yu-Yu* so you get a job right away. Maybe a special one for me?
LA CHATA: *Y para la* New Girl, a *Yu-Yu* for her too.
NEW GIRL: *Ah sí, un Yu-Yu.*

(All the women get very excited. They surround Eugenia and sit on the floor except for La Cubana who stands up from her seat and starts walking out the door.)

LA CUBANA: I already have a job.

(The women sit on the floor in a semi-circle, holding hands, and intensely watch Eugenia as she rummages through her shopping bag.)

EUGENIA: *(Takes out an herb from her bag.) Yerba santa para la garganta ... no.*
LA CUBANA: *(Pausing just before she gets to the door.)* Don Félix told me that Sarita already has a job for me as a lady's companion in Bel Air and I start ...

(Eugenia gives La Cubana a powerful look and a soft gesture of her hand to sit down. La Cubana sits down quietly on a chair nearest the door.)

EUGENIA: *(It is a different Eugenia speaking in a rich, serious voice.)* Alma, *piénsalo bien ¿de veras, quieres trabajar?*
EVITA*: (Very excited.) Sí, sí,* Doña Eugenia. She wants a job with a nice lady and kids. She's good with kids and I want ...
EUGENIA: *(Sternly to Evita.) No le hablo a usted.* Alma Gutiérrez, *¿quieres trabajar?*
EVITA: *(Pauses, then with strength and belief.) Sí.*

(Lights go down in the back room and come up in the front room.)

SARITA: Something is going on here, I can feel it.

(She stands very still and sniffs the air until the end of the song. Don Félix bursts through the front door with confetti sticking to his sticky hair and all over his clothes, a few colorful paper streamers here and there.)

DON FÉLIX: *(Walking to his desk.)* What a wedding. *Ay,* honey, you should have been there. The bride, this big she was ... *(Stretches his arms out to indicate width of bride.) Una gorda sabrosa y chichones hasta aquí ... (Stretches his hands out to indicate huge breasts.) Ay,* her skin so smooth. She was delicate. When she got excited, she trembled all over *y el novio, un hueso,* a real skinny runt, he was. *(Laughing.)* I hope he's going to be all right. *(Don Félix sits at desk absorbed in the yellow pages of phone book. Sarita starts to pace back and forth in front of his*

desk. Don Félix finally looks up.) Something bothering you, honey?
SARITA: *(Still pacing.)* No!

(Don Félix continues to look for phone number.)

DON FÉLIX: You sure nothing's bothering you, honey?
SARITA: (Still pacing.) Absolutely nothing's bothering me, honey! (To audience.) First, the New Girl bites me. Then, I lose a job on *Eight is Enough* because I am too exotic. Without any warning whatsoever, Lola quits her job with Mrs. Camden. Mrs. Camden calls and yells at me. Mrs. Homes returns Alma, insults us and now wants me to find her a cheery Chinese person or a docile Mexican with no relatives. La Cubana is now well into an advanced state of paranoia and is seeing things. Chata is getting drunk. María is mad at me because I don't believe in St. Anthony. Lola's mad at me because, because, well, skip that one. *(Turns back to Don Félix.)* The jobs aren't corning in. Mrs. Camden is screaming for a replacement today and where are you? Behind the body shop marrying Laurel Hardy.
DON FÉLIX: Ay, honey, is that all? First of all, Mrs. Camden you don' have to worry about because we already have the money. She'll just have to wait for a replacement and the rest you just make up so M.B.'s.
SARITA: M.B.'s! M.B.'s! I ... I *(Sarita turns and talks to audience with her back to Don Félix.)* I don't believe this. His solution every problem is an M.B. A make believe.
DON FÉLIX: *(Talking to the back of Sarita as if she were facing him.)* Give them an illusion. Make up some hope, honey, make up a job.
SARITA: *(To audience.)* He does that just before they leave for the day. He makes up a perfect job for each of them so they'll come back next day. When they do come

back, of course, the make believe job is no longer available. It's all bullshit! But they keep coming back and coming back. What I can't figure out is, do they really believe it or do they want him to think they believe it so they keep him coming back?

DON FÉLIX: *(To Sarita's back.)* I know you think it's bullshit. Every body's gotta have a dream, honey. It keeps them together, like all those huddled masses that came to Ellis Island. They had their dreams, some of them even thought that the streets in this country were paved with gold.

(Lights up slowly in the back room. Women, except for La Cubana, sitting on floor around Eugenia, holding hands. Every now and then Eugenia says the name of an ingredient, making up Yu-Yu.)

SARITA: *(To audience.)* M.B.'s should be for big dreams, not for some piddly maid's job to keep your family on this side of starvation.

DON FÉLIX: Now, take me for example. I got a dream that I'll be businessman of the year. I'll be the speaker at the Rotary Club luncheon. *(He has made microphones out of paper cups placed on his desk pen set. The effect is of a speaker on a podium. He taps a glass of water on his desk, taps the microphones.)* Testing, one, two, three, testing, one, two, three. As a young boy in Guatemala, we didn't have a lot. *(He takes a pause. The phone rings and shatters his dreams. He answers it.)* Félix Sánchez Domestic Agency, Don Félix speaking. Oh, Carlos, *sí hombre.*

(La Cubana enters front room and goes up to Sarita.)

LA CUBANA: *Oyes*, Sarita, *a mí me prometieron ese trabajo de* ladies companion. It's my job.
SARITA: What job?
LA CUBANA: My job as a ladies companion.
SARITA: Ladies companion? *(Looks at heaven.)* Give me a break, will you?

(She walks to her desk as the other phone rings.)

LA CUBANA: *(Running after her.) Sí, sí,* my lady's companion job.
SARITA: *(Hand on phone about to pick it up.)* Believe me, Margarita, I haven't had a call for a lady's companion since the Bronte sisters left town.
LA CUBANA: *(Reaches over, picks up the receiver of the ringing phone and slams it down. Ring stops.)* No! *Yo se,* you're on their side. They all hate me because I have a green card *y la* Doña Eugenia make *Yu-Yu por Almita* to find job. *Por eso,* you're giving *Almita* my job, my lady's companion job.
SARITA: Calm down. Where did you get the idea I had a lady's comp ...

(Looks at Don Félix who has quickly gotten off the phone. He looks at them both sheepishly.)

LA CUBANA: Tell her, Don Félix, how you promised me the job with the rich, lonely old lady in Bel Air.
DON FÉLIX: *(Suddenly in an awful hurry.) Sí, sí, con su pe miso, voy al baño.*
SARITA: *(Angrily to Don Félix, enunciating every word.)* Which "rich," "lonely," "old lady," in Bel Air?
DON FÉLIX: *(To Sarita.)* M.B. honey, M.B. *(In stage whisper.)* Use your imagination.

(Don Félix exits to bathroom.)

SARITA: *(Gritted teeth.)* An M.B.

LA CUBANA: M.B.?

SARITA: *A, sí, sí,* M.B., which means, *"Muy bien,"* which means, as you know, "very good." I remember now thinking it was a terrific job for you, Margarita, but unfortunately the old lady ... she ... she died. This morning. So, she won't be needing you for the job.

LA CUBANA: She didn't die! My old lady didn't die! You're just giving the job to *Almita!*

SARITA: I swear to you the old lady is dead. And that's the truth.

LA CUBANA: *¡Cerda! ¡Mentirosa! ¡Puñetera!* ¡Bullshit!

SARITA: *Ay,* Margarita, such language from a ladies companion. Remember who you are.

LA CUBANA: I know who I am. I am Cuban *y* I have a green card, *¿y tú?* You are *pocha.* Mexican trying to be *gringa.* That's why the television people no want you, they know, they see, television people they see everything, they watching you. Even when the television off, they watching you. They see how you lie, how you don't stand up for Almita, how you are afraid to speak up to the *gringas.* The television people no want you to be on the shows because you dark face, *pocha prieta,* who don't tell the truth.

SARITA: Okay, okay, you want the truth? There is no lady's companion job. There is no job. Don Félix just made it up and even if there a lady's companion job, you, you would be the last person to get it. You're fat, lazy, overbearing, obnoxious, a hypochondriac, paranoid and crazy.

LA CUBANA: No! No! You lying.

SARITA: Oh yes, and you smell bad.

LA CUBANA: No, no.

SARITA: Yes, yes, let's have the "truth." You want to know what you smell like?

LA CUBANA: *No es cierto, mentirosa.*

SARITA: You smell of sweat, urine, boogers and cheap perfume.

LA CUBANA: *No, no, mentiras, no más mentiras.*

SARITA: Yes, yes, you do, you stink! I've sent you on countless interviews. People think you're a joke, a big smelly joke. God only knows, I've tried, I've tried, I have really tried. Nobody wants you either.

(They are both stunned. Sarita, with hand over her mouth as she watches La Cubana sink slowly into the chair by her desk, tears streaming down her face. Her lower lip trembling, gently but firmly and rhythmically, she pounds her clenched fist against the desk, muttering ...)

LA CUBANA: *No, no es cierto, mentiras, nomás se burlan de mí, todo el mundo se burla de mí; me quitan todo.*

SARITA: Oh, please ... I didn't mean it, you got me so angry. It just came out. *(Sarita crouches down and gently takes La Cubana's fist to stop the pounding. La Cubana turns and looks at Sarita. For a moment the two women look at each other. Lights softly up back room as we see more Yu-Yu ceremony.)* Don't pay any attention to me. You know, for an idiot, no one can out do me.

LA CUBANA: Only me. Everybody always make fun of me. Since I was a little, little girl, *todo el mundo se burla de mí.*

SARITA: Margarita, not the whole world, don't exaggerate, and not when you were a little, little girl.

LA CUBANA: *Sí,* that's true.

SARITA: There was always somebody holding you, kissing you, calling you *la consentida.*

LA CUBANA: *Mi papi* use to call me *Amorcita, o Corazón o Mi Reina.* We used to go to the beach every Sunday and make a *barbacoa*, a goat, a pig.
SARITA: Ah, geez, look at you. You got snot coming down your nose, mascara running, here.

(Hands La Cubana Kleenex from desk. La Cubana wipes her eyes and blows her nose loudly.)

LA CUBANA: Sarita, I will never be a lady's companion?
SARITA: I ... I don't know.
LA CUBANA: But they say in this country anything is possible.
SARITA: Yeah, look at Charo, *"Cuchi, cuchi,"* uhhh sick!
LA CUBANA: And I am Cuban, I am somebody.
SARITA: Absolutely!
LA CUBANA: *Sí,* absolutely.
SARITA: Margarita, what exactly do lady's companion do?
LA CUBANA: Oh, many things. They talk, they are friends, they take care of each other. I show you. I will be the companion and you can be the lady.
SARITA: *(With a cockney accent, scratching herself)* "Me mother was a lady."
LA CUBANA: *(Bringing Sarita a paper cup from the desk.)* Here, Sarita, you are the lady and I bring you your morning coffee.
LA CUBANA: *Andale,* Sarita, you start.
SARITA: Okay, okay. *(Sarita concentrates for a moment.)* "Ah, good morning, Margarita." (Takes a pretend sip of coffee.) "Oh, delicious coffee."
LA CUBANA: It's Colombian. Would you like me to take you to the park? It's a beautiful day.
SARITA: "Not just yet, maybe later. How are you feeling Margarita?"

LA CUBANA: *Ay,* lady, it's the cancer. Last night alone in my bed, I felt it like, *ay* ... like feathers on my arms ... *(She strokes her upper arms sensuously.)* On my neck, on my thighs, and even, even there. *(Quickly points to her genital area.)*

SARITA: "Oh, that nasty cancer!" Wait a minute, hold it. You can't talk to the lady about cancer. Nobody's going to hire you if you keep talking about cancer. People don't like to hire people with cancer. So, don't talk cancer, okay?

LA CUBANA: *Sí,* okay.

SARITA: Anyway, it really isn't cancer, Margarita. It's, it's, well, I feel that way a lot. Especially after I see a Robert Redford movie and have to go home alone.

LA CUBANA: *Ah, sí... (Pause.)* So the lady, do the lady again, Sarita.

SARITA: Okay, okay, I'll do the lady.

LA CUBANA: Ah lady, I like Ricardo Montalban, *ay* "the rich Corinthian," he looks just exactly like my husband.

SARITA: "The astronaut?"

LA CUBANA: *Sí,* he is on a secret mission.

(María comes to doorway of front room.)

SARITA: "Another one!"

LA CUBANA: *Sí,* he can't even come to see me. Maybe he don't want me anymore.

SARITA: "Margarita, he just doesn't want to ... to ... blow his cover; it must be very difficult for him, without you." What am I saying ? Hold it, time out. Listen, Margarita, two things you have to remember, number one, don't talk cancer, number two, don't talk about your astronaut husband. No secret missions, none of that stuff okay?

LA CUBANA: *Sí,* lady, okay?

SARITA: All right, now, go on, go on.

(Sarita takes another sip of her coffee, holding her cup in a lady-like fashion with an exaggerated pinkie sticking out. She turns and sees María, dismisses her with a "Hmmmmmph!")

LA CUBANA: *A ver, ah sí,* is it time for the park now, lady?

MARÍA: *Jose y María, ¿qué está pasando Aquí?*

LA CUBANA: Sarita is pretending she is the lady and I am the companion.

MARÍA: *(In disbelief, pointing to Sarita.)* She is the lady?

SARITA: *Sí, pobre, pero de tan buena familia.*

(We hear car horn honking, just as Mrs. Levine walks through the front door, harried and smoking one of her Shermans.)

MRS. LEVINE: Oh, María, thank God you're here. I need a replacement right away. *(Car horn beeps.)* Those guys in the car are going to drive me crazy! *(She turns and goes out the door.)*

LA CUBANA*: (To Mrs. Levine, as she is leaving.)* Ah, you saw them, too? María, María, *ya ves,* she saw those men in the car, too. The ones I saw this morning, the ones that are after me.

SARITA: Margarita, Margarita, rule number three, we don't talk about strange men in cars who are after us, you don't see them, okay?

LA CUBANA: *Sí,* lady, but ...

MARÍA: *(Interrupting.) Sí, sí,* Margarita, and go to the back and tell, ah, tell ... *ay,* Sarita, who would be good for this job? She don't need English.

SARITA: Almita, she needs it.

MARÍA: *Sí, pues,* Margarita, go tell Almita to get ready, *y qué si Dios quiere le tengo un trabajo. (Lights go up in the*

back room. *La Cubana runs to the back and runs into Don Félix on his way to the front.)* Mrs. Levine, she always needs a replacement, the girls just leave her.
SARITA: Well, Alma stays through anything. I am going to make sure she gets this job.

(Sarita goes to back room and runs into Don Félix who is going into the front room. We hear a car horn again and off stage voice of Mrs. Levine.)

MRS. LEVINE: Robert! Bernard! Knock it off.

(Mrs. Levine comes through the front door, takes a few steps into the front room, the horn blows again. Phone rings, María answers. Mrs. Levine sticks her head out the door and yells at the kids as Don Félix walks up to her.)

MRS. LEVINE: I told you two to knock it off.
DON FÉLIX: Ah, lovely Mrs. Levine. Such a pleasure to see you again.
MRS. LEVINE: Oh, I'll bet it is. If you could find somebody that would even stay a week. Nobody has stayed a week.

(During Mrs. Levine's last speech, New Girl has sneaked out of the back room. Phone rings, Don Félix answers it. María gets off the phone.)

MARÍA: The same money, Mrs. Levine?
MRS. LEVINE: Yes. No, ten dollars more if she stays the week.
MARÍA: Ah, I have the just right girl for you. Excuse *un momento.*

(María goes to the back room. The car horn beeps again. Mrs. Levine sticks her head out the door and yells at the boys as New Girl cautiously approaches Mrs. Levine.)

MRS. LEVINE: Knock it off, boys. Do you hear me, Robert? Don't stick your leg out the window ... the traffic. Do you hear me? Get your leg back in the car.

(Mrs. Levine closes the front door, turns around and finds herself face to face with New Girl.)

NEW GIRL: *Perdóneme, Señora, me fijé qué usted busca a alguien qué le ayude en la casa y pues yo soy trabajadora buena. Yo sé hacer todo en la casa. Por favor, señora.*

(Car horn beeps.)

MRS. LEVINE: Oh, I am sorry. I don't speak Spanish too well. I just took one year in high school. *(In a very slow, broken Spanish with a heavy American accent.) Yo me llamo* Stephanie. *(Car horn beeps.) Ninos. Muy mal.* Excuse me. *(Mrs. Levine* sticks her head out the front door and yells.) If you boys don't stop that, I am taking all of your privileges away, do you hear me?

(Mrs. Levine closes the front door, turns around and faces the New Girl.)

NEW GIRL: *(Talking rapidly.) Yo me llamo Elsa María Cristina López de Moreno. A mí me encantan los niños. En mí país yo tengo tres hermanitos, viven con mí mamá. Mi papá se murió y me he propuesto a mantenerlos.*

(Car horn beeps again.)

MRS. LEVINE: I got your name, I think, but I missed all the rest. I just took one year. All I can remember is the lesson on Isabel.
NEW GIRL: Isabel?
MRS. LEVINE: *(Slowly.) ¡Hola, Isabel! ¿Cómo está usted? Yo está bien. Yo voy a la biblioteca.* Of course, I can say other Spanish phrases*: niños watchando* T.V.? ... *lavando los* windows? ... Vacuuming *aquí ... (Car horn beeps.)* Excuse me, *yo spanko los niños.*

(Mrs. Levine goes out the front door. New Girl waits for her by the front door. Don Félix is still on the phone as lights get brighter and voices get louder in the back room. Evita putting the finishing touches on Alma's face and hair. Sarita brushes off Alma's skirt.)

SARITA*: ¡Apurate! ¡Apurate!*
LA CHATA: Sarita, what's all the fuss for? *La* Mrs. Levine, she's lucky to get anybody. I am telling you, Sarita, those kids *son diablitos,* it ain't such a good job.
SARITA: I want Alma to look responsible, neat, professional. Then Mrs. Levine and her kids will respect her.
LA CHATA: I am telling you, those kids don't respect nothing.
CLARA: Hmmmph! Carmela left Mrs. Levine *porque los* kids, they tie firecrackers around the toilets.
LA CHATA: *Sí,* Alma, cuidado when you sit down, eh? *Ay* Evita, you put too much pencil on her eyebrows. She looks like she got one line straight across.
SARITA: *Sí,* Chata 's right, here Evita, wipe it off. *(Evita wipes off the eyebrow pencil. Alma stands very still as the women appraise her. She has on her own skirt and blouse*

but all of Sarita's accessories, except for her own shawl. Sarita gives Alma a long critical look. All the women look at Sarita for the final judgement. All except Lola, who just sits there with arms crossed across her chest.) Hmmmm, something is wrong, I know. Here, Alma, take my sweater. Give me your shawl. *(They exchange.)* Much better. Now don't forget what I told you. Don't look sad. Pretend you're Hazel. Don't mention your relatives and don't get nervous. María, don't forget to say what a good cook she is.

CHATA: All this fuss, for *La* Levine.

CLARA: *A lo menos,* it's a job.

MARÍA: *Mira,* Alma, *los* weekends off *y te dan* $85, *si duras la semana.*

ALMA: *Qué bien, sí, sí, yo lo duro. (All women wish Alma good luck in Spanish. Sarita, María, Alma start to leave the back room, suddenly Alma stops.) ¡Mi Yu-Yu ! ¿Dónde está mi Yu-Yu ?*

(Eugenia gets the Yu-Yu and hands it to Alma. They get to the front room just as Mrs. Levine returns to the front room.)

MARÍA: Mrs. Levine, this is Alma Gutiérrez. I have good references on her.

MRS. LEVINE: *Hola, yo me llamo* Stephanie.

(Alma and Mrs. Levine shake hands. A very dejected New Girl leaves the front room.)

ALMA: *Mucho gusto, señora.*

(Car horn beeps.)

MRS. LEVINE: *Niños, muy malos.*

(Alma looks out the front door, looks back at Mrs. Levine.)

ALMA: *Ay qué chulos, muy bonitos. (Car horn beeps. Alma opens the door, sticks her head out and yells out the door.) Oigan chavalitos, les voy a dar una buena patada si no se me portan bien.*

(All honking stops. Alma puts her head in the door as Eugenia comes into the front room with Alma 's paper bag.)

MRS. LEVINE: Oh, María, could she come home with us now?
MARÍA: Oh, I am sure.

(Eugenia brings paper bag to Alma, hugs her as Mrs. Levine signs another contract and makes out and gives check to María. Sarita goes to the back room. Visually, we see Sarita tell the women that Alma got the job. The women all cheer. Chata pours herself another drink. In the front room, María, Eugenia wave goodbye to Alma and Mrs. Levine as they exit. New Girl returns to front room with broom and vigorously attacks cleaning the front room. Eugenia and María look at check. Don Félix gets off the phone and grabs the check from María as Sarita comes into front room.)

SARITA: Hey, María, we did it. Did you see Alma's face? She looked so proud and confident. I gave away half my clothes, but we did it.
MARÍA: It was God and Doña Eugenia's *Yu-Yu* .
SARITA: Sure it was.

MARÍA: *Sí,* sure it was. Doña Eugenia say Almita would find job with nice lady and kids. She makes special *Yu-Yu* .

SARITA: Oh, *Yu-Yu* , *shmu yu.*

MARÍA: Sarita, Lola is right. You really are a ... you don't respect the old ways.

SARITA: Listen, I believe in hard work. I can't do it all the time, but I know that's what gets you what you want. Not *Yu-Yus.*

DON FÉLIX: Sometimes it does, sometimes it doesn't. Me, I believe this ... *(Kisses Mrs. Levine 's check.)* But I don't like to any chances. That's why I am going to ask Doña Eugenia to make me a special *Yu-Yu* for the disco opening tonight.

SARITA: God save us from the *Yu-Yu* disco ... *(Sees the New Girl passionately scrubbing the walls.)* What is going on here? What's with Miss Peru?

NEW GIRL: *No se nota, pero yo soy muy fuerte. Yo soy trabajado buena. Por favor, señorita Sarita, necesito un trabajo. Mire, mire, yo se ... (Very slowly in broken English.)* I don pay *atencion, watchando* T.V., *lavando los* windows, one ... two ... three …

(Eugenia, María, Don Félix watch in amazement as New Girl continues counting. Slowly lights change as Sister appears and a younger Sarita appears, and a younger Sarita jumps and down, waving her arm at Sister.)

YOUNG SARITA: Sister! Sister, I know, I know the answer ... Franci Zúñiga, the statues of the Latina women, on page 324, were done by Francisco Zúñiga and he is Mexican. The statues are made of bronze, not pink marble and Mr. Zúñiga made them to sit outside on the earth. They're tough, they sit outside, through the rain, the wind, the snow, even tornadoes. They look soft, like my Grandma's lap, like you could hug them, but they are hard

and strong and heavy ... 2, 4, 6 even 100 strong men couldn't move them, not even Mr. Amador's truck.
SISTER: That's enough, Sarita.
YOUNG SARITA: They would need a bulldozer.
SISTER: I said that's enough, Sarita. Now, class, turn to page 375 and look at those extraordinary statues of Michael Angelo.

(Sister disappears. Lights dim, music from back room radio gets louder. La Cubana and Evita are dancing to Cuban music, with Lola, Clara and La Chata looking on. La Chata is drinking, Clara is knitting, Lola is sitting there with arms crossed, lost in thought.)

LA CHATA: *Chiiii, mira esa Cubana chiflada, sí, sabe bailar.*
CLARA: How fine Almita looks. That was smart of Sarita to make Almita look good.
LOLA: Smart? *¿Eso también quieres? ¿Qué Sarita le viste al gusto de los gringos?* She don't stand up for Alrnita when they insult her and then your *preciosa* Sarita dressed her up, so she won't look too Latina for the *gringos.*
CLARA: Sarita was helping.
LOLA: *(Interrupting.) No entiendes.* She is so ashamed that she don't think Almita looked good enough to clean the *gringa's* toilet.
LA CHATA: Ay, Lola, *¿qué te pasa?*

(Lola angrily gets up and goes to the bathroom slamming the door shut.)

CLARA: Hmmmmmmph! She needs a job.
CHATA: *¡Ay tú!* Work, work, maybe she's having trouble with Roberto. *(Sipping from her cup, she becomes*

reflective.) Comadre, men are nothing but trouble. That *pinchi gordo* of mine, even took my T.V. when he left me.
CLARA: Hmmmmmmph! Maybe you're lucky. My Xavier stays, but he runs around, *viejo vago,* but I don't pay attention. I work, I have my boy.

(Music has stopped, Evita flops down on the chair next to La Chata as La Cubana.fixes herself some beans with white bread from the table with bean pot.)

LA CHATA: *(To Evita.) Oyes,* Evita, this *gringo,* Mr. Hodges, he don't give you trouble?
EVITA: *Claro qué sí, todos los hombres* give trouble.
CLARA: *Todos son eguales.*
EVITA: *Pero los gringos son cobardes,* Men here, they are afraid, afraid of their hearts, their feelings, of the women. Doña Eugenia give me this … *(Fishes down into the front of her blouse and pulls out a little Yu-Yu bag.)* I put this under Mr. Hodges pillow for ten day then we will be married.
CLARA: Hmmmmmmph! Evita, forget it.
EVITA: *Sí,* you will see, in the church in a white satin dress with little, little pearls here. *(Touches her neckline area.)* With … with sleeves to there. *(Points to spot on upper arms.)* Long white gloves *con botones de* pearls, *toda de blanco, toditita de blanco voy a estar.*
CLARA: Hmmmmmmph!
EVITA: And on my head, a crown, a crown of pearls, the bridesmaids in long pink velvet dresses with powder blue sashes, carrying yellow tea roses and baby's breath and the grooms, all twelve of them, in white pants with a blue stripe down the leg and powder blue jackets.
LA CHATA: *Ay,* no, Evita, white jackets, more simple.
EVITA: White jackets then. I will keep it simple. But my *mamá, mamá* will wear a yellow lace dress with an orchid

corsage. *(Turns to Clara.)* And you, Doña Clara, if you would come, I would for get you an orchid corsage and you could sit next to *mamá*, please?

CLARA: Maybe I could get the day off.

LA CHATA: *(Getting very melancholy.)* The day I met my first husband Emilio, was two days after my sixteenth birthday. I shaved my eyebrows to look like Lola Beltrán. I cut off my *trenzas* and did my hair like María Félix in *El Rapto.* I was living with my sister mother on Soto Street. I walked down the block to the little *mercado* and there he was ... *¡hijo! ¡Guapísimo estaba! Y me dice, "Mamacita, ¿a dónde vas?"* Ay, he was a real lady killer. *Divino estaba. Me puso loca* and pretty soon he did me the favor and I got the big belly. My uncle Rufino told him he was gonna cut off his balls if he didn't marry me. So, we got married, but not by the priest. So, mamá said we weren't really married. She cried, poor thing *(Crosses herself.)* and that no good Emilio didn't even have the pantalones to stick around after Consuelo was born. *(Tums to Clara.)* Clara, I really had feelings for Emilio. All the rest, the guy from Pep Boys, the Samoan bartender, what was his name?

CLARA: Nickie, big Nickie.

LA CHATA: Ah is, big Nickie, even that *gordo,* when they left I feel lonely, bad. But I don't feel them in my heart like Emilio. *Ay, comadre,* people always leave me. *Pero,* it's the ones that leave me and stay in my heart, like Emilio and Consuelo, that hurts.

(Clara drops knitting and embraces Chata.)

CLARA: And me? I am not in your heart? I am here. I don't leave.

LA CUBANA: I met my husband when I was living in Miami at the space center.

*(María, Eugenia and New Girl come into the back room.
Eugenia takes New Girl to far comer of the back room.)*

EUGENIA: *No te preocupes, mi hija.* Sarita *te va a
ayudar y yo voy a hacer un Yu-Yu muy fuerte para qué te
encuentres un trabajito.*

*(Eugenia and New Girl secretly sit in far comer of the room
as Eugenia makes Yu-Yu for New Girl.)*

MARÍA: *(To Clara.) ¿Qué le pasa a Chata?*
CLARA: Hmmmmmmph! *Los hombres son diablos.*
MARÍA: *No todos,* some husbands is very good.
Pobrecito, my husband works so hard *y tambien es muy
dulce con la niña.*
EVITA: *Ay sí,* María, *qué suerte tienes,* your husband is so
good. Always happy.
CLARA: *Si,* María, *es verdad. ¿Cómo le haces?*
LA CHATA: *Ay* you, how do you think she does it?
MARÍA: *(Interrupting.)* I pray to *Santa Bárbara.*
LA CHATA and EVITA: *¡Santa Bárbara!*
MARÍA: Yes, you pray to *Santa Bárbara* and she will send
you a good man.
LA CHATA: With big fingers?
MARÍA: Big fingers?
LA CHATA: *Si,* if they have big fingers that means they
have a big *cosa ...*
EVITA: No, Chata, it's the feet, if they have big feet.
MARÍA: *¡No! ¿Si? Ay,* Chata, you can't ask *Santa
Bárbara* to bring you a man *con ...*
CLARA: Hmmmmmph! It's the nose!

(Lights start to dim and go up in the front.)

LA CHATA: *¿Ah, tú qué sabes?* It's the fingers.

LA CUBANA: On the moon it gets bigger *porque no tiene* gravity to hold it back.

EVITA: My cousin Chuyita is married to this man with big feet and she say ...

(We hear another, "¡No! ¿Sí?" from María as lights go down in the back room and up in the front room. Sarita is on the telephone.)

SARITA: Yes, *Eight is Enough.* Well, I wondered if they had made any decision. Yes, I'll hold.

(Second phone rings. Don Félix answers it.)

DON FÉLIX: Félix Sánchez Domestic Agency. Mr. Félix Sánchez speaking, ah, lovely Mrs. Camden, so good to ... *(Sarita gets Don Félix 's attention, shakes her head and points to herself indicating that she isn't in.)* Yes, yes, but of course, the contract? Oh, no refund; yes, of course. One of our many counselors will be happy to help you through this difficult situation. Goodbye, Mrs. Camden. We look forward to seeing you.

SARITA: *(Still on hold.)* Oh, please, tell me she isn't coming.

DON FÉLIX: I am afraid so, honey.

SARITA: Why don't you just give her a refund?

DON FÉLIX: Me? Refund? Just get her a replacement, honey.

(Don Félix leaves for back room.)

SARITA: *(Mimicking Don Félix.)* Just get her a replacement, honey ... one of your many counselors will help. *(Into telephone.)* Hello, not yet? Yes, I'll call back. *(Slams receiver down and takes a deep breath.)* I wish I were Betty in *Father Knows Best,* or I wish I were in *Mayberry* with Sheriff Taylor, Barney, Goober, Aunt Bea, Opie. We'd all be in the kitchen, eating one of Aunt Bea's famous pies, What's that, you say you took first prize with this pie over at Mt. Pilot?"

(María enters front room.)

MARÍA: Sarita, Don Félix wants ...
SARITA: Oh, María, you're just in time. *(Clearing path for Aunt Bea.)* "Careful, don't drop it now, Aunt Bea." Look, María, a peach pie, *(Pad of paper on Sarita 's desk had become the pie. They both look at it intently.)* all warm from the oven with a tender, flakey, golden crust. Oh wait, "Yes, Aunt Bea, María would love a scoop of vanilla ice cream right there on top." Wouldn't you, María?

(Sarita looks up and sees Ms. Harris as María, is still concentrating on pad.)

MS. HARRIS: Uh, make mine chocolate. I'd have to have chocolate.
SARITA: With peach pie?
MS. HARRIS: With anything. I am really into chocolate.
MARÍA: I am María, this is Sarita, she is always playing the games, making us laugh, ha, ha. Can we help you Mrs ...
MS. HARRIS: Oh hey, it's Cindy, Cindy Harris. We're neighbors. I'm into Public Relations. We're just down the street. I just got this great promotion. My girlfriend Silvia, she's the one who told me about you, she went into the hot tub business with her boyfriend, who is a total jerk. Anyway, I got her job. But my boss, he's a real sweetie,

says I am going to have to put in a lot more time, so I need somebody to look after my two kids, since my ex, the ultimate Virgo, will only take them on weekends. I really can't afford anybody, but Silvia said most of your women were ... well, you know, illegal.

SARITA: We're not responsible for ...

MS. HARRIS: Oh, hey, listen, it doesn't bother me. I mean I wouldn't dream of asking, it's not my business. Everybody's gotta do what they gotta do. I mean, as far as I am concerned, she doesn't even have to speak English. It would be nice, but I hear that's more expensive. I just want somebody young, clean, bright. I mean, I don't want one of those fat ones with the gold teeth. I always see those kind at the bus stop. God, I don't see how anybody can let themselves go like that and I guess they think the gold teeth are pretty. Anyway, I've never had a maid before, I mean, what do we do? Do you just send somebody? Could I get her today? Could I get somebody for $50 a week?

MARÍA: *(Taking a form and starting to fill it in.)* I explain everything, but first, I must put the little cross in this little box for child care. Cooking?

MS. HARRIS: Not much, they're into Mrs. Paul's Frozen Fish sticks. Do you think you have somebody?

SARITA: Hmmmm, no English, not fat, clean, young, bright for $50 a week. I don't know.

MS. HARRIS: Today? For $55?

MARÍA: Sarita, the New Girl. She is young, clean and she don't got gold teeth. She would go for $55, since this would be the first time she work ...

SARITA: *(Interrupting.)* The first time she's worked for a single parent. She's always worked in large families. She's great with kids, but she wouldn't go for less than $65 a week, too bad. She's very clean, energetic, bright, got her own teeth too.

MS. HARRIS: I could go to $60.

SARITA: And you wouldn't be sorry, she's perfect and a Taurus. They're great with kids, right María?

MARÍA: *Ah sí, sí,* the New Girl is the best one for you and she is from Peru!

(Lights come up slowly in back room. Evita and La Cubana are showing Don Félix, Lola and New Girl some new disco steps. On the radio "Disco Inferno." As Eugenia, La Chata and Clara sit on the side line Clara is mending Don Félix's disco pants on her lap.)

MS. HARRIS: New girl? From Peru? She didn't just get here, did she? Because Sylvia said they're not any good when they first come here.

EVITA: *(Dancing with La Cubana.)* See, this one's the "Latin Hustle."

SARITA: Oh, no, I can assure you she's been here a while. No problem, I'll get her, you'll see for yourself.

LA CHATA: *Ay,* I don't like this music. I like the Cuban music better or ...

MARÍA*: Ah sí, sí,* no problem, I explain contract.

(Lights dim but not out, front room. Exit Sarita.)

LA CHATA: *(Picking up one of Don Félix 's disco chains from chair next to her.)* Don Félix, how come you have this little gold razor blade on a chair?

CLARA: *(Shaking out Don Félix 's pants.)* *Aquí sus pantalones, no debe romperlos otra vez.*

SARITA: *(Entering back room.)* Quick, I think we got Miss Peru a job.

DON FÉLIX: Make sure María gets a check. I better go.

(Fast exit into front room.)

SARITA: *(To New Girl.) A ver, ¿Cómo se llama otra vez?*
NEW GIRL: Elsa María Cristina López de Moreno.
SARITA: *No, no más dile a la señora,* Elsa Moreno.
NEW GIRL: *Sí,* Elsa Moreno.
SARITA: Okay, now we have to make her look like she's been here a couple of years.
LOLA: *¿Y por qué?* Why we have to do that, because you say it?
SARITA: Why? Because the client doesn't want someone who just fell off the turnip truck, that's why!
LOLA: *Ah sí,* you always please the *gringo* lady, *pero yo no!*
LA CHATA: (To Clara.) *Ay comadre, fíjate,* they're using turnip trucks to bring them in now.

(Radio volume gets louder with "Latin Hustle.")

SARITA: Evita, you fix her hair. Margarita, get some lipstick. *A ver, Elsa, quítale la falda y ponle la mía ...*

The women all gather around New Girl and Sarita. Lola sits disapprovingly to the side. La Chata is too tipsy to stand, but yells instructions from the side.

LA CHATA: It's better with the belt.
EVITA: *Ay, ¿dónde está mi hair spray?*

(Finds spray and sprays.)

LA CHATA: Here, put one of Don Félix's disco chains on her for luck.
LA CUBANA: *Ay,* Evita, why you spray my face?
LA CHATA: This one with gold razor blade. It ain't going to help Don Félix if he gets into a fight.

EVITA: *Pues,* if you will remove your big Cuban *nalgas.*

EUGENIA: *(To New Girl.) Mi hija, no te pongas nerviosa, todas las cosas van a salir bien.*

LA CHATA: My *Gordo* love to fight, that's why my daughter didn't like him.

LA CUBANA: *Mira, no me faltes respeto, eh.*

CLARA: *Es más* ladylike without the belt.

EVITA: *Qué* cute.

LA CHATA: *Ay qué* mi Consuelo. She was such a cute baby. Look just like her father.

SARITA: Elsa, *si te pregunta la señora, le dices qué estas aquí más qué dos annños,* okay.

ELSA: *Sí, sí. Más qué* two *años.*

LA CHATA: Smart too, she wants to be somebody.

CLARA: *Qué barbaridad,* too much lipstick.

LA CHATA: She's going to the Brymann School for to be a dental assistant.

EVITA: *Mira,* Sarita, *la* Cubana *se freakió con el lipstick and el blusher.*

CLARA*: ¡Mira no más, cómo le pintó la cara a está pobre criatura!*

SARITA: *Ay* Margarita, you went crazy with the blusher. Here wipe it off.

LA CUBANA: *Así, me gusta, se ve muy apasionada.*

SARITA: She's not supposed to look passionate, she's supposed to look bright and responsible.

LA CHATA: Every day she say I ain't gonna be like you, cleaning houses, getting drunk. I ain't nothing like you, she say.

LOLA: *¿Qué dices,* Chata?

LA CHATA: *Mi hija, ay mi* Consuelo, *y la perdí.* "I ain't gonna be like you," *así me dice.*

LOLA: *Ay,* Chata, *es mejor qué tomes un cafe. Horita te lo traigo.*

(As Lola goes to get Chata's coffee, women stand back from tight circle. We see an Americanized version of New Girl, with a new slick hair style, make-up and Sarita 's clothes. Off to the side we see a different Sarita, with New Girl's clothes. Sarita looks stunned at New Girl as others stand back and exclaim, "Qué guapa," "Qué bien se ve," as New Girl struts around the room.)

EVITA: *Ahi va la* New Girl.
LA CHATA: *(Looking at New Girl.)* Consuelo.
SARITA: No, it's not right. I made a mistake.
LOLA: You make terrible mistake. Didn't you have eyes to see she was beautiful the way she was?

(Don Félix enters back room.)

DON FÉLIX: Hurry up, honey, I got her to sign the contract and give me the check and she hasn't even seen the merchandise. *(Sees New Girl and whistles.) Ay,* honey, we shoulda asked for more money.

(Doña Eugenia gives New Girl a hug. New Girl shows her the Yu-Yu around her neck, then drops it into her blouse.)

EUGENIA: *(To New Girl.) Buena suerte. Qué te vaya bien, hija. Mucha cuidado, mi hija.*
NEW GIRL: *Muchas gracias a todas.*
DON FÉLIX: *Andele, señorita.*

(Presenting his arm to her.)

NEW GIRL: *(With arm on Don Félix's hand, looks back at Sarita, with one hand reaching out to wave.)* Seño Sarita, *muchas gracias, lo agradezco mucho.*

(All women except CHATA stand around the door as though they could still see her.)

SARITA*: (to Eugenia)* She was beautiful the way she was.
EVITA: *Ay,* Sarita, she looks much better now.

(We see New Girl going into front room with Don Félix, timidly shaking hands with Ms. Harris, María interpreting and giving final instructions.)

CLARA: No, I like her the way she was. She had more ...
LOLA: *Dignidad.*
CLARA: *Sí, eso es.*
LA CUBANA: Now she looks good. She looks Cuban.
EVITA: *Ay tú,* Cuban, she don't look Cuban. I know what Cubans look like *porque* I been looking at one all day and I am telling you she don't look that bad.
LOLA: *(To Sarita.)* Are you happy now? You and all your changes. I am tired of all these changes.
LA CHATA: *Ya perdí mi* Consuelo.
EUGENIA: *Andale,* Chata, *tómate el cafecito.*
CLARA: Hmmmmph! *Mira, Lolita, esto no es nada.* You want to hear about changing, I will tell you. That no good daughter *de la* Chata, Consuelo, she changed her name on the papers for the school.
LOLA: Consuelo changed her name?
LA CHATA: *Si, pues,* María Consuelo Sandoval de García. *Ahora se llama,* Connie Gar.
SARITA: Your daughter is now Connie Gar?

CLARA: Connie Garr *(Trilling the r's.)* Two R's ...
Garrrrr.
LA CHATA: You shut up.

*(We hear front room phone ring and Don Félix answers.
We see New Girl saying goodbye to María and then starts
to leave out the front door with Ms. Harris. Second phone
line rings and María answers.)*

MS. HARRIS: *(Going out the door.)* Elsa Moreno. I'll
just call you Elsie.
NEW GIRL: Si, Elsie.

(Exit New Girl with with Ms. Harris.)

LA CHATA: *Ay,* I'm gonna be sick.
CLARA: *¿Ya ves? ¿Ya ves? ¿Qué te dije?* Evita, get a
wet towel.

*(Evita goes to bathroom as Lola and Clara make La Chata
drink coffee. Doña Eugenia massages her head, La
Cubana fans her and María enters the back room.)*

MARÍA: Sarita, you got a phone call, it's your agent.

*(Sarita starts to take it on the back room phone and
changes her mind, goes to the front room.)*

EUGENIA: *Buena suerte, mi hija.*

*(Sarita goes into the front room. Don Félix is on the the
other phone.)*

DON FÉLIX: *(Into the phone.) Sí, sí, pues mira, las pagué la semana pasada.*
SARITA: *(Into the phone.)* Hello ... I did? *(Don Félix looks over at Sarita, nods his head in affirmation.)* I'll be there, that's great, thank you, okay, goodbye.
DON FÉLIX: Okay, Carlos. I'll be right over. *(Hangs up phone.)* You got the part?
SARITA: Yes, I got the part.
DON FÉLIX: Honey, I gotta change for the disco. I can see it now, your name in lights over the Million Dollar Theatre: Sara Gómez. No. Sarita Gómez. No, no, something special like Estrellita Gómez. No, *ay,* I'm late. *(He turns to exit, takes a few steps, then turns.)* Estrellita Espan ... Eh! Eh, think about it.

(Don Félix exits to back room, lights change as Sister appears.)

SISTER: Sara, Sara Gómez.
SARITA: *(Drops her shawl and becomes a twelve year old Sarita.)* Yes, Sister.
SISTER: Is this your paper?

(Shows Sarita paper.)

SARITA: Yes, Sister.
SISTER: It's a very good paper. Why did you sign it Donna Reed? And last week it was Gidget. Sara Gómez is a beautiful name.
SARITA: It's a dumb name. It's Mexican.
SISTER: Oh, Sarita.
SARITA: Ah, Sister, you don't understand. I seen it on television.
SISTER: You *saw* it on television.

SARITA: Yes, I saw it on television on *Father Knows Best*. There's Kathy, Betty and Bud, and then there's *Mr. Ed*, the talking horse, David and Ricky Nelson. Even on *Leave It to Beaver* the people have names like June and Ward Cleaver, Eddie Haskel ... I never saw anybody named Jesúsita, Rubén or Sara Gómez.

SISTER: A rose by any other name would smell as sweet. Can't you see that Sara Gómez is a special name?

SARITA: No. When you think about it, Sister, "the Beaver" is a real weird name for a kid. I'll bet he's going to have trouble with it when he grows up.

SISTER: Sara, read your history books, then you will see what a rich, fertile heritage you have. Why, just look at California, filled with Hispanic names: San Francisco, Santa Barbara, Los Angeles, San Fernando ...

SARITA: San Fernando ... Whittier Boulevard.

SISTER: Father Junipero Serra ... Ramona.

SARITA: *Cholo* wagons ... Graffitti ... Gangs ...

SISTER: El Camino Real, San Luis Obispo.

SARITA: Homeboys, Low riders, Chebbies.

SISTER: Sara, Sara, listen to me. The first governor, the very first governor of California was a man named Pío Pico.

SARITA: Sara Pico. *(Trying it out.)* No, I'm staying with Donna Reed. *(Sister disappears.)* No, Sara Gómez, SARITA GÓMEZ!!!!

(Phone rings. Sarita answers. María and Lola coming into front room.)

MARÍA: Lola, Lola, *¿ya te vas?*

LOLA: *Sí,* I go before *la* Mrs. Camden comes *y tú amiguita* Sarita dresses up somebody for her.

MARÍA: *Ay* Lola, *no digas eso.* Sarita's trying to help ...

LOLA: *Sí,* I see how she helps by taking away what we are.

SARITA: *(On phone.)* Shsssh! Yes, Mrs. Walker, a good basic cook. Nothing fancy.

LOLA: *Sí* nothing fancy. *(Going to Sarita and phone.)* We got fancy, too, Mrs. Sarita can make us anything you want.

SARITA: Be quiet. I am sorry, Mrs. Walker.

LOLA: She'll dye our hair, change our names, anything you want, Mrs.

SARITA: *(With hand over mouthpiece.)* Will you shut up?

LOLA: No, I will not shut up, *gringa!* *¡Gavacha!*

SARITA: And don't call me names.

LOLA: *Gringa, gavacha, imbécil.*

MARÍA: *(Taking Lola aside.)* *Ay,* Lola, *¿qué te pasa?*

SARITA: Hello, hello, Mrs. Walker? She hung up.

MARÍA: *Ay, tanta rabia,* it's very bad for your heart.

SARITA: *(Slamming down phone.)* Well, I hope you're satisfied. That might have been a good job for Clara you just lost us.

LOLA: *¡Qué bien! ¡Me alegro!* One less chance for you to take away our *dignidad,* our pride.

SARITA: Don't point your finger at me. You haven't done anything all day but bitch and moan and walk out on your job. Did you come here for work? Well, pride doesn't get you work. Haven't you learned that?

LOLA: No. *Ay, Dios* must have saved me from that lesson. But not you, you have no pride. *(Sarita hangs up phone.)* New Girl, the way she was, *ay,* I think of my country, going to the fields to bring Roberto his food every day. On my bare feet, the sun on my back, the earth smell *y entonces* I would see him there in the fields. *Esa vista me mataba:* his beautiful brown body, strong, *disfrutando el trabajo.* My heart would stop, this feeling would enter my body, *ay,* I don't know how to say, *me invadía.* He look up *y me dice, "¿Qué trais, mujer?"* and I stand there, shy, my head a little away so he don't see my face. But I feel at the moment, every day, *en* these moments, that I belong here on this earth. *(Points to floor.)* I belong to him, my family, God. That is pride.

(La Cubana, Evita, holding up Chata. Eugenia carrying the shopping bags, comes into the front room.)

MARÍA: *Estabas* young and in love, touched by the noble fever.

LA CHATA: *Ay, comadre,* you would have been better for a touch of typhoid.

EVITA: *Vamos a llevar a Chata a su casa.*

LA CHATA: *Ay qué mi chavalona de Guatemala, yo soy pura Mexicana.*

EVITA: Tell Don Félix, I'll meet him at the disco.

LA CHATA: *Disco no ... (Starts to sing.) "Mexico lindo y querido, si me muero lejos de ti. Qué digan estoy dormido y qué me traigan aquí." (Sees Sarita.) Un* party to celebrate Sarita's T.V. job. Sarita, ask for cash, no checks.

MARÍA: *Ay, sí,* Sarita, Don Félix told us. I am so stupid.

EUGENIA: *Ya ves, yo te hice un Yu-Yu.*

LA CUBANA: She going to be big movie star and I will be her companion.

EVITA: *Y yo le voy a hacer su* make-up.

LOLA: *Ay sí,* congratulations, Sara Smith. Aren't you going to change your name, dye your hair, change your eyes, insult yourself, your family ...

(All women mumble, "Ay Lola," "No seas asi." Mrs. Camden enters. Chata falls down on the couch. Evita, La Cubana, Doña Eugenia gather by the couch and stand very still.)

MARÍA: Mrs. Camden!

MRS. CAMDEN: Well, I see my maid is here, Sara.

LOLA: I am not your maid.

MARÍA: *(Taking Lola away to other end of front room.)* *Cálmate,* Lola, *pórtate con dignidad.*

MRS. CAMDEN: Oh, you people. What you are doing is criminal and unethical and I'm not about to put up with it.

SARITA: Mrs. Camden, I will get you a replacement.

MRS. CAMDEN: You people don't seem to understand that when a busy person pays for competent, reliable help, they expect a competent, reliable person, *comprende?*

LA CHATA: *(Sitting up from couch.)* *Mira tú, vieja pinchi ...*

(Evita puts her hand over La Chata's mouth and pushes her back down on the couch as La Cubana sits nearly on top of her. Eugenia next. They giggle.)

MRS. CAMDEN: Ah, let me tell you something ... *(Looking at every one.)* You people think you are so downtrodden. Well, you bring it all on yourselves. Most of you know nothing about running a modern house. The repair bills I've had to pay for all the appliances you people have broken would support your families in Mexico. Most of you can't even take a simple phone message ... no sense of responsibility.

SARITA: Mrs. Camden, I think ...

LOLA: *(Tearing herself away from María's grip and interrupting Sarita.)* And you, and you come here to insult us. Don't worry, Sarita will find you a replacement, she is very good for that.

MARÍA: *(Taking Lola firmly aside.)* *Tranquila, tranquilamente.*

MRS. CAMDEN: That maid *(Pointing to Lola.)* with no previous warning, quit. It is customary to give two weeks notice. She didn't even call.

LOLA: You look at me like I'm a machine. So I act like machine. Machine don't give notice.

MRS. CAMDEN: Oh, we treated you very well, you took advantage of it. *(Addressing all women, even Sarita on the phone.)* Understand, please, that she had her own room and bath with her own T.V.. It is a very lovely room. I am sure she has never seen anything like it before in Mexico. She had nothing, so out of the goodness of my heart I bought her some nice uniforms. She eats the same food we eat. I gave her the advantages and protection of my home and this is the way she thanks us?

(La Cubana gets up from La Chata and stands by window, every now and then looking out.)

LOLA: Why, no one in your house call me by my name. I hear you, your husband, the children, all of you speak about me as your Mexican maid. Always you say, "Ask the maid, tell the maid." Each day you make me more nobody, more dead. You put me in nice white uniform so I won't offend your good taste. You take away my name, my country. You don't want a person, you want a machine. My name is Lola. I am from Guatemala.

MRS. CAMDEN: She is an illegal. She is an alien. And if I wanted to, I could call immigration on her so fast …

SARITA: It would what, Mrs. Camden?

LA CUBANA: *(Looking out window.)* Be quiet, they'll hear you.

SARITA: Mrs. Camden?

LOLA: This legal-illegal is the business of governments, but God put me, a human being, in this world. I am here because my children must eat.

(Clara and Don Félix in his disco outfit enter front room.)

CLARA: Sara, don't forget I am looking for work.
DON FÉLIX: Ah, you must be the lovely Mrs. Camden we've heard so much about.
MRS. CAMDEN: *(Looking at Clara.)* Sara, is this my replacement?
SARITA: No. No, Mrs. Camden.
CLARA: Sarita!
SARITA: We will give you a refund, Mrs. Camden.
DON FÉLIX: No refund. No, Sarita, *¿estas completamente loca?* No refund, Mrs. Camden.
MRS. CAMDEN: And who are you?
SARITA: *¡Juan Revolta!*

(Phone rings. María answers.)

LA CUBANA: *Ay,* Don Félix, please look. They are after us. *Ay, apurate. Ven aver.*

(She rushes up to Don Félix and pulls his arm.)

MARÍA: Don Félix, it's for you. An emergency, Carlos say.
DON FÉLIX: *(Going to phone.)* No refund. No refund.
MRS. CAMDEN: You'll hear from my lawyers. You, whatever you are, and your illegal aliens.

(Sarita clutches her chest and has trouble breathing.)

SARITA: Oh, oh, you! *(Pointing to Mrs. Camden.)* You, you. All my life, you, you hypocrite! You talk "legal," you hired her because you didn't want to pay the salary a legal person gets.

MRS. CAMDEN: Why should I? My taxes support your people's welfare.

SARITA: You! Your support? No! You depend! You're cheap, you're greedy. You want their labor, their cheap abundant labor. You don't care about the "legalities," *sí, your* "legalities," *chinga tus* "legalities." If you did care, you wouldn't be here whining for me to get you a maid.

MRS. CAMDEN: Whining? This person is crazy. I don't deal with your kind. Mr. Sánchez? Mr. Sánchez!

DON FÉLIX: *(On the telephone.) Sí, sí,* ah, just a moment, Mrs. Camden.

MRS. CAMDEN: Mr. Sánchez.

DON FÉLIX: *(On telephone.) Un momento,* Carlos. Yes, Mrs. Camden.

MRS. CAMDEN: Mr. Sánchez, what can we do to solve this matter?

DON FÉLIX: Do not worry, Mrs. Camden, I will take care of this matter myself. I will personally deliver to your home a fresh maid.

MRS. CAMDEN: In the morning promptly at 10.

DON FÉLIX: Yes, exactly at 10. It's been a pleasure serving you. *(Continues on telephone.)* Carlos, when did you give them the money?

MRS. CAMDEN: I am glad to see someone takes pride in their work.

(Turns and starts to walk to front door.)

SARITA: Pride! Pride? *(Sarita goes after Mrs. Camden ready to tear her apart. As Sarita takes a swing at Mrs. Camden's back, Lola grabs Sarita's arm, throwing her off balance, which causes Mrs. Camden to turn around.)* Let me go, let me go, I say. You pink, colorless pig!

MRS. CAMDEN: This person is crazy!

MARÍA: Hurry, lady, hurry. You must leave.

(Fast Exit, Mrs. Camden.)

LOLA: Sarita, I only wanted you to stand up for us, not to kill the woman. *Andale, un abrazo. (Sarita collapses into Lola's arms.) Ahora, sí, eres una latina completamente latina.*
MARÍA: *(Crossing herself) Ay Dios mío de mi vida,* you were going to kill her, Sarita. That's a sin. *Un pecado muy grave.*

(Doña Eugenia, who has been holding on to Clara during fight, goes to Sarita and comforts her with Lola. Clara goes to Chata and wakes her.)

CLARA: Chata! Wake up.
LA CHATA: *¿Qué? ¿Qué pasó?*
EVITA: *¡La* Sarita *se freakió!*
DON FÉLIX: *Esta seguro,* Carlos. I gave them the money myself.
LA CUBANA: Look, they are getting out of their cars.

(Evita goes the window.)

EVITA: *¿Quienes son?* Don Félix! *¡La migra!*
DON FÉLIX: *(Looking up from phone.) No. No puede ser.* I fixed it. fixed it. *(To telephone.)* Carlos, *hombre,* call my lawyers. *(DON FÉLIX drops the phone and runs to the window and looks.)* Sarita! *¡Viene la migra!* Immigration!

(General commotion as lights start to dim. Lola is torn out of Sarita's embrace by Chata. Women run towards back room exit. Except La Cubana who stands still holding

green card. Don Félix is at file cabinet putting papers into briefcase. Sarita walks slowly to stage apron.)

(As lights get dimmer we hear voices of immigration officers herding the women. Women's screams and protests are heard. Some women call Sarita with requests to call relatives. Chata singing "Mexico Lindo." Don Félix, carrying briefcase, and La Cubana run after Sarita onto stage apron as curtain falls behind them. Sarita has back to them as she faces audience.)

DON FÉLIX: Don't worry, honey. They can't touch you. You're free to go and my lawyer says they can't hold me. I didn't break the law. I didn't bring them up here.
LA CUBANA: And me, what about me, Sarita?
DON FÉLIX: Honey, you got a green card. You got no problems. I'll see you tomorrow, Sarita. Sarita! They'll all be back. They just put them on the bus and drop them on the other side. When they get the money, they'll be back. You'll see. *(Putting his arm around Margarita, they walk off the stage.)* Listen, Margarita, tomorrow there's this job with an old lady ...

(Sarita walks over and sits on the bus bench. Flute music, helicopter lights and sounds, barbed wire fence as we see creeping towards the fence another New Girl and her coyote.)

END OF PLAY

The Cuban Swimmer
1984

CHARACTERS in order of appearance:
MARGARITA SUÁREZ, the swimmer
EDUARDO SUÁREZ, her father, the coach
SIMÓN SUÁREZ, her brother
AÍDA SUÁREZ, her mother
ABUELA, her grandmother
Voice of MEL MUNSON
Voice of MARY BETH WHITE
Voice of RADIO OPERATOR

SETTING: *The Pacific Ocean between San Pedro and Catalina Island.*

TIME: *Summer.*
Live conga drums can be used to punctuate the action of the play.

SCENE 1

Pacific Ocean. Midday. On the horizon, in perspective, a small boat enters upstage left crosses to upstage right, and exits. Pause. Lower on the horizon, the same boat, in larger perspective, enters upstage right, crosses and exits upstage left. Blackout.

SCENE 2

Pacific Ocean. Midday. The swimmer, Margarita Suárez, is swimming. On the boat following behind her are her father, Eduardo Suárez, holding a megaphone, and Simóne her brother, sitting on top of the cabin with his shirt off, punk sunglasses on, binoculars hanging on his chest.

EDUARDO: *(Leaning forward, shouting in time to Margarita's swimming.)* Uno, dos, uno, dos y uno, dos,.keep your shoulders parallel to the water.
SIMÓN: I'm gonna take these glasses off and look straight into the sun.
EDUARDO: *(Though megaphone.)* Muy Bien, muy bien…but punch those arms in, baby.
SIMÓN: *(Looking directly at the sun through binoculars.)* Come on, come on, zap me. Show me something. *(He looks behind at the shoreline and ahead at the sea.)* Stop! Stop! *Papi!* Stop!

(Aída Suárez and Abuela, the swimmer's mother and grandmother, enter running from the back of the boat.)

AÍDA AND ABUELA: *Qué? Qué es?*

AÍDA: *Es un* shark?
EDUARDO: Eh?
ABUELA: *Qué es un shark dicen?*

(Eduardo blows whistle. Margarita looks up at the boat.)

SIMÓN: *No Papi*, no shark, no shark. We've reached the halfway mark.
ABUELA: *(Looking into the water.) A dónde está ?*
AÍDA: It's not in the water.
ABUELA: Oh, no? Oh, no?
AÍDA: No! *A poco* do you think they're gonna have signs in the water to say you are halfway to Santa Catalina? No. It's done very scientific. *A ver, hijo,* explain it to your grandma.
SIMÓN: Well, you see, *Abuela* – *(He points behind.)* there's San Pedro. *(He points ahead.)* And there's Santa Catalina. Looks halfway to me.

(Abuela shakes her head and is looking back and forth, trying to make the decision, when suddenly the sound of a helicopter is heard.)

ABUELA: *(Looking up.) Virgencita de la Caridad del Cobre. Qué es eso?*

(Sound of helicopter gets closer Margarita looks up.)

MARGARITA: *Papi, Papi!*
(A small commotion on the boat, with everybody pointing at the helicopter above. Shadows of the helicopter fall on the boat. Simón looks up at it through binoculars.)
Papi-Qué es? What is it?

EDUARDO: *(Through megaphone.)* Uh … uh … uh, *un momentico ... mi hija* …Your *Papi*'s got everything under control, understand? Uh … you just keep stroking. And stay … uh … close to the boat.

SIMÓN: Wow, *Papi!* We're on TV, man! Holy Christ, we're all over the fucking U.S.A.! It's Mel Munson and Mary Beth White!

AÍDA: *Por Dios!* Simón, don't swear. And put on your shirt.

(Aída fluffs her hair, puts on her sunglasses and waves to the helicopter. Simón, leans over the side of the boat and yells to Margarita.)

SIMÓN: Yo, Margo! You're on TV, man.

EDUARDO: Leave your sister alone. Turn on the radio.

MARGARITA: *Papi, Qué está pasando?*

ABUELA: *Qué es la televisión dicen?* (She shakes her head.) *Por qué cómo yo no puedo ver nada mis espejuelos.*

(Abuela rummages through the boat, looking for her glasses. Voices of Mel Munson and Mary Beth White are heard over the boat's radio.)

MEL'S VOICE: As we take a closer look at the gallant crew of *La Havana* … and there … yes, there she is … the little Cuban swimmer from Long Beach, California, nineteen-year-old Margarita Suárez. The unknown swimmer is our Cinderella entry … a bundle of tenacity, battling her way through the choppy, murky waters of the cold Pacific to reach the Island of Romance … Santa Catalina … where should she be the first to arrive, two-thousand dollars and a gold cup will be waiting for her.

AÍDA: Doesn't even cover our expenses.

ABUELA: *Qué dice?*

EDUARDO: Shhhh!

MARY BETH'S VOICE: This is really a family effort, Mel, and—

MEL'S VOICE: Indeed it is. Her trainer, her coach, her mentor, is her father, Eduardo Suárez. Not a swimmer himself. It says here, Mr. Suárez is head usher of the Holy Name Society and the owner-operator of Suárez Treasures of the Sea and Salvage Yard. I guess it's one of those places—

MARY BETH'S VOICE: If I might interject a fact here, Mel, assisting in this swim is Mrs. Suárez, who is a former Miss Cuba.

MEL'S VOICE: And a beautiful women in her own right. Let's try and get a closer look.

(Helicopter sound gets louder. Margarita, frightened, looks up again.)

MARGARITA: *Papi!*

EDUARDO: *(Through the megaphone.) Mi hija,* don't get nervous...it's the press. I'm handling it.

AÍDA: I see how you're handling it.

EDUARDO: *(Through the megaphone.)* Do you hear? Everything is under control. Get back to your rhythm. Keep your elbows high and kick and kick and kick and kick...

ABUELA: *(Finds her glasses and puts them on.) Ay sí, es la television ... (She points to helicopter.) Qué lindo mira ... (She fluffs her hair, gives a big wave.) Aló América! Viva mi Margarita, viva todo los Cubanos en los Estado Unidos!*

AÍDA: *Ay por Dios,* Cecelia, the man didn't come all this way in his helicopter to look at you jumping up and down, making a fool of yourself.

ABUELA: I don't care. I'm proud.

AÍDA: He can't understand you anyway.

ABUELA: *Viva ... (She stops.) Simón, cómosé dice viva?*

SIMÓN: Hurray.

ABUELA: Hurray for *mi Margarita y* for all the Cubans living *en* the United States, *y un abrazo ... Simón, abrazo ...*

SIMÓN: A big hug.

ABUELA: *Sí*, a big hug to all my friends in Miami, Long Beach, Union City, except for my son Carlos, who lives in New York in sin! He lives...*(She crosses herself.)* in Brooklyn with a Puerto Rican woman in sin! *No decente...*

SIMÓN: Decent.

ABUELA: Carlos, *no decente*. This family, *decente*.

AÍDA: Cecilia, *por Dios*.

MEL"S VOICE: Look at that enthusiasm. The whole family has turned out to cheer little Margarita on to victory! I hope they won't be too disappointed.

MARY BETH'S VOICE: She seems to be making good time, Mel.

MEL'S VOICE: Yes, it takes all kinds to make a race. And it's a testimonial to the all-encompassing fairness...the greatness of this, the Wrigley Invitational Women's Swim to Catalina, where among all the professionals there is still room for the amateur ... like these, the simple people we see below us on the ragtag *La Havana*, taking their long-shot chance to victory. *Vaya con Dios!*

(Helicopter sound fading as family, including Margarita, watch silently. Static as Simón turns radio off. Eduardo walks to bow of boat, looks out on the horizon.)

EDUARDO: (To himself.) Amateurs.

AÍDA: Eduardo, that person insulted us. Did you hear, Eduardo? That he called us a simple people in a ragtag boat? Did you hear…?
ABUELA: (Clenching her fist at the departing helicopter.) Mal-Rayo los parta!
SIMÓN: *(Same gesture.)* Asshole!

(Aída follows Eduardo as he goes to side of boat and stares at Margarita.)

AÍDA: This person comes in his helicopter to insult your wife, your family, your daughter …
MARGARITA: (Pops her head out of the water.) *Papi?*
AÍDA: Do you hear me, Eduardo? I am not simple.
ABUELA: *Sí.*
AÍDA: I am complicated.
ABUELA: Sí, demasiada complicada.
AÍDA: Me and my family are not so simple.
SIMÓN: Mom, the guy's an asshole.
ABUELA: (Shaking her fist at helicopter.) Asshole!
AÍDA: If my daughter ws simple, she would not be in that water swimming.
MARGARITA: Simple? *Papi … ?*
AÍDA: *Ahora*, Eduardo, this is what I want you to do. When we get to Santa Catalina, I want you to call the TV station and demand an apology.
EDUARDO: Cállete mujer! Aqui mando yo. I will decide what is to be done.
MARGARITA: *Papi*, tell me what's going on.
EDUARDO: Do you understand what I am saying to you, Aída?
SIMÓN: (Leaning over the side of the boat, to Margarita.) Yo Margo! You know that Mel Munson guy on TV? He called you a simple amateur and said you didn't have a chance.

ABUELA: (Leaning directly behind Simón.) Mi hija, insultó a la familia. Desgraciado!

AÍDA: (Leaning in behind *Abuela*.) He called us peasants! And you father is not doing anything about it. He just knows how to yell at me.

EDUARDO: (Through megaphone.) Shut up! All of you! Do you want to break her concentration? Is that what you are after? Eh?

(Abuela and Aída, and Simón shrink back. Eduardo paces before them.)

Swimming is rhythm and concentration. You win a race *aquí. (Pointing to his head.)* Now... *(To Simón.)* you, take care of the boat. Aída *y Mama*...do something. Anything. Something practical.

(Abuela and Aída get on knees and pray in Spanish.)

Hija, give it everything, eh? ... *por la familia. Uno ... dos* ... You must win.

(Simón goes into the cabin. The prayers continue as lights change to indicate bright sunlight, later in the afternoon.)

SCENE 3

Tableau for a couple of beats. Eduardo on bow with timer in one hand as he counts strokes per minute. Simón is in the cabin steering, wearing his sunglasses, baseball cap on backward. Abuela and Aída are at the side of the boat,

*heads down, hands folded, still muttering prayers in
Spanish.*

AÍDA and ABUELA: *(Crossing themselves.)* En la nombre
del Padre, del Hijo y del Espíritu Santo amén.
EDUARDO: *(through megaphone.)* You're stroking
seventy-two!
SIMÓN: *(Singing.)* Mama's stroking, Mama's stroking
seventy-two…
EDUARDO: *(Through megaphone.)* You comfortable
with it?
SIMÓN: *(Singing.)* Seventy-two, seventy-two, seventy-
two for you.
AÍDA: *(Looking at the heavens.)* Ay, Eduardo, ven acá,
we should be grateful that *Nuestro Señor* gave us such a
beautiful day.
ABUELA: *(Crosses herself.)* Sí, gracias a Dios.
EDUARDO: She's stroking seventy-two, with no problem.
(He throws a kiss to the sky.) It's a beautiful day to win.
AÍDA: ¡Qué hermoso! So clear and bright. Not a cloud in
the sky. ¡Mira! ¡Mira! Even rainbows on the water…a
sign from God.
SIMÓN: *(Singing.)* Rainbows on the water … you in my
arms …
ABUELA and EDUARDO: *(Looking the wrong way.)*
Dónde?
AÍDA: *(Pointing toward Margarita.)* There, dancing in
front of Margarita, leading her on …
EDUARDO: Rainbows on … *Ay coño!* It's an oil slick!
You … you … *(To Simón.)* Stop the boat. *(Runs to bow,
yelling.)* Margarita! Margarita!

*(On the next stroke, Margarita comes up all covered in
black oil.)*

MARGARITA: *Papi! Papi ... !*

(Everybody goes to the side and stares at Margarita, who stares back. Eduardo freezes.)

AÍDA: *Apúrate,* Eduardo, move ... what's wrong with you ... *no me oiste,* get my daughter out of the water.
EDUARDO: *(Softly.)* We can't touch her. If we touch her, she's disqualified.
AÍDA: But I'm her mother.
EDUARDO: Not even by her own mother. Especially by her own mother ... You always want the rules to be different for you, you always want to be the exception. *(To Simón.)* And you ... you didn't see it, eh? You were playing again?
SIMÓN: *Papi,* I was watching ...
AÍDA: *(Interrupting.)* *Pues,* do something Eduardo. You are the big coach, the monitor.
SIMÓN: Mentor! Mentor!
EDUARDO: How can a person think around you?

(He walks off to bow, puts head in hands.)

ABUELA: *(Looking over side.)* *Mira cómo todos los* little birds are dead. *(She crosses herself.)*
AÍDA: Their little wings are glued to their sides,
EDUARDO: Christ, this is like the LaBrea tar pits.
AÍDA: They can't move their little wings.
ABUELA: *Esa niña tiene qué moverse.*
SIMÓN: Yeah, Margo, you gotta move, man.

(Abuela and Simón gesture for Margarita to move. Aída gestures for her to swim.)

ABUELA: *Anda niña muvéte.*
AÍDA: Swim, *hija*, swim or the *aceite* will stick to your wings.
MARGARITA: *Papi?*
ABUELA: *(Taking megaphone.)* Your *Papi* say "move it!"

(Margarita with difficulty starts moving.)

ABUELA, AÍDA and SIMÓN: *(Laboriously counting.)* *Uno, dos ... uno, dos ... anda ... uno , dos.*
EDUARDO: *(Running to take the megaphone from Abuela.) Uno, dos ...*

(Simón races into the cabin and starts the engine. Abuela, Aída and Eduardo count together.)

SIMÓN: *(Looking ahead.) Papi*, it's over there!
EDUARDO: Eh?
SIMÓN: *(Pointing ahead and to the right.)* It's getting clearer over there.
EDUARDO: *(Through megaphone.)* Now pay attention to me. Go to the right.

(Simón, Abuela, Aída and Eduardo all lean over side. They point ahead and to the right, except Abuela who points to the left.)

FAMILY: (Shouting together.) *Para yà! Para yà!*

(Lights go down on boat. A special light on Margarita, swimming through the oil, and on Abuela, watching her.)

ABUELA: *Sangre de mi sangre*, you will be another to save us. *En Bolondron*, where you great-grandmother Luz Suárez was born, they say one day that it rained blood. All the people, they run into their houses. They cry, they pray *pero* your great-grandmother Luz she had *cojones* like a man. She run outside. She look straight at the sky. She shake her fist. And she say to the evil one, *"Mira ... (Beating her chest.) coño, Diablo, aquí estoy si me quieres."* And she opened her mouth, and she drunk the blood.

(Blackout.)

SCENE 4

Lights up on boat. Aída and Eduardo are on deck watching Margarita swim. We hear the gentle, rhythmic lap, lap, lap of the water, then the sound of inhaling and exhaling as Margarita's breathing becomes louder. Then Margarita's heartbeat is heard, with the lapping of the water and the breathing under it. These sounds continue beneath the dialogue to the end of the scene.

AÍDA: *Dios mío.* Look how she moves through the water...
EDUARDO: You see, it's very simple. It is a matter of concentration.
AÍDA: The first time I put her in water she came to life, she grew before my eyes. She moved, she smiled, she loved it more than me. She didn't want my breast any longer. She wanted the water.
EDUARDO: And of course, the rhythm. The rhythm takes away the pain and helps the concentration.

(Pause. Aída and Eduardo watch Margarita.)

AÍDA: Is that my child or a seal…
EDUARDO: Ah, a seal, the reason for that is that she's keeping her arms very close to her body. She cups her hands, and then she reaches and digs, reaches and digs.
AÍDA: Tó think that a daughter of mine …
EDUARDO: It's the training, the hours in the water. I used to tie weights around her little wrists and ankles.
AÍDA: A spirit, an ocean spirit, must have entered my body when I was carrying her.
EDUARDO: *(To Margarita.)* Your stroke is slowing down.

(Pause. We hear Margarita's heartbeat with the breathing under, faster now.)

AÍDA: Eduardo, that night , the night on the boat…
EDUARDO: Ah, the night on the boat again … the moon was …
AÍDA: The moon was full. We were coming to America …. *Qué romantico.*

(Heartbeat and breathing continue.)

EDUARDO: We were cold, afraid, with no money, and on top of everything, you were hysterical, yelling at me, tearing at me with your nails. *(Opens his shirt, points to the base of his neck.)* Look, I still bear the scars … telling me that I didn't know what I was doing … saying that we were going to die …
AÍDA: You took me, you stole me from my home…you didn't give me a chance to prepare. You just said we have to go now, now! Now, you said. You didn't let me take

anything. I left everything behind … I left everything behind.

EDUARDO: Saying that I wasn't good enough, that your father didn't raise you so that I could drown you in the sea.

AÍDA: You didn't let me say even a good-bye. You took me, you stole me, you tore me from my home.

EDUARDO: I took you so we could be married.

AÍDA: That was in Miami. But that night on the boat, Eduardo …. We were not married, that night on the boat.

EDUARDO: *No pasó nada!* Once and for all get it out of your head, it was cold, you hated me, and we were afraid …

AÍDA: *Mentiroso!*

EDUARDO: A man can't do it when he is afraid.

AÍDA: Liar! You did it very well.

EDUARDO: I did?

AÍDA: *Sí.* Gentle. You were so gentle and then strong… my passion for you so deep. Standing next to you … I would ache … looking at your hands I would forget to breathe, you were irresistible.

EDUARDO: I was?

AÍDA: You took me into your arms, you touched my face with your fingertips … you kissed my eyes … *la esquina de la boca y ...*

EDUARDO: *Sí, sí,* and then …

AÍDA: I look at your face on top of mine, and I see the lights of Havana in your eyes. That's when you seduced me.

EDUARDO: Shhh, they're gonna hear you.

(Lights go down. Special on Aída.)

AÍDA: That was the night. A woman doesn't forget those things … and later that night was the dream … the dream of a big country with fields of fertile land and big, giant

104

things growing. And there by a green, slimy pond I found a giant pea pod and when I opened it, it was full of little, tiny baby frogs.

(Aída crosses herself as she watches Margarita. We hear louder breathing and heartbeat.)

MARGARITA: Santa Teresa. Little flower of God, pray for me. San Martin de Porres,pray for me. Sant Rosa de Lima, *Virgencita de la Caridad del Cobre*, pray for me … Mother pray for me.

SCENE 5

Loud howling of wind is heard, as lights change to indicate unstable weather, fog and mist. Family on deck, braced and huddled against the wind. Simón at the helm.

AÍDA: *Ay Dios mío, qué viento.*
EDUARDO*: (Through megaphone.)* Don't drift out … that wind is pushing you out. *(To Simón.)* You! Slow down. Can't you see your sister is drifting out?
SIMÓN: It's the wind, *Papi.*
AÍDA: Baby, don't go so far …
ABUELA: *(To heaven.) Ay Gran Poder de Dios, quita este maldito viento.*
SIMÓN: Margo! Margo! Stay close to the boat.
EDUARDO: Dig in. Dig in hard … Reach down from your guts and dig in.
ABUELA: *(To heaven.) Ay Virgen de la Caridad del Cobre, por los más tú quieres a pararla.*
AÍDA: *(Putting her hand out, reaching for Margarita.)* Baby, don't go far.

(Abuela crosses herself. Action freezes. Lights get dimmer, special on Margarita. She keeps swimming, stops, starts, again, stops , then, finally exhausted, stops altogether. The boat stops moving.)

EDUARDO: What's going on here? Why are we stopping?
SIMÓN: *Papi,* she's not moving! Yo Margo!

(The family all run to the side.)

EDUARDO: *Hija! ... Hija!* You're tired, eh?
AÍDA: *Por supuesto* she's tired. I like to see you get in the water, waving your arms and legs from San Pedro to Santa Catalina. A person isn't a machine, a person has to rest.
SIMÓN: Yo, Mama! Cool out, it ain't fucking brain surgery.
EDUARDO: *(To Simón.)* Shut up, you. *(Louder to Margarita.)* I guess your mother's right for once, huh? ... I guess you had to stop, eh? ... Give your brother, the idiot, a chance to catch up with you.
SIMÓN: *(Clowning like Mortimer Snerd.)* Dum dee dum dee dum oops, ah shucks ...
EDUARDO: I don't think he's Cuban.
SIMÓN: *(Like Ricky Ricardo.)* *Oye*, Lucy! I'm home! Ba ba lu!
EDUARDO: *(Joins in clowning, grabbing Simón in a headlock.)* What am I gonna do with this idiot, eh? I don't understand this idiot He's not like us, Margarita. *(Laughing.)* You think if we put him in your bathing suit with a cap on his head ... *(He laughs hysterically.)* You think anyone would know ... huh? Do you think anyone would know? *(Laughs.)*

SIMÓN: *(Vamping.) Ay, mi amor.* Anybody looking for tits would know.

(Eduardo slaps Simón across the face, knocking him down. Aída runs to Simón's aid. Abuela holds Eduardo back.)

MARGARITA: *Mia Culpa! Mia culpa!*

ABUELA: *Qué dices hija?*

MARGARITA: *Papi,* it's my fault, it's all my fault ... I'm so cold, I can't move ... I put my face in the water ... and I hear them whispering ... laughing at me ...

AÍDA: Who is laughing at you?

MARGARITA: The fish are all biting me ... they hate me ... they whisper about me. She can't swim, they say, She can't glide. She has no grace ... Yellowtails, bonita, tuna, man-o'-war. Snub-nose sharks, *los baracudos* ... they all hate me ... only the dolphins care ... and sometimes I hear the whales crying ... she is lost, she is dead. I'm so numb. I can't feel. *Papi! Papi!* Am I dead?

EDUARDO: *Vamos* baby, punch those arms in. Come on ... do you hear me?

MARGARITA: *Papi ... Papi ...* forgive me ...

(All is silent on the boat. Eduardo drops his megaphone, his head bent down in dejection, Abuela, Aída, Simón, all leaning over the side of the boat, Simón slowly walks away.)

AÍDA: *Mi hija, qué tienes?*

SIMÓN: Oh, Christ, don't make her say it. Please don't make her say it.

ABUELA: Say what? *Qué cosa?*

SIMÓN: She wants to quit, can't you see she's had enough?

ABUELA: *Mira, para eso. Esta niña* is turning blue.

MARGARITA: *Papi?*

SIMÓN: *(To Eduardo.)* She won't come out until *you* tell her.

AÍDA: Eduardo ... answer your daughter.

EDUARDO: *Le dije* to concentrate ... concentrate on your rhythm. Then the rhythm would carry her ... ay, it's beautiful thing, Aída. It's like yoga. Like meditation, the mind over matter ... the mind controlling the body ... that's how the great things in the world have been done. I wish you ... I wish my wife would understand.

MARGARITA: *Papi?*

SIMÓN: *(To Margarita.)* Forget him.

AÍDA: *(Imploring.)* Eduardo, *por favor.*

EDUARDO: *(Walking in circles.)* Why didn't you let her concentrate? Don't you understand, the concentration, the rhythm is everything. But no, you wouldn't listen. *(Screaming to the ocean.)* Goddamn Cubans, why, God, why do you make us go everywhere with our families? *(He goes to back of boat.)*

AÍDA: *(Opening her arms.)* Mi hija, ven, come to Mami. *(Rocking.)* Your mami knows.

(Abuela has taken the training bottle, puts it in a net. She and Simón lower it to Margarita.)

SIMÓN: Take this. Drink it. *(As Margarita drinks, Abuela crossed herself.)*

ABUELA: *Sangre de mi sangre.*

(Music comes up softly. Margarita drinks, gives the bottle back, stretches out her arms, as if on a cross. Floats on her back. She begins a graceful backstroke. Lights fade on

boat as special lights come upon Margarita. She stops. Slowly turns over and starts to swim, gradually picking up speed. Suddenly as if in pain she stops, tries again, then stops in pan again. She becomes disoriented and falls to the bottom of the sea. Special on Margarita at the bottom of the sea.)

MARGARITA: *Ya no puedo* ... I can't ... A person isn't a machine ... *es mia culpa* ... Father forgive me ... *Papi! Papi!* One, two, *Uno, dos. (Pause.) Papi! A dónde está? (Pause)* One, two, one, two. *Papi! Ay, Papi!* Where are you ...? Don't leave me ... Why don't you answer me? *(Pause. She starts to swim, slowly.) Uno, dos, uno, dos.* Dig in, dig in. (Stops swimming.) *Por favor, Papi!* (Starts swimming again.) One, two, one, two. Kick from your hip, kick from you hip. (Stops swimming. Starts to cry.) Oh God, please ... (Pause.) Hail Mary, full of grace ... dig in, dig in ... the Lord is with thee ... dig in, dig in ... Blessed art thou among women ... *Mami*, it hurts. You let go of my hand. I'm lost ... And blessed is the fruit of thy womb, now and at the hour of our death. Amen. I don't want to die, I don't want to die.

(Margarita is still swimming. Blackout. She is gone.)

SCENE 6

Lights up on boat, we hear radio static. There is a heavy mist. On deck we see only black outline of Abuela with shawl over her head. We hear the voices of Eduardo, Aida and radio operator.

EDUARDO'S VOICE: *La Havana!* Coming from San Pedro. Over.

RADIO OPERATOR''S VOICE: Right. DT6-6, you say you've lost a swimmer?

AÍDA'S VOICE: Our child, our only daughter ... listen to me. Her name is Margarita Inez Suárez, she's wearing a black one-piece bathing suit cut high in the legs with a white racing stripe down the sides, a white bathing cap with googles and her whole body covered with a ... with a ...

EDUARDO'S VOICE: With lanolin and paraffin.

AÍDA'S VOICE: *Sí ... con* lanolin and paraffin.

(More radio static. Special light on Simón, on the edge of the boat.)

SIMÓN: Margo! Yo Margo! *(Pause.)* Man don't do this. *(Pause.)* Come on ... Come on ... *(Pause.)* God, why does everything have to be so hard? *(Pause.)* Stupid. You know you're not supposed to die for this. Stupid. It's his dream and he can't even swim. *(Pause.)* Punch those arms in. Come home. Come home. I'm your little brother. Don't forget what Mama said. You're not supposed to leave me behind. *Vamos.* Margarita, take your little brother, hold his hand tight when you cross the street. He's so little. *(Pause.)* Oh, Christ, give us a sign ... I know! I know! Margo, I'll send you a message ... like mental telepathy. I'll hold my breath, close my eyes, and I'll bring you home. *(He takes a deep breath, a few beats.)* This time I'll beep ... I'll send out sonar signals like a dolphin. *(He imitates dolphin sounds.)*

(The sound of real dolphins takes over from Simón, then fades into sound of Abuela saying the Hail Mary in Spanish as full lights come up slowly.)

SCENE 7

Eduardo coming out of cabin, sobbing. Aída holding him.
Simón anxiously scanning the horizon. Abuela looking
calmly ahead.

EDUARDO: *Es mi culpa. (He hits his chest.)*
AÍDA: *Ya, ya viejo* ... it was my sin ... I left my home.
EDUARDO: Forgive me, forgive me. I've lost our
daughter, our sister, our granddaughter, *mi carne, mi*
sangre, mis ilusiones. (To heaven.) Dios mío, take me ...
take me, I say ... Goddamnit, take me.
SIMÓN: I'm going in.
AÍDA and EDUARDO: No!
EDUARDO: *(Grabbing and holding Simón, speaking to*
heaven.) God, take me, not my children. They are my
dreams, my illusions ... and not this one, this one is my
mystery ... he has my secret dreams. In him are the parts
of me I cannot see.

(Eduardo embraces Simón. Radio static becomes louder.)

MEL'S VOICE: Tragedy has marred the face of the
Wrigley Invitational Women's Race to Catalina. The
Cuban swimmer, little Margarita Suárez, has reportedly
been lost at sea. Coast Guard and divers are looking for her
as we speak. Yet in spite of this tragedy the race must go
on because ...
MARY BETH'S VOICE: *(Interrupting loudly.)* Mel!
MEL'S VOICE: *(Startled.)* What!
MARY BETH'S VOICE: Ah ... excuse me Mel ... we
have a winner. We've just received word from Catalina
that one of the swimmers is just fifty yards from the
breakers ... it's, oh, it's Margarita Suárez!

MEL'S VOICE: What? I thought she died!

(Special light on Margarita taking off bathing cap, trophy in hand, walking on the water.)

MARY BETH'S VOICE: Ahh … unless … unless this is a tragic … No … there she is, Mel. Margarita Suárez! The only one in the race wearing a black bathing suit cut high in the legs with a racing stripe down the side.

(Family cheering, embracing.)

SIMÓN: *(Screaming.)* Way to go, Margo!
MEL'S VOICE: This is indeed a miracle! It's a resurrection! Margarita Suárez, with a flotilla of boats to meet her, is now walking on the waters, through the breakers … onto the beach, with crowds of people cheering her on. What a jubilation! This is a miracle!

(Sound of crowds cheering. Pinspot on Abuela.)

ABUELA: *Sangre de mi Sangre* you will be another to save us … to say to the evil one, *Coño Diablo, aquí estoy si me quieres.*

(Lights and cheering sounds fade.)

(Blackout.)

END OF PLAY

PROPERTY LIST

Scene 1

Boat
Megaphone
Binoculars
Whistle
Radio

Scene 3

Timer

Scene 5

Training bottle
Net

Scene 7

Trophy

Dog Lady
1984

CHARACTERS in order of appearance:

RAPHAEL
ORLANDO, the mailman
ROSALINDA Luna, the runner
MARÍA PILAR, Luna, Rosalinda's mother
LUISA RUIZ, (Doña Luisa) the Dog Lady
JESSE Luna, Rosalinda's younger sister
MRS. AMADOR, a neighbor

SETTING:
Los Angeles: a small barrio off the Hollywood freeway.

TIME:
Summer.

First Day

Early summer morning. The residential section of Castro Street. There is a large sun, and the sunlight has the particular orange hue that indicates the Santa Ana weather condition.

We see two front yards, enclosed by a low stone or cement fence. One yard is very neat, tidy almost manicured, with a rotating sprinkler watering the green lawn. The other yard is jungle-like, with strange plants in odd places, rubber tires, all kinds of other rubbish, and a sign in front that reads: "CURANDERA-HEALER". Each yard has a mailbox and on the far side of the neat house, there is a jacaranda tree.

Leaning against the fence is Raphael, a dark, brutal-looking young man of eighteen or nineteen. He has smoldering dark eyes. He is wearing a Cuban T-shirt, khaki pants, a dark felt hat. He is staring at the neat house.

RAPHAEL: *(Like music.)* Rosalinda!

(Enter Orlando, the mailman carrying his bag. Raphael runs away before Orlando can see him.)

ORLANDO: *(Walking.)* Neither rain, nor sleet, nor snow … Says nothing about the heat … not one word about the heat. *(He opens the mailbox of the messy yard and rummages through his bags.) Nada, ni modo,* nothing for you, Doña Luisa. *(Reading sign.)* "Curandera … healer." *(Shakes his head.)* It takes all kinds. *(Rosalinda comes out of the neat house. She is 18 years old, wearing a jogging shorts outfit. She is quite pretty and feminine. She does some warm-up stretches.) Hola* Rosalinda, *ay qué* hot! … It's a scorcher … it's a sauna … you could fry eggs on the sidewalk … it's so hot that … You gonna run? Today?

ROSALINDA: I'm gonna win. Orlando.

ORLANDO: You're gonna die! This heat could affect your brain.

ROSALINDA: *(Getting into starting position.)* I'm going to run around the world. Today Africa, tomorrow India and Saturday …

ORLANDO: On you mark. Get set. The whole barrio's behind you … Go! *(Rosalinda runs off. Yelling to Rosalinda.)* May all the Angels come down and blow you over the finish line. *(Walking off.)* Wish we had some rain, some sleet, some snow.

(Exit Orlando. The sun moves up a fraction in the sky to indicate passage of time. In front of the neat yard of the Luna family we see María Pilar Luna, Rosalinda's mother, wearing a fresh housedress and apron. She is standing on the newly swept cement path that leads to her front porch. She has a very determined look as her eyes scan the street. The Luna's neighbor, Luisa Ruiz, is slowly making her way through the rubble and rubbish in her front yard. She is dressed in a torn, stained, dingy white bathrobe. Although her lips are painted a bright red, her hair has not been combed. The overall effect is that she looks not unlike her front yard.)

MARÍA PILAR: Rosalinda! Rosalinda!

LUISA RUIZ: *Buenos días,* María Pilar. It's a beautiful Santa Ana day, *qué no?*

MARÍA PILAR: *Buenos días,* Doña Luisa. *Sí, sí* it's a beautiful day. Rosalinda! *Ay, dondé está, esa muchacha?* Rosalinda!

LUISA RUIZ: Are you looking for Rosalinda?

MARÍA PILAR: No, I'm doing this for the good of my health.

LUISA RUIZ: Oh. Maybe a tea of wild pepper grass.

MARÍA PILAR: I'm only joking, Doña Luisa, I'm already under the doctor's care, thank you.

LUISA RUIZ: Oh. You're welcome.

MARÍA PILAR: Rosalinda! Rosalinda!

LUISA RUIZ: Where is she?

MARÍA PILAR: *Ay,* Doña Luisa, believe me, if I knew where Rosalinda was, I wouldn't be calling for her. Rosalinda!

LUISA RUIZ: Sometimes if you whistle, they come. *El* Bobo only comes when I whistle.

MARÍA PILAR: El Bobo?

LUISA RUIZ: The big one. He's a … a … Labrador retriever. He only comes when I whistle. Once the people complained so I got one of them ultrasonic dog whistles, but when I blow it, Mr. Mura says it opens up his garage door.

MARÍA PILAR: Doña Luisa, my daughter is not a dog to be whistled for.

LUISA RUIZ: Oh. Now *El* Pepe, he's the cockapoo, they're not so independent, you know. He comes whenever you just call him.

MARÍA PILAR: Rosalinda! *(Holding her stomach.) Ay,* this screaming is making me acid. *(She yells toward the house.)* Jesse! Jesse! *Andale,* baby, get me the Rolaids. They're on top of *la llelera.* You hear me, Jesse?

LUISA RUIZ: You just say "Pepe, Pepe" and he just comes running, wagging his tail, happy to see you. Not like Esmerelda, she's the collie that stays in the window all the time.

MARÍA PILAR: Jesse! The Rolaids!

JESSE: *(Offstage.)* I can't find them, Mom.

MARÍA PILAR: On top of *la* refrigerator, I said.

JESSE: *(Offstage.)* There's only bananas on top of the refrigerator.

MARÍA PILAR: *Ay San Fernando de Los Flojo*s, when will you cure that lazy child? *Con permiso,* Doña Luisa.

(She starts to leave. Grabbing Mana Pilar by the sleeve, Luisa Ruiz points to the window of her own house.)

LUISA RUIZ: There she is. There's Esmerelda. You see her? Eh, you see her?

MARÍA PILAR: Yes, yes Doña Luisa, I can see her.

LUISA RUIZ: I call her *"La Princesa,"* she's a real snob, that one, just like royalty. Sits there all day.

MARÍA PILAR: That's because the dog is blind, Doña Luisa. And you should …

LUISA RUIZ: *(Interrupting.)* They gave her to me that time I was an extra in the movies ... the man said that she was the daughter of Lassie and she had belonged to *La* Liz Taylor.

MARÍA PILAR: You should take that animal to the veterinarian and …

LUISA RUIZ: *(Interrupting.)* It's the cataracts in her eyes. I can cure that. I know there is something I can use to cure that.

MARÍA PILAR: *(walking briskly to house.)* Jesse! Jesse! *María de Jesús.*

(Jesse comes out the back door. She looks disheveled.)

JESSE: Mom! Don't call me that.

MARÍA PILAR: *Ay,* if your Sainted Father *qué Dios lo tenga en la Gloria … (Crosses herself.)* could see you now. Jesse, *por favor*, stand up straight and comb your hair.

(She exits into house.)

JESSE: What for? I'm not going anyplace. I never go anyplace. Nobody even knows that I'm alive. *(Jesse slumps her way to Luisa Ruiz, who is busy studying the sky.)* I'm just drifting.
LUISA RUIZ: *(Looking at sky.)* Like a cloud.
JESSE: *(Looking at sky.)* Yeah.
LUISA RUIZ: *(No longer looking up.)* It was such a little cloud.
JESSE: *(Still looking at sky.)* A baby cloud, all fat and happy …
LUISA RUIZ: But it got bigger and bigger ...
JESSE: *(Looking up.)* It didn't know what to do, what to say. It wasn't ready ....
LUISA RUIZ: … and bigger until it blinded her.
JESSE: *(Looking at Luisa Ruiz.)* Huh?
LUISA RUIZ: The clouds in Esmerelda's eyes.
JESSE: The cataracts.
LUISA RUIZ: I put the pollen of the yellow passion flower on them, which is very strong, Jesse, they say within the flower are the symbols of the crucified Christ.
JESSE: I knew you were talking about the cataracts.
LUISA RUIZ: But it had no effect. I made a tea of that weed they call Juan Simón .... *(Raphael appears, lurking around the edge of the yard.)* It had no effect, but I still have the ginseng root in the shape of a cross.... *(She starts walking back to her house, mumbling to herself.)* The ginseng root with the leaf of the aloe plant.... *(She exits.)*
JESSE: *(Yelling to Raphael.)* My sister's not home! She's not interested in you. She's going to see the world. So you can stop hanging around the house. *(Jesse and Raphael*

stand, stare at each other for a beat. Jesse picks up a rock. Exit Raphael. Jesse shouts after him.) And you can stop calling on the phone and hanging up. I know it's you ... *(Softly.)* I recognize your breathing.

First Night

Lights change to night. The stage is dark, except for a large three-quarter moon and the small light in the bedroom window of the Luna house. We hear crickets and the howling of a dog. Enter Rosalinda from the house, in sweatshirt and pants.

ROSALINDA: *(Running in place.)* I'm going to run around the world, over oceans and islands and continents. I'm going to jump over the Himalayas, skip the Spanish Steps and dip my toes in the Blue Nile. I 'm going to see places I've never seen and meet people I've never known, Laplanders, Indonesians, Ethiopians.... *(Pointing and waving to imaginary people.)* Ay, mira Los Japoneses, y Los Chinitos and who are those giants? *Ay Dios, Los Samoans!* And I will speak many tongues like the Bible .... *(Shaking hands with imaginary people.)* Mucho gusto, yo soy Rosalinda. je suis Rosalinda, comment allez-vous? Io sono Rosalinda. Jumbo! Me Rosalinda from America. *(Jesse appears in window. The alarm clock in Jesse's hand goes off.)* Shhhh! Somebody might hear me.
JESSE: Somebody might mug you.
ROSALINDA: I'm too fast. *(She gets into starting position.)*
JESSE: Jeez, I wish we had a stopwatch. It's hard with this alarm clock .... Which way are you going tonight?
ROSALINDA: The northern route. Over the Pole.

JESSE: Say hello to the Eskimos.

ROSALINDA: Oh please, Jesse, hurry up.

JESSE: OK, OK. When the little hand hits twelve ... on your mark ... get set ... go!

ROSALINDA: *(Running.)* There's Fresno ... San Francisco ... Portland.... *(She exits.)*

JESSE: Weird. *(Enter Raphael. Seeing him, Jesse hides behind window curtain. Raphael paces up and down in front of the house, looking at the window. He picks up a small stone and throws it through window. Loudly.from behind curtain.)* Hey!

RAPHAEL: Psst ... Rosalinda ... Rosalinda ...

JESSE: *(In a breathy, sexy voice.)* Yeeesss?

RAPHAEL: Rosalinda, I know you got things on your mind with your big race on Saturday *pero* a man can only be ignored so much. *(Pause)* Listen, Rosalinda, *me voy a declarar. Sí,* I'm going to declare myself. *(Pause.)* "Rosalinda": a poem by Raphael Antonio Piña.

You are once
You are twice
You are three times a lady
And that is why you'll always
Be my one and only baby.
When I see you running
Running through the barrio
With your legs so brown and fine
Oh Rosalinda, Rosalinda,
Won't you be mine?

JESSE: *(Throwing a shoe out the window.)* Oh Christ.

RAPHAEL: *Ay,* Rosy, don't be mean.

JESSE: Her name isn't Rosy. So stop calling her Rosy. She's not gonna answer to Rosy.

RAPHAEL: Oh, you again.

JESSE: *Ay* Rosalinda! Quick somebody hold me back, I'm about to declare myself.

RAPHAEL: Listen you ... you ...

JESSE: My name is Jesse. I live here too ya know.

RAPHAEL: Where is Rosalinda?

JESSE: She's not home. She's running. She's in training and she doesn't see boys when she's training.

RAPHAEL: I'm not a boy, I'm a man.

JESSE: Oh yeah! ... Well ... eh ... er . . you're not her type. *(Raphael starts to exit.)* Hey Raphael!

RAPHAEL: Yeah.

JESSE: You know your poem?

RAPHAEL: Yeah.

JESSE: It wasn't bad.

RAPHAEL: Thanks .... Good night Jesse. *(He exits.)*

JESSE: Good night Raphael Antonio Pina.

ROSALINDA: *(Offstage.)* Mexico City, Acapulco, Puerto Vallarta, La Paz, Santa Rosalia, Encinada ... *(She enters.)* Tijuana, San Diego, *La* Orange County, Los Angeles ... Castro Street. *(Looking up at Jesse.)* How did I do?

JESSE: Huh ... ? I ... I lost track.

(Rosalinda sighs and gets into starting position again.)

ROSALINDA: OK, one more time.

JESSE: Go!

ROSALINDA: *(Running.)* Santa Barbara, San Jose, San Francisco ... (She exits running. Rosalinda's voice is heard sounding further and further away, as lights slowly change to day. Continued; offstage.)* Seattle, Portland, Vancouver, Alaska, the Bering Strait, Russia ...

Second Day

Early morning. Same large sun as First Day. María Pilar, wearing a fresh housedress and apron, is standing in front

*of her house, scanning the street. Luisa Ruiz, wearing the
same outfit as on First Day, is coming out of her house.*

MARÍA PILAR: Rosalinda! Rosalinda!
LUISA RUIZ: *Buenos días,* María Pilar.
MARÍA PILAR: *Buenos días,* Doña Luisa.
LUISA RUIZ: It's a beautiful day *con mucho viento.*
Some people call it the Santa Ana wind. Some people call
it the Devil Wind. Some people call it *El Siroco.* And
some people--
MARÍA PILAR: *Sí, sí,* it's a very windy day. Rosalinda!
Running, running, that's all that girl thinks about. *Ay* and
my stomach secreting the acid all morning.
LUISA RUIZ: Running, running that's all *El* Bobo and
Pepe think about too. They wake up, sniff the air and off
they go. I think it's something they smell in Mrs. Amador's
rose garden. Maybe it's a dead bird. *(She sniffs the air.)*
No. Maybe Mrs. Amador is making *chicharrones ... (She
sniffs the air.)* No. *(She sniffs more thoughtfully.)* It must
be that patch of wild peppermint. They say the scent is
very invigorating. Maybe that's where *La* Rosalinda is.
MARÍA PILAR: Doña Luisa, my daughter does not have
the custom to go smelling things in other people's garden.
LUISA RUIZ: Oh.
MARÍA PILAR: She runs to practice.
LUISA RUIZ: Oh.
MARÍA PILAR: She runs because this Saturday she is
entered in Our Lady of a Thousand Sorrows Marathon.
LUISA RUIZ: No! ... *Sí?*
MARÍA PILAR: *Sí,* Father Estefan himself went from
door to door to collect money for her entrance fee.
LUISA RUIZ: Oh, *pero* he didn't ask me for money. He
never came to my door.
MARÍA PILAR: *Válgame Dios,* three hundred young girls
from all the Catholic Diocese in California. *Ay,* I don't

know what those priests can be thinking. All that running shakes up a woman's insides.

LUISA RUIZ: He never came to my door.... I didn't give anything .... This Saturday? ... That's tomorrow.

MARÍA PILAR: They are making them run from Elysian Park to the Mission downtown.

LUISA RUIZ: Oh. That's far ... *El* Bobo could run that far.

MARÍA PILAR: It's not for dogs. It's for Catholic girls.

LUISA RUIZ: Maybe it's not too late for me to give ...

MARÍA PILAR: I cannot give to her the things she wants. I am a woman alone. Now if her Sainted Father, *qué Dios lo tenga en la Gloria ... (Crosses herself.)* were down here with us today ...

LUISA RUIZ: But it is important to give.

MARÍA PILAR: To give, *ah sí,* to give, *mira no más*, it's easy for you to say give ... and for him, my husband ... *(Raising her hand to heaven.) charlando* up there, playing the big macho with all the angels and the saints ... does he listen when Rosalinda says she wants to be educated ... she wants to see the world? Does he lift a finger? Does he put in a good word for us? No, *se hace sordo*, he pretends not to hear me. *Gracias a Dios,* Rosalinda knows how to work. She gets that from me.

LUISA RUIZ: She looks so pretty working at *La* Dairy Queen in her white uniform, just like a nurse. She always gives me free cones, soft-serve she calls it. She goes up to that big steel machine, she presses the red button, and *zas!* Out comes the ice cream, like a clean white snake it comes round and round and round. Rosalinda twirls the cone. She never spills a drop. When it just gets so high she stops, just like that. She never spills a drop. Then she leans over the counter, with -a-big smile, and says, "This is for you, Doña Luisa." That girl knows how to give.

MARÍA PILAR: I cry, I beg him, "*Juanito, mi amor,*" I say, "help us. It's our duty as parents to provide for our children. *Por favor, Papacito lindo*, I'm already sewing ten hours a day just to put food in our mouths." Did I hear from him? Nothing. *Ni una palabra. Condenado viejo* .... It took Father Estefan to put her in this race. Just think if she wins *el gran premio* it is a trip to Rome and all the expenses paid ... but he ... *(Indicating husband in heaven.)* didn't even help me with the entrance fee or the Nike running shoes. Father Estefan himself had to go door-to-door.

LUISA RUIZ: *(To María Pilar's husband in heaven.)* I swear he never came to my door.

MARÍA PILAR: She has to run like a dog to get somewhere in life. *Ay*, this acid is killing me. Jesse!

LUISA RUIZ: Run like a dog ...?

MARÍA PILAR: Jesse, the Rolaids. *(Jesse is coming out the back door, looking more disheveled than usual.)*

JESSE: I can't find them Mom.

MARÍA PILAR: *María de Jesús!* Look at you! *Por favor,* do something. Comb your hair. Stand up straight. Be a *señorita.*

(Exit María Pilar into house. Jesse walks up to the fence and Luisa Ruiz.)

JESSE: Please stop calling me that! It's weird .... I was real cute until I was twelve ... people always pinching my cheeks. *(Pinching her own cheeks.)* "Ay qui preciosa!" "Ay qui belleza." But now it's all this pressure.

LUISA RUIZ: Run like a dog ....

JESSE: Yeah, far away .... No, wouldn't do any good, I think it's some kinda contagious disease, no matter where you go people expect you to comb your hair and stand up straight. I try, but my hair keeps falling into my face and my body just has this ... terminal slouch ... it's like I got a-hunchback's blood ... or--

MARÍA PILAR: *(Offstage.)* Jesse! Jesse! What is this *porquería* under your bed?

JESSE: Maybe I wasn't meant to be a *señorita*.

MARÍA PILAR: *(Offstage.)* Dr. Pepper, Twinkies, Cheetos ...

(Jesse sighs and slumps her way into the house.)

LUISA RUIZ: She has to run like a dog .... *(She exits slowly toward her house.)*

MARÍA PILAR: *(Offstage.)* Snickers, Ding-Dongs, Ho-Ho's, Susie-Qs, a pizza!

(María Pila r's voice fades. Light changes to night.)

Second Night

Moon is fuller than First Night, but not yet full. There is a soft, low-energy sound under this scene, like something vibrating.

Luisa Ruiz, wearing a dark kimono, is standing in front of her doorway. She is holding her hands in front of her body, with a red flannel cloth over them. Raphael appears, lurking around the edges of the yard. Seeing Luisa Ruiz, he hides behind the jacaranda tree. As Rosalinda comes out of her house in her running outfit, Luisa Ruiz beckons to her with both hands and the red flannel cloth. This gesture is slow, as though she is hypnotizing Rosalinda.

LUISA RUIZ: *Ancho y profundo en pasos en el corawn en al Espíritu Santo. Espíritu Bendito. (Rosalinda slowly*

*waves to Luisa Ruiz and stands before her. Luisa Ruiz
makes the sign of the cross on Rosalinda. Rosalinda kneels
in front of Luisa Ruiz, who then opens her hands and
carefully holds out a special Yu-Yu amulet--a small red
flannel bag, the size of a large book of matches, which is
filled with special herbs and potions and hung around the
neck by a drawstring. Luisa Ruiz holds the Yu-Yu high
above her own head.) Niño Santo Lobo. (She brings the
Yu-Yu down and hangs it around Rosalinda's neck as she
starts her chant over and around Rosalinda.)
Cristo Santo de Los Lagos y las Montañas dice--
(She claps.)
Madre Santa de las Valles dice--
(Clap.)
Padre Santo de la Sombra y el Sol dice--
(Clap.)
Virgencita de la Niebla dice--
(Clap.)
Niño Santo de las Criaturas dice--
(Clap.)
Santa Ana de Los Vientos Secos dice--
(Clap.)
Santo de la Chupa Rosa dice--
(Clap.)
Espíritu Santo de la Mariposa dice--
(Clap.)
San Bernardo de Los Perros dice--
(Clap.)
Dios te bendiga
Cristo Santo te bendiga.*

*(We hear a dog howl. Raphael exits. Low-energy sound
fades into sound of TV cartoons as lights change to day.)*

Third Day

Early morning. Same large sun as First and Second Days. Sound of TV cartoons continues. María Pilar comes out from her house.

MARÍA PILAR: Rosalinda! *(Yells toward house.)* Jesse! Jesse! Turn off those cartoons, you hear me? I want you to go after your sister.
JESSE: *(In the window.)* Mom ... it's seven o'clock. It's Saturday.
MARÍA PILAR: Now,Jesse. Do you hear me?
JESSE: Jeez, what's the big deal?

(Jesse disappears from window. Sound of cartoons goes off.)

MARÍA PILAR: Your sister has to come back here and have a good breakfast. Then we have to go to *la* special mass for the runners where Father Estefan is going to bless her feet before the race. *Andale,* Jesse. Hurry up.

(Jesse comes out, looking very sleepy, wearing her pajamas with a skirt on top.)

JESSE: I don't believe this.
MARÍA PILAR: You don't believe anything *y mira no más,* how you look. At your age I was up at five. I was already washed, dressed and making *tortillas* for all the men in the house.
JESSE: *(Rolling up pj legs.)* Take it easy, Mom, I'm going. *(She exits.)*

MARÍA PILAR: *(Calling after Jesse.)* And stop at the market and get some orange juice for your sister. Tell them to charge it to my account ... and tell them I'll pay them next week. *(To husband in heaven.)* *Ay,* Juanito, you better keep your eye on that child.

ORLANDO: *(Enters.)* Reader's Digest ... bill from Dr. Mirabel. ... *Buenos días,* María Pilar. *(Handing her mail.)* Well today's the big day ... eh. And the whole barrio's gonna be there. How's Rosalinda?

MARÍA PILAR: *Ay* Orlando, how do I know? I am only her mother, I am the last person to know where she is or how she is. Have you seen Rosalinda?

ORLANDO: Now don't start worrying, she's just warming up for the big race ... whew! Qué hot ... looks like it's going to be another scorcher.

MARÍA PILAR: Running, running. The whole thing is affecting my nerves.

ORLANDO: It's the Santa Ana winds, they affect people.

MARÍA PILAR: Por favor Orlando, if you see her tell her to come home.

ORLANDO: Of course María Pilar, "Go home at once," that's what I'll tell her. *(Turning to go.)* See you at the race. *(He exits.)*

MARÍA PILAR: *(Walking to house.)* Big race or no big race a person should tell their mother, a person should eat their breakfast.

(Exit María Pilar. Sun moves up a fraction in sky to indicate passage of time. Rosalinda zooms past the house. Enter Jesse, running, carrying a paper bag; one of her pj legs has fallen down.)

JESSE: *Amaa! Amaa!*

MARÍA PILAR: *(Comes out of house.)* Ay por Dios, Jesse, walk *coma una dama ... un* lady.

JESSE: Ma, wait'll I tell you what Rosalinda did.

MARÍA PILAR: And where's your sister? Did you tell her about *la* special mass?

JESSE: I tried, Mom, but she just barked at me. OK. I'm walking down Castro Street. I'm right in front of Arganda's Garage. When Manny Arganda slides out from under a '68 Chevy, stands up and says, "Hey Essé, what's with jur seester?" I tell him to drop dead. He says, "OK. Esse, hab a nice dey." He thinks he's so cool.

MARÍA PILAR: Jesse.

JESSE: OK, OK. That's when I see Rosalinda, with Pepe and Bobo. I yell at her, I say, "Rosalinda, Mom says to come home," that's when she barked at me. Then she turns around and runs up to this car.... It was a black Impala with a little red racing stripe all along the side and real pretty red letters on the door that said "Danny Little Red Lopez."

MARÍA PILAR: *Por favor* Jesse.

JESSE: OK, OK. So she runs up to the car, and Mom ... you won't believe this ... she jumps over the car! ... The black Impala, she jumps over it! ... Just like *la* Wonder Woman ... and she wasn't even breathing hard.

MARÍA PILAR: Jesse, why do you lie?

JESSE: Mom, it's exactly what happened. And when I went to the market they said Rosalinda charged a pound of chopped meat and bones.

MARÍA PILAR: That's ridiculous. Your sister never eats meat. Didn't you tell her to get home and about the mass?

JESSE: I couldn't catch her. She's so fast. The last time I saw her she's standing by the stoplight going like this ....

(Does an imitation of a dog running in place. Paws out, tongue out like a dog, panting.)

MARÍA PILAR: Ave María Santisima, I told her never to bounce like that. She's gonna break her eggs.

JESSE: Not eggs, chopped beef.

MARÍA PILAR: I'm talking about her ovaries.

JESSE: Ovaries?

MARÍA PILAR: She's going to ruin her ovaries running like that.

JESSE: Ah Mom, I'm sure ...

MARÍA PILAR: *La verdad!* Any doctor will tell you bouncing and riding a motorcycle is going to break your eggs.

JESSE: Uuggh. Disgusting. I'm going in for a soda.

MARÍA PILAR: No *señorita,* not before your breakfast.

JESSE: Eeewww Mom, please, I don't want breakfast. I just want a soda.

MARÍA PILAR: All right baby, all right. You stay here in case your sister runs by and I'll get you the soda ... but don't drink it too fast. If you drink ice-cold soda too fast it gives you bad gas.

JESSE:. Mom!

MARÍA PILAR: Ah *sí,* you laugh *pero* I've known people who have died of these things. *(Exits to house.)*

JESSE: Oh yeah? When I'm eighteen I'm going to ride a big black Harley Davidson motorcycle that has "*La* Jesse" painted on the side of the gas tank. I'll be jumping over cars, zooming along dusty, bumpy desert trails, and doing loop-dee-loos on the Ventura Freeway. All this, while drinking an ice ... cold ... soda real fast before breakfast! *(We hear the sound of a pack of dogs barking and see Rosalinda running from U.L. to U.R.—a flash of her flying, wild black hair as she runs by. Jesse runs after Rosalinda.)* Rosalinda! Rosalinda! *(As she exits.)* Rosalinda Mom says for you --*(More barking. Off- stage.)* Rosalinda wait ... !

(María Pilar runs out the back door with a bottle of soda and a glass in her hands.)

MARÍA PILAR: Jesse ... ! Rosalinda ... ! Come back here. This is no time to be playing. *(María Pilar runs around the back of the house and comes out in front. Enter Mrs. Amador. She is out of breath, her hair is askew. She is splattered with mud and rose petals. She carries a broken rosebush. She leans against the fence, trying to catch her breath.) Señora! Qué le pasa? (Out of breath, Mrs. Amador struggles to speak.) Andale* Mrs. Amador, make an effort. Speak to me.

MRS. AMADOR: Rosalinda ... ! The dogs ... !

MARÍA PILAR: *Qué? Qué? Qué dices de* Rosalinda?

MRS. AMADOR: Rosalinda *y los perros* destroyed my rose garden!

MARÍA PILAR: No ... No ...

MRS. AMADOR: *Si, si,* all my roses. *La* Yellow Rose *de* Texas ... *las* tea roses, *La* Eleanor Roosevelt ... *La* Jacqueline Kennedy ... *y está* ... *(Holding up broken rosebush.) La* Mamie Eisenhower. *(The sound of dogs barking is heard.) Here they come ... here they come ...*

(Rosalinda runs through, U.R. to U.L., followed by a worn out Jesse.)

JESSE: *(Running to her mother.)* Mom, Mom you should see Rosalinda! She's chasing cars down Castro Street! She's ... !

MRS. AMADOR: *(Interrupting.)* You should see what she did to, my rose garden!!

MARÍA PILAR: I'm telling you it was those dogs next door.

MRS. AMADOR: *Pero* Rosalinda was with them! She was one of them. All wild-looking she was *así, mira ... (Baring her teeth, imitating Rosalinda's wild look.) Ay!* And blood all around her mouth. (Crossing herself.) It makes me tremble to think of it.

MARÍA PILAR: Blood around her mouth.
JESSE: Aw Mom, that was just from the raw meat she was eating.

(Enter Orlando, in a state of disarray, strap on mailbag broken, pants leg torn.)

ORLANDO: *La* Rosalinda *se freakió.*
MARÍA PILAR: Where is she!? Where did she go?
JESSE: She's OK, Mom, she's over at the park catching frisbees between her teeth. She's really good. You should see her.
MRS. AMADOR: She's on drugs. I've seen it. They go crazy.
JESSE: She's not crazy.
MARÍA PILAR: *(Crying.)* She can't even take Contac.
MRS. AMADOR: That's how they start. First the Contac and then the --*(Luisa Ruiz enters to her front yard.)*
LUISA RUIZ: Pepe! Pepe! Bobo!

(Enter Raphael running.)

RAPHAEL: Jesse! Jesse! Rosalinda's in ... *(Seeing Luisa Ruiz and pointing at her.)* She's the one! *La* Dog Lady! She gave her something. She put a curse on her. She turned her into a dog! I seen her do it.
MARÍA PILAR: *(To Luisa Ruiz.)* What have you done to my daughter?
MRS. AMADOR: Drugs! She gave her drugs. She's a pusher.
RAPHAEL: I seen her. She put something around her neck. And said spooky words over her.
MARÍA PILAR: *(Taking Luisa Ruiz by the shoulders, shaking her.)* What did you do to Rosalinda? What did you give her?

MRS. AMADOR: Speed! I bet that's what she gave her.

ORLANDO: *(Pulling María Pilar away from Luisa Ruiz.)* Give her a chance to talk. *Orale,* Doña Luisa. Did you give Rosalinda something?

LUISA RUIZ: She had to run like a dog ... I gave her the Spirit ... the Dog Spirit. It won't hurt her.

MRS. AMADOR: *(Crossing herself.)* Devil's work. *Ave, Dios,* she's a *bruja,* a witch. Where's my cross? *(Searching for cross at her neck.)* Jesse! Don't look at her. *(Pulling Jesse's face away.)* Nobody look at her eyes.

(All shield their eyes, except Orlando.)

ORLANDO: *Cálmanse! Y* stop talking nonsense.

MRS. AMADOR: *Qué* nonsense and *qué nada!* Didn't Father Estefan himself say that she made the dog in the window blind with all them herbs she put in the dog's eyes? Didn't he? Didn't he?

MARÍA PILAR: *Sí, sí,* he said to keep away from her. *(Crying.)* She's turned my daughter into a dog.

JESSE: Mom!

(Raphael, shielding his eyes, pulls a switchblade and points it at Luisa Ruiz's throat.)

RAPHAEL: Turn her back, Dog Lady.

ORLANDO: Raphael ... put it away. Now everybody calm down. It's just these damn Santa winds. It drives people crazy.

JESSE: She's not crazy.

MARÍA PILAR: *Por favor* Doña Luisa, you're a powerful woman .... I beg you, bring me back my daughter.

(Luisa Ruiz rummages in her pockets and pulls out an ultrasonic dog whistle. As she pulls it out, everybody stands back. She blows it. Mrs. Amador crosses herself, gasps, and points across the street.)

MRS. AMADOR: *Ay! Mira* Mr. Mura's garage door opened all by itself.

(They all turn around and look in shocked silence. Raphael drops his knife. One by one all cross themselves, except for Luisa Ruiz and Jesse. Jesse stands up on the fence and looks up and down the street.)

JESSE: Here she comes. Wow! Rosalinda that was great.

(Rosalinda enters running. She continues running in place. Her hair is messy and wild. She is splattered with mud and rose petals. She has a keenly determined look in her eyes and holds a frisbee between her teeth.)

MARÍA PILAR: Rosalinda, where were you? And why didn't you come when I called? *(Rosalinda drops frisbee at María Pilar's feet.)* No *señorita*, I'm not playing games with you.
MRS. AMADOR: *(Passing her hands before Rosalinda's face.)* Rosalinda ... how do you feel?
JESSE: Fine! She feels fine!
ORLANDO: You're all right, eh Rosalinda?
JESSE: Of course she's all right.
MARÍA PILAR: Rosalinda, I want you to go to bed.
JESSE: Not now, she'll be late for the race, Ready? Rome, here comes Rosalinda.

(Exit Rosalinda, running. The others look at one another. Then all run offstage after Rosalinda, except for Luisa Ruiz, and Raphael, who lags slowly behind.)

RAPHAEL: *(Exiting slowly.)* A man can only take so much. She's never home, she's a lot of trouble, running, jumping, barking. Women!

(Luisa Ruiz stands onstage alone for a beat. We hear the sound of dogs barking. She goes to the alleyway.)

LUISA RUIZ: Pepe! Bobo! No, you can't go ... it's only for Catholic girls. We're not invited. *(She runs offstage after the dogs.)*

Third Night

There is a full moon. The sound of a Mariachi band playing "Guadalajara," and other party sounds. María Pilar in front of her house, in a party dress, hanging a banner proclaiming "Rosalinda Number One." Enter Mrs. Amador carrying a big plate.

MRS. AMADOR: *Tamales estilo Jalisco.*
MARÍA PILAR: Just think, she's going to Rome and all the expenses paid.
MRS. AMADOR: What about the woof! woof!

(Rosalinda comes out of the house. Mrs. Amador jumps back and looks at Rosalinda very cautiously.)

ROSALINDA: She hasn't come yet? She said she would come.

MARÍA PILAR: Now don't get excited, if Doña Luisa said she would come, then she will come.

MRS. AMADOR: *Sí*, don't get excited. Nothing to get excited about.

ROSALINDA: Oh Mom, isn't it wonderful! I'm going to see the world. *(Looking up at the sky.)* I'm going to see the universe .... I am going to dance on Venus, skate on Saturn's rings, dive into the Milky Way and wash my hair with stars.

MRS. AMADOR: Is she getting excited?

(Rosalinda and María Pilar are looking up to the sky. Seeing them, Mrs. Amador very cautiously starts to look up.)

MARÍA PILAR: *Ay* Juanita ... I feel your soft brown eyes on me ... on Rosalinda ... on Jesse ... Jesse? Rosalinda, where's Jesse?

ROSALINDA: *(Still gazing at the sky.)* I don't know Mom.

MRS. AMADOR: *(Eyeing the sky with great suspicion.)* Is some-body there?

(Mrs. Amador continues to stare straight up to the sky throughout the rest of this scene. Enter Orlando and Raphael, both very dressed up. Raphael carries a big bouquet of flowers.)

ORLANDO: *Orale,* Rafa, give her the flowers.

RAPHAEL: Now?

MARÍA PILAR: *Ay* look Rosalinda, it's Orlando and Raphael .... *Pasen, pasen ... ay,* where is Jesse? Rosalinda. I'll get her.

(Rosalinda goes toward house as Luisa Ruiz comes out of her house in a faded cocktail dress, a large flower in her hair.)

MARÍA PILAR: *Ay qué bonita se ve, me da tanto gusto aver La* Doña Luisa.
LUISA RUIZ: Oh! Thank you, María Pilar. *(She looks up to the sky.)* It's a beautiful night.
MARÍA PILAR: *Sí.* God works in mysterious ways, Doña Luisa.

(Enter Jesse. She has been transformed into a beautiful young princess. She stands next to Rosalinda. Raphael stands before them, holding the bouquet of flowers, awestruck at Jesse. All stare at Jesse in silence except for Mrs. Amador, who is still staring at the sky.)

ORLANDO: Look at *La* Jesse!
MARÍA PILAR: *Ay* Juanito. *(She crosses herself.)* She combed her hair.
LUISA RUIZ: She looks just like a princess.
ORLANDO: *(Nudging Raphael.)* Now Rafa! Now. *(Raphael, staring at Jesse, tears the bouquet of flowers in half, giving half to Rosalinda and half to Jesse.) Y la fiesta pues?* I am gonna ... dance with you, Doña Luisa.

(Orlando takes Luisa Ruiz arm-in-arm and exits into the house as María Pilar moves to Mrs. Amador, who is still staring into the sky, holding plate of tamales.)

MARÍA PILAR: *Andale,* Mrs. Amador, it's time for the *tamales.*
MRS. AMADOR: *(Still looking at the sky.)* Is somebody watching us*?*

(María Pilar takes Mrs. Amador into the house, followed by Raphael.)

ROSALINDA: I'm proud of you Jesse.
JESSE: *(To Rosalinda.)* You're going to see the world ... all those places ... all the things that will happen to you.
ROSALINDA: I'll be back.
JESSE: You'll be different.
ROSALINDA: We're sisters forever.
JESSE: Rosalinda? ... Can I see it? *(Rosalinda brings out the Yu-Yu from under her blouse.)* Can I touch it? ... Did ... did you really turn into a dog?
ROSALINDA: *(Taking Yu-Yu off her neck, holding it in her hands.)* You have to work very hard.
JESSE: I know.

(Rosalinda puts Yu-Yu around Jesse's neck. She exits into the house. Jesse turns around and stares at the moon. She slowly walks up Castro Street toward the moon as lights slowly fade and we hear María Pilar's voice.)

MARÍA PILAR: *(Offstage.)* Jesse! Jesse!

END OF PLAY

140

PROPERTY LIST

First Day

Onstage
Rotating sprinkler
Strange plants
Rubber tires
Rubbish
Sign: "CURANDERA – HEALER"
2 mailboxes
Jacaranda tree

Offstage
Mailbag (Orlando)
Alarm clock (Jesse)
Shoe (Jesse)

First Night
Onstage
Small stone

Second Night

Onstage
Yu-Yu amulet

Third Day
Offstage
Paper bag (Jesse)
RockBottle of soda and glass (María Pilar)
Broken Rosebush (Mrs. Amador)
Switchblade (Raphael)
Ultrasonic dog whistle (Luisa Ruiz)
Frisbee (Rosalinda)

Roosters
1987

CHARACTERS in order of appearance:
GALLO Morales
ZAPATA, dancer/rooster
HECTOR Morales
ANGELA Ester Morales
JUANA Morales (Juanita la Morenita Sabrosita)
CHATA Morales
ADAN
SHADOW #1
SHADOW #2
SAN JUAN, dancer/rooster

SETTING: *An agricultural valley in the American Southwest.*

TIME: *Summer.*

ACT 1

SCENE 1

Stage and house are dark. Slowlyy a narrow pinspot of light comes up. We hear footsteps. Enter Gallo, a very, very handsome man in his forties. He is wearing a cheap dark suit, with a white open-neck shirt. He carries a suitcase. He puts the suitcase down. He faces the audience.

GALLO: Lord Eagle, Lord Hawk, sainted ones, spirits and winds, Santa María Aurora of the Dawn ... I want no resentment, I want no rancor .... I had an old red Cuban hen. She was squirrel-tailed and sort of slab-sided and you wouldn't have given her a second look. But she was a queen. She could be thrown with any cock and you would get a hard-kicking stag every time. I had a vision, of a hard-kicking flyer, the ultimate bird. The Filipinos were the ones with the pedigree Bolinas, the high flyers, but they had no real kick. To see those birds fighting in the air like dark avenging angels ... well like my father use to say, *"Son nobles ... finos .... "* I figured to mate that old red Cuban. This particular Filipino had the best. A dark burgundy flyer named MacArther. He wouldn't sell. I began borrowing MacArthur at night, bringing him back before dawn, no one the wiser, but one morning the Filipino's son caught me. He pulled out his blade. I pulled out mine. I was faster. I went up on manslaughter. ... They never caught on.... thought I was in the hen house trying to steal their stags .... It took time -- refining, inbreeding, crossbreeding, brother to sister, mother to son, adding power, rapid attack ... but I think we got him.

(Gallo stands still for a beat, checks his watch, takes off his jacket and faces C. A slow, howling drumbeat begins. As it gradually goes higher in pitch and excitement mounts, we see narrow beams of light, the first light of dawn, filtering through chicken wire. The light reveals a heap of chicken feathers which turns out to be an actor/dancer who represents the rooster Zapata. Zapata stretches his wings, then his neck, to greet the light. He stand, and struts proudly, puffs his chest and crows his salutation to the sun. Gallo stalks Zapata, as drums follow their movements.)

Ya, ya, mi lindo ... yeah, baby ... you're a beauty, a real beauty. Now let's see whatcha got. *(He pulls out a switchblade stiletto. It gleams in the light as he tosses it from hand to hand.)* Come on baby boy. Show Daddy whatcha got. *(Gallo lunges at Zapata. Zapata parries with his beak and wings. This becomes a slow, rhythmic fight-dance. Gallo grabs Zapata by his comb, bending his head backwards until he is forced to sit. Gallo stands behind Zapata, straddling him. With one hand Gallo holds Zapata's comb, with the other he holds the knife next to Zapata's neck.)* Oh yeah, you like to fight? Huh? You gonna kill for me baby boy?
Huh? *(Gallo sticks the tip of the knife into Zapata. The rooster squawks in pain.)* Sssh! Baby boy, you gotta learn. Daddy's gotta teach you. *(Gallo sticks it to Zapata again. This time the rooster snaps back in anger.)* That's right beauty.... Now you got it.... Come on, come. *(Gallo waves his knife and hand close to Zapata's face. The rooster's head and eyes follow.)* Oh yeah ... that's it baby, take it! Take it! *(Suddenly Zapata attacks, drawing blood. Gallo's*

body contracts in orgasmic pleasure/pain. Loudly.) Ay
precioso! ... Mi lindo ... You like that, eh? Taste good,
huh? *(Gallo waves the gleaming knife in a slow hypnotic
movement which calms the rooster.)* Take my blood, honey
... I'm in you now ... Morales blood, the blood of kings ...
and you're my rooster ... a Morales rooster. *(He slowly
backs away from the rooster. He picks up his suitcase, still
pointing the knife at Zapata.)* Kill. You're my son. Make
me proud. *(Gallo exits.)*

*(Zapata puffs his chest and struts U. Lights go up a little
on U.L. area as the rooster goes into the chicken wire
henhouse. He preens and scratches. Enter Hector, a
young man of about twenty. He is very handsome. He
wears gray sweatpants and no shirt. On his forehead is a
sweatband. His hair and body are dripping wet. He has
been running. Now he is panting as he leans on the
henhouse looking at Zapata.)*

HECTOR: I saw what you did to those chicks. Don't look
at me like you have a mind, or a soul, or feelings. You kill
your young ... and we are so proud of your horrible animal
vigor ... But you are my inheritance ... *Abuelo*'s gift to me
... to get me out. Oh, *Abuelo*, Grandfather ... you should
have left me your courage, your sweet pacific strength.

*(A ray of light hits D.R. In a semi-shadow, we see a
miniature cemetery, with small white headstones and white
crosses. We see the profile of a young angel/girl with
wings and a pale dress. Angela is kneeling next to a bare
desert tree with low scratchy branches. She has a Buster
Brown haircut and a low tough voice. She is fifteen, but
looks twelve.)*

ANGELA: *(Loudly.)*
Angel of God
My Guardian Dear
To whom God's love
Commits me here
Ever this day be
At my side
To light and guard
To rule and guide
Amen.
(Her paper wings get caught in a tree branch.) Aw, shit!
(She exits.)

SCENE 2

As the light changes we hear the clapping of women making tortillas. Lights come up full. Center is a faded wood-frame house, with a porch that is bare except for a table and a few chairs. The house sits in the middle of a desert agricultural valley somewhere in the Southwest. Everything is sparse. There is a feeling of blue skies and space. One might see off on the horizon tall Nopales or Century cactus. Juana, a thin, wornout-looking woman of thirty-five, comes out of the house. She is wearing a faded housedress. She goes to mid-yard, faces front and stares out.

JUANA: It's dry. Bone dry. There's a fire in the mountains ... up near Jacinto Pass. *(The clapping stops for a beat, then continues. Juana starts to go back into the house, then stops. She sniffs the air, sniffs again,* and again.) *Tres Rosas* ... I smell *Tres Rosas*. *(She hugs her body and rocks.) Tres Rosas ... Ay*, St. Anthony let him come home ... Let him be back. *(The clapping stops. Chata enters from the house. She is a fleshy woman of forty, who give, new meaning to the word blowsy. She has the lumpy face of a hard boozer. She walks with a slight limp. She wears a black kimono, on the back of which is embroidered in red a dragon and the words "Korea, U.S.S. Perkins, 7th Fleet." A cigarette hangs from her lips. She carries a bowl containing balls of tortilla dough.)* I smell *Tres Rosas* ... The brilliantine for his hair ... He musta been here. Why did he go?

CHATA: Men are shit.

JUANA: Where could he be?

CHATA: First day out of jail! My brother never comes home first day. You should know that. Gotta sniff around ... gotta get use to things. See his friends.

JUANA: *Sí*, that's right ... He just gotta get used to things. I'll feel better when I see him ... I gotta keep busy.

CHATA: You been busy all morning.

JUANA: I want him to feel good, be proud of us.... You hear anything when you come in yesterday?

CHATA: Who's gonna know anything at the Trailways bus station?

JUANA: You ain't heard anything?

CHATA: Juanita, he knows what he's doing. If there was gonna be any trouble he'd know. *Ay, mujer*, he's just an old warrior coming home.

JUANA: Ain't that old.

CHATA: For a fighting man, he's getting up there. *(Juana slaps tortillas. Chata watches her.)* Who taught you to make tortillas?

JUANA: I don't remember. I never make 'em. Kids don't ask.

CHATA: Look at.this. You call this a tortilla? Have some pride. Show him you're a woman.

JUANA: Chata, you've been here one day, and you already--

CHATA: Ah, you people don't know what it is to eat fresh handmade tortillas. My grandmother *Hortensia*, the one they used to call *"La India Condenada"* ... she would start making them at five o'clock in the morning. So the men would have something to eat when they went into the fields. *Hijo!* She was tough ... Use to break her own horses ... and her own men. Every day at five o'clock she would wake me up. *"Buenos pinchi dias,"* she would say. I was twelve or thirteen years old, still in braids ... "Press your hands into the dough," *"Con fuerza,"* "Put your stamp on it." One day I woke up, *tú sabes, con la sangre.* "Ah! So you're a woman now. Got your cycle like the moon. Soon you'll want a man, well this is what you do. When you see the one you want, you roll the tortilla on the inside of your thigh and then you give it to him nice and warm. Be sure you give it to him and nobody else." Well, I been rolling tortillas on my thighs, on my *nalgas*, and God only knows where else, but I've been giving my tortillas to the wrong men ... and that's been the problem with my life. First there was Emilio. I gave him my first tortilla. *Ay Mamacita*, he use to say, these are delicious. *Aye*, he was handsome, a real lady-killer! After he did me the favor he didn't have the *cojones* to stick around ... took my TV set too. They're all shit ... the Samoan bartender, what was his name ...

JUANA: Nicky, Big Nicky.

CHATA: The guy from Pep Boys--

JUANA: Chata, you really think he'll be back?

CHATA: His son's first time in the pit? With "the" rooster? A real Morales rooster? Honey, he'll be back. Stop worrying.

JUANA: Let's put these on the griddle. Angela, Hector ... breakfast.

SCENE 3

Angela slides out from under the house, wearing her wings. She carries a white box which contains her cardboard tombstones, paper and crayons, a writing tablet and a pen. She too sniffs the air. She runs to the little cemetery and looks up, as Hector appears at the window behind her.

ANGELA: *Tres Rosas* ... Did you hear? Sweet Jesus, *Abuelo*, Queen of Heaven, all the Saints, all the Angels. It is true. It is certain. He is coming, coming to stay forever and ever. Amen.

HECTOR: Don't count on it!

ANGELA: *(To Heaven.)* Protect me from those of little faith and substance.

HECTOR: I'm warning you. You're just going to be disappointed.

ANGELA: *(To Heaven.)* Guard me against the enemies of my soul.

HECTOR: Your butt's getting bigger and bigger!

ANGELA: And keep me from falling in with low companions.

HECTOR: Listen, little hummingbird woman, you gotta be tough, and grown-up today.

(Angela digs up her collection can and two dolls. Both dolls are dressed in nuns' habits. One, the St. Lucy doll, has round sunglasses. She turns a box over to make a little tea table on which she places a doll's teapot and cups.)

ANGELA: As an act of faith and to celebrate her father's homecoming, Miss Angela Ester Morales will have a tea party.

150

HECTOR: No more tea parties.

ANGELA: Dancing in attendance will be that charming martyr St. Lucy.

HECTOR: He will not be impressed.

ANGELA: Due to the loss of her eyes and the sensitivity of her alabaster skin, St. Lucy will sit in the shade. *(She seats St. Lury in the shade and picks up the other doll.)*

HECTOR: Who's that?

ANGELA: St. Teresa of Avigon, you will sit over here. *(She seats St. Teresa doll.)*

HECTOR: Just don't let him con you Angela.

ANGELA: *(Pouring pretend tea.)* One lump or two, St. Lucy? St. Teresa has hyperglycemia, and only takes cream in her tea. Isn't that right St. T'eresa?

HECTOR: He's not like *Abuelo*.

(Angela animates the dolls like puppets and uses two different voices as St. Lucy and St. Teresa.)

ANGELA: *(As St. Teresa)* Shouldn't we wait for St. Luke?

HECTOR: Stop hiding. You can't be a little girl forever.

ANGELA: *(As St. Lucy.)* St. Luke! St. Luke! Indeed! How that man got into Heaven I'll never know. That story about putting peas in his boots and offering the discomfort up to God is pure bunk. I happen to know he boiled the peas first.

HECTOR: I don't want you hurt. It's time to grow up.

ANGELA: *(As St. Teresa.)* St Lucy! I can only think that it is the loss of your eyes that makes you so disagreeable. Kindly remember that we have all suffered to be saints.

HECTOR: Are you listening to me, Angie?

ANGELA: *(As St. Lucy.)* Easy for you to say! They took my eyes because I wouldn't put out! They put them on a plate. A dirty, chipped one, thank you very much indeed! To this day no true effort has been made to find them.

HECTOR: Excuse me! ... Excuse me, St. Teresa, St. Lucy, I just thought I should tell you ... a little secret ... your hostess, Miss Angela Ester Morales, lies in her little, white, chaste, narrow bed, underneath the crucifix, and masturbates.

ANGELA: Heretic! Liar!

HECTOR: Poor Jesus, up there on the cross, right over her bed, his head tilted down. He sees everything.

ANGELA: Lies! Horrible lies!

HECTOR: Poor saint of the month, watching from the night table.

ANGELA: I hate you! I hate you! Horrible, horrible, Hector.

JUANA: *(From offstage.)* Breakfast!

(Hector leaves the window. Angela sits on the ground writing on a tombstone.)

ANGELA: *(Lettering tombstone.)* Here lies Horrible Hector Morales. Died at age twenty, in great agony, for tormenting his little sister.

JUANA: *(Offstage.)* You kids ... breakfast!

HECTOR: *(Pops up at window.)* Just be yourself. A normal sex crazed fifteen-year-old girl with a big, gigantic, enormous butt. *(He exits.)*

ANGELA: *(To Heaven.)*
Send me to Alaska
Let me be frozen
Send me a contraction
A shrinking antidote
Make me little again
Please make my legs
Like tiny pink Vienna sausages
Give me back my little butt.

152

(Juana and Chata bring breakfast out on the porch and set it on the table.)

JUANA: Angie! Hector! We ain't got all day. *(Angela goes to the breakfast table with the St. Lucy doll and the collection can.)* And take your wings off before you sit at the table. Ain't you kids got any manners? *(Angela removes her wings, sits down, bows her head in prayer. Chata stares at St. Lucy. St. Lucy stares at Chata. Juana shoos flies and stares at the distant fire.)* I hope he's on this side of the fire.
CHATA: That doll's staring at me.
ANGELA: She loves you.

(Lights fade on the women, come up on the henhouse. Adan, a young man of twenty, is talking to Zapata -- now a real rooster, not the actor/dancer -- and preparing his feed.)

ADAN: *Hola Zapata ... ya mi lindo ... mi bonito. En Inglés. Tengo qué hablar en* English *... pinchi* English *... verdad Zapata? En Español* más *romantico pero* Hector *say I must learned di* English. *(Zapata starts squawking.) Qué te pasa? Orita vas a comer.*

(Hector enters.)

HECTOR: English, Adan ... English.
ADAN: No English ... *pinchi* English.
HECTOR: Good morning, Adan.
ADAN: *A qué la fregada!* ... Okay this morning in the fields, I talk English *pero* this afternoon for fight I talk *puro Español.*
HECTOR: Good morning, Adan.

ADAN: *Sí, sí*, good morning, *muy fine* ... Hector *el Filipino* he say ... *(He moves away from Zapata, so bird will not hear him.)* He say to tell you *qué* Zapata no win. *Por qué Filipino* bird fight more *y* your bird first fight *y* your first fight *y* you not no ex ... ex ...
HECTOR: Experience.
ADAN: *Sí eso*, he say you sell bird to him *y* no fight ... He say is not true Morales bird *por qué* Gallo not here. *El Filipino* say if you fight bird ... bird dead. If bird still alive after Filipino bird beat him ... Bird still dead *por qué* nobody pay money for bird that lose.
HECTOR: But if he wins, everybody wants him.
ADAN: I say, *ay di* poor Hector. His *abuelo* leave him bird. He can no sell. *El Filipino* say, "Good!" Inside, in my heart I am laughing so hard *por qué* he not know Gallo gonna be here. We win, we make much money.
HECTOR: It's my bird, I have to do it myself.
ADAN: *You tonto! You stupido! You mulo!* Like donkey.... He help you, he the king ... he you papa. For him all birds fight.
HECTOR: No!
ADAN: Why? Why for you do this? You no even like bird. Zapata he knows this, he feel this thing in his heart. You just want money to go from the fields, to go to the other side of the mountains ... to go looking to go looking for what? On the other side is only more stupid people like us.
HECTOR: How could you think I just wanted money? I want him to see me.
ADAN: Sorry ... I am sorry my friend ... I know ... I stay with you *y* we win *vas a ver!* Okay Zapata! We win *y est a noche estamos tomando* Coors, Ripple, Lucky Lager, *unas* Buds, Johnny Walkers, oh *sí, y las* beautiful *señoritas. (He gives Zapata his food.)* Eat Zapata! Be strong.
HECTOR: I almost forgot, look what I have for you ... fresh, warm homemade tortillas.

ADAN: Oh, how nice.

HECTOR: Yes, how nice. Aunt Chata made them.

ADAN: Oh, much nice.

HECTOR: Today she woke up at five o'clock, spit a green booger the size of a small frog into a wad of Kleenex. She wrapped her soiled black "7th Fleet" kimono around her loose, flaccid, tortured, stretch-marked body and put her fat-toed, corned yellow hooves into a pair of pink satin slippers. She slap-padded over to the sink where she opened her two hippo lips and looked into the mirror. She looked sad. I looked at those lips ... those lips that had wrapped themselves warmly and lovingly around the cocks of a million *campesinos*, around thousands upon thousands of *Mexicanos, Salvadoreños, Guatemaltecos.* For the tide of brown men that flooded the fields of this country, she was there with her open hippo whore's lips, saying "Bienvenidos," "Welcome," "Hola," "Howdy." Those are legendary lips, Adan.

ADAN: Yes ... muy yes.

HECTOR: What a woman, what a comfort. Up and down the state in her beat-up station wagon. A '56 Chevy with wood panels on the sides, in the back a sad, abused mattress. She followed the brown army of pickers through tomatoes, green beans, zucchinis, summer squash, winter squash, oranges, and finally Castroville, the artichoke capital of the world, where her career was stopped by the fists of a sun-crazed *compañero.* The ingratitude broke her heart.

ADAN: Oh my gooseness!

HECTOR: She was a river to her people, she should be rewarded, honored. No justice in the world.

ADAN: *Pinchi* world. *(He and Hector look to mountains.)* You look mountains. In my country I look mountains to come here. I am here and everybody still look mountains.

ADAN: No, my friend, we are here, we belong ... *la tierra.*

JUANA: *(From offstage.)* Hector, I ain't calling you again. *(Light up on the porch. Juana and Chata are sitting at the table. Angela is sitting on the steps. She has her wings back on. St. Lucy and the collection can are by her side. She is writing on her tablet.)* Oh Gallo, what's keeping you?
CHATA: Men are shit! That's all. And it's Saturday. When do they get drunk? When do they lose their money? When do they shoot each other? Saturdays, that's when the shit hits the fan.

(Enter Hector and Adan with Zapata in a traveling carrier.)

JUANA: It's because I'm so plain.
HECTOR: We're better off without him.
CHATA: *Buenos dias* Adan. *Un cafecito?*
ADAN: Ah. Good morning, Mrs. Chata, *no gracias*, ah good morning, Mrs. Morales *y* Miss Angelita.

(Angela sticks out her donation can. Adan automatically drops coins in.)

JUANA: Angela!
ADAN: No, is good, is for the poor. Miss Angela, she good lady ... eh, girl. *(He pats Angela on the head.)*
JUANA: Why don't you leave the bird, so your father can see him when he gets home.
HECTOR: He's my bird. He can see it later.
JUANA: I can't believe you would do this to your own father. Birds are his life ... and he's so proud of you.
HECTOR: This is news. How would he know, he hasn't seen me in years.
JUANA: It isn't his fault.

HECTOR: It never is.

JUANA: Your father is with us all the time, he got his eye on us, he knows everything we're doing.

ANGELA: Everything!

JUANA: I brag about you kids in my letters ... His friends they tell him what a smart boy you are ... that you're good-looking like him ... He's proud ... "A real Morales," that's what he says.

HECTOR: And did he call me a winner? A champ? A prince? And did you tell him I was in the fields?

ANGELA: What did he say about me, Mama?

HECTOR: Nothing, you're a girl and a retard. What possible use could he have for you? Grow up!

CHATA: No, you grow up.

(Angela buries herself in Chata's lap.)

JUANA: Hector, please, Hector, for me.

HECTOR: No, Mother. Not even for you.

JUANA: You give him a chance.

HECTOR: What chance did he give us? Fighting his birds, in and out of trouble. He was never here for us, never a card, a little present for Angela. He forgot us.

JUANA: You don't understand him. He's different.

HECTOR: Just make it clear to him. *Abuelo* left the bird to me, not to him, to me.

JUANA: Me, me, me. You gonna choke on this me, me. Okay, okay, I'm not going to put my nose in the bird business. I just ask you for me, for Angie, be nice to him.

HECTOR: As long as we all understand the "bird business," I'll be nice to him even if it kills me, Mother.

JUANA: Now you're feeling sorry for yourself. Just eat. You can feel sorry for yourself later.

HECTOR: Why didn't I think of that? I'll eat now and feel sorry for myself later.

JUANA: Now, you kids gotta be nice and clean, your papa don't like dirty people.

CHATA: Me too, I hate dirty people.

JUANA: Angie, you take a bath.

HECTOR: Oh, Angela, how ... how long has it been since you and water came together? *(Angela hits him.)* Oww!

JUANA: You put on a nice clean dress, and I don't wanna see you wearing no dirty wings.

HECTOR: Right, Angie, put on the clean ones.

JUANA: You say please and excuse me ... and you watch your table manners ... I don't want to see any pigs at my table.

HECTOR: *(Making pig noises.)* What a delicious breakfast! Cold eggs, sunny-side up. How cheery! How uplifting! Hmm, hmmm! *(He turns so Angela can see him. He picks up the eggs with his hands and stuffs them in his mouth.)* Look, Angela, refried beans in a delicate pool of congealed fat. *(Still making pig noises, he picks up gobs of beans, stuffs them into his mouth.)*

CHATA: *A qué la fregada!* Hector, stop playing with your food. You're making us sick.

JUANA: *(Looking at watch.)* 7:20, you got ten minutes before work. *(Hector drums his fingers on the table.)*

HECTOR: Nine minutes ... I will now put on the same old smelly, shit-encrusted boots, I will walk to the fields. The scent of cow dung and rotting vegetation will fill the air. I will wait with the same group of beaten-down, pathetic men ... taking their last piss against a tree, dropping hard warm turds in the bushes. All adding to this fertile whore of a valley. At 7:30 that yellow mechanical grasshopper, the Deerfield tractor, will belch and move. At this exact moment, our foreman, John Knipe, will open his pig-sucking mouth, exposing his yellow, pointy, plaque-infested teeth. He yells, "Start picking, boys." The daily war begins ... the intimidation of violent growth ... the expanding melons and squashes, the hardiness of potatoes,

the waxy purple succulence of eggplant, the potency of ripening tomatoes. All so smug, so rich, so ready to burst with sheer generosity and exuberance. They mock me ... I hear them ... "Hey Hector," they say, "show us whatcha got," and "Yo Hector we got bacteria out here more productive than you." ... I look to the ground. Slugs, snails, worms slithering in the earth with such ferocious hunger they devour their own tails, flies oozing out larvae, aphids; bees, gnats, caterpillars their proliferation only slightly dampened by our sprays. We still find egg-sacks hiding, ready to burst forth. Their teeming life, their lust, is shameful ... Well it's time ... Bye Ma. *(He exits.)*
JUANA: *(Yelling.)* Hector! You gotta do something about your attitude. *(To herself.)* Try to see the bright side. *(Juana and Chata exit into the house, leaving Angela on the porch steps. Adan runs up to her.)*
ADAN: Psst! Miss Angelita! ... di ... di cartas?
ANGELA: Oh, the letters ... that will be one dollar.
ADAN: One dollar! Adan very poor man ... *(Angela sticks the donation can out and shakes it. Adan reaches into his pockets and drops coins into the can.)* Oh, *sí*, you are very good.

(Angela puts on glasses and pulls out a letter.)

ANGELA: *(Reading letter.)* Adored *Señora* Acosta: The impulses of my heart are such that they encourage even the most cautious man to commit indiscretion. My soul is carried to the extreme with the love that only you could inspire. Please know that I feel a true passion for your incomparable beauty and goodness. I tremulously send this declaration and anxiously await the result. Your devoted slave, Adan.
ADAN: *(Sighing.)* Ay, qué beautiful.

ANGELA: P. S. With due respect *Señora*, if your husband should be home, do not turn on the porch light.
ADAN: Ah, thank you ... thank you very much.

(Adan hurriedly exits. Angela gathers her St. Lucy doll and her donation can, and exits quickly. Chata enters from the house wearing "colorful" street clothes. She looks around, then swiftly exits. Hector enters, picks up Zapata, hurries off. The stage darkens, as if smoke from the distant fire has covered the sun. Drum howls are heard. In the distance we hear a rooster crow and sounds of excited chickens as the henhouse comes to life. Gallo appears.)

GALLO: Easy hens, shush! My beauties. *(He puts his suitcase down, cups his hands to his mouth, and yells to the house.)* Juana! Juana! Juana! *(Juana opens the door.)* How many times, in the fever of homesickness, have I written out that name on prison walls, on bits of paper, on the skin of my arms ... Let me look at you ... my enduring rock, my anchor made from the hard parts of the earth -- minerals, rocks, bits of glass, ground shells, the brittle bones of dead animals.
JUANA: I never seen you so pale, so thin ...
GALLO: I'm home to rest, to fatten up, to breathe, to mend, to you.
JUANA: How long? How long will you stay?
GALLO: Here. Here is where I'll put my chair ... I will sit here basking in the sun, like a fat old iguana catching flies, and watching my grandchildren replant the little cemetery with the bones of tiny sparrows. Here. Here I will build the walks for my champions. Morales roosters. The brave and gallant red Cubans, the hard and high-kicking Irish Warhorses, the spirited high-flying Bolinas.
JUANA: Don't say nothing you don't mean ... you really gonna stay?

160

GALLO: *(Gently.)* Here. Here is where I'll plant a garden of herbs. Blessed laurel to cure fright, wild marjoram for the agony of lovesickness, cempauchie flowers for the grief of loneliness.

(Gallo gently kisses Juana, picks her up and carries her into the house. The door slams shut. Angela enters, her wings drooping behind her. She trips over Gallo's suitcase. She examines it. She smells it.)

ANGELA: Tres Rosas! *(Angela looks at the house. She sits on the suitcase, crosses her arms over her chest as if she were ready to wait an eternity. The shadows of two strangers fall on her.)* What do you want?

SHADOW #1: Nobody's home to you, rancor.

SHADOW #2: Just go in, tell him we got something for him.

ANGELA: Nobody's home to you, resentment.

SHADOW #1: Who are you supposed to be?

ANGELA: *(Holding St. Lucy doll.)*
I am the angel of this yard
I am the angel of this door
I am the angel of light
I am the angel who shouts
I am the angel who thunders.

SHADOW #1: She is pure crazy.

SHADOW #2: Don't play with it, it's serious.

ANGELA:
You are the shadow of resentment
You are the shadow of rancor
I am the angel of acid saliva
I will spit on you.

SHADOW #1: There's time.

SHADOW #2: Yeah, later.

(Angela spits. The shadows leave. Angela crosses her hands over her chest and looks to Heaven.)

ANGELA: Holy Father ... Listen, you don't want him, you want me. Please take me, claim me, launch me and I will be your shooting star woman. I will be your comet woman. I will be your morning-star woman.

SCENE 4

Lights become brighter. Angela exits under the house. The door opens. Gallo comes out in T-shirt and pants and goes to his suit-case. Juana comes to the door in slip and tight robe.

GALLO: I never sent him to the fields.
JUANA: I know.
GALLO: I never said for you to put him there.
JUANA: No, you never said ...
GALLO: Then why is my son in the fields? (*They look at each other. Gallo looks away.*) Don't look at me. I see it in your eyes. You blame me. Just like the old man.
JUANA: *Abuelo* never said a word against you.
GALLO: I never let him down with the birds, nobody could match me. They were the best.
JUANA: He knew that ...
GALLO: So, he left the bird to Hector.
JUANA: He wanted him out of the fields. We didn't know when you would be out or maybe something would happen to you.
GALLO: He let the boy into the fields, that was his sin. He allowed a Morales into the fields.
JUANA: He was old, tired, heartbroken.

162

GALLO: Heartbroken, he wasn't a woman to be heartbroken.

JUANA: His only son was in jail.

GALLO: Yes, we know that, the whole valley knows that. You ... what did you do? Didn't you lay out your hard, succulent, bitch's teat at the breakfast table? So he would have the strength to stand behind a hoe, with his back bent and his eyes on the mud for ten hours a day.

JUANA: Hard work never killed anybody.

GALLO: *Ay, mujer!* Can't you think what you've done, you bowed his head down.

JUANA: What was I suppose to do? There ain't no other work here. I can't see anything wrong with it for a little while.

GALLO: The difference between them and us, is we never put a foot into the fields. We stayed independent -- we worked for nobody. They have to respect us, to respect our roosters. *(Hector and Adan enter. They are both very dirty. Hector has Zapata, in his carrier. Adan has a carrier containing a second rooster. Gallo and Hector stare at each other.)* Well ... you are taller. This offshoot ... this little bud has grown.

HECTOR: Yeah, well .. that must be why you seem ... smaller.

GALLO: Un abrazo!

HECTOR: I'm dirty. I'm sweaty.

GALLO: I see that.

HECTOR: I'm afraid I smell of the fields.

GALLO: Yes.

HECTOR: Of cheap abundant peon labor ... the scent would gag you.

GALLO: It's going to kill you.

HECTOR: Mama says hard work never killed anyone ... isn't that right, Mother?

JUANA: It's only for a little while. Your papa thinks that--

GALLO: I'll tell him what I think. Now what about those tamales you promised me?

JUANA: Ah *sí, con permiso* ... I got some work in the kitchen.

ADAN: Oh *sí*, Mrs. Juana, *los tamales ... qué rico.*

JUANA: *(Smiling at Adan.)* I hope they're the kind you like. *(She exits into house.)*

GALLO: *Hijo*, you always take the bird with you into the fields?

HECTOR: No, not always.

GALLO: This bird has to look like he's got secrets ... no one but us should be familiar with him.

HECTOR: This is Adan.

ADAN: *Es un honor*, Mr. *El Gallo. (Angela sticks her head out from under the house. Adan and Gallo shake hands and greet each other.)*

GALLO: *(Referring to Zapata.)* Let him out ... he needs a bigger carrier ... he's a flyer.

ADAN: *Como Filipino* birds?

GALLO: Yes but this baby boy he's got a surprise. He's got a kick.

ADAN: Like Cuban bird?

GALLO: He'll fight in the air, he'll fight on the ground. You can put spurs or razors on that kick and he'll cut any bird to ribbons. You can put money on that.

ADAN: *Hijo! Señor* ... how you know? He never fight. Maybe he only kick in cage.

GALLO: I know because I'm his papa ... *(Pointing to the other carrier.)* That your bird?

ADAN: *Sí, pero* no good ... no fight. San Juan, he run away.

GALLO: I'll make him fight. Just let him out.

ADAN: Mr. *El* Gallo, you give this *pendejo* bird too much honor. *Gracias Señor, pero* this poor bird, he no can fight.

GALLO: Is it the bird, or you who will not fight?

HECTOR: The bird is too young. He doesn't want him to fight.

GALLO: I've never seen a bird that won't fight, but there are men who are cowards.

HECTOR: He is not a coward.

ADAN: This is true, *pero* I am not *El* Gallo. In my country all men who love *di* rooster know Mr. *El* Gallo. They tell of *di famoso día de los muertos* fight in Jacinto Park.

GALLO: Ah, you heard about that fight. You remember that fight, Hector?

HECTOR: No.

GALLO: First time you saw a real cockfight ... *Abuelo* took you.... How could you forget your first cockfight? *(To Adan.)* Go on, take your bird out. I'll make him fight.

(Gallo takes a drink from a bottle, then blows on San Juan. As he does this, lights go down almost to black. Pinspot comes up C. as other lights come up to a dark red. During this process, we hear Gallo's voice – "Ready," then a few beats later "Pit!" On this cue two dancer/roosters jump into the pinspot. This rooster dance is savage. The dancers wear razors on their feet. The Zapata dancer jumps very high. The poor San Juan dancer stays close to the ground. Throughout the dance, we hear drums and foot—stomping. At every hit, there is a big drum pound. During the fight, Hector appears on the porch.)

HECTOR: *(To himself.)* It was in Jacinto Park ... the crowd was a monster, made up of individual human beings stuck together by sweat and spittle. Their gaping mouths let out screams, curses, and foul gases, masticating, srnacking, eager for the kill. You stood up. The monster roared. Quasimodo, your bird, in one hand. You lifted him high, "Pit!" went the call. "Pit!" roared the monster. And

you threw him into the ring ... soaring with the blades on
his heels flashing I heard the mighty rage of his wings and
my heart soared with him. He was a whirlwind flashing
and slashing like a dark avenging angel then like some
distant rainbow star exploding he was hit. The monster
crowd inhaled, sucking back their hopes ... in that vacuum
he was pulled down. My heart went down the same dark
shaft, my brains slammed against the earth's hard crust ...
my eyes clouded ... my arteries gushed ... my lungs
collapsed. "Get up," said *Abuelo*, "up here with me, and
you will see a miracle." You, Father, picked up
Quasimodo, a lifeless pile of bloody feathers, holding his
head oh so gently, you closed your eyes, and like a great
wave receding, you drew a breath, that came from deep
within your ocean floor. I heard the stones rumble, the
mountains shift, the topsoil move, and as your breath
slammed on the beaches, Quasimodo sputtered back to life.
Oh *Papi*, breathe on me.

*(Angela appears and stands behind her brother. Her wings
are spread very far out. Drums and stomping crescendo as
Zapata brutally kills San Juan.)*

(Blackout.)

ACT 2

SCENE 1

*Early afternoon. The table is set up in the middle of the
yard in a festive way, with tablecloth, flowers, a bowl of
peaches, and bottles of whiskey and wine. Gallo is in the
henhouse with Adan. Hector is in the bathroom, Juana and*

*Chata are in the kitchen. Angela is by the little cemetery
writing on a tombstone.*

ANGELA: Here lies Angela Ester Morales died of acute
neglect. Although she is mourned by many, she goes to a
far, far, better place, where they have better food.

*(Angela slides under the house as Juana comes out wearing
a fresh housedress and carrying a steaming pot.)*

JUANA: *(Yelling.)* Hector! Angela! You kids wash up,
it's time to eat.

*(Juana hurries back into the house, almost knocking Chata
down as she comes out with a tray of tortillas. She is
heavily made up, wearing tight clothes, dangling earrings,
high-heeled shoes. A cigarette dangles from her mouth.)*

CHATA: Why are you eating out here?
JUANA: He wants it. Says he don't wanta hide in the
house.
CHATA: Begging for trouble.
JUANA: What can I do, he's the *man*. *(She goes into the
house.)*
CHATA: Ah, they're all shit! Just want trouble. Soup's
on! *(Chata pours herself a quick shot of whiskey, shoots it
down and makes a face. Juana comes out with another
pot.)*
JUANA: You better tell 'em that the food's ready. *(Chata
goes to henhouse.)* Hector!
HECTOR: *(Coming out on porch.)* What?
JUANA: It's time. to eat ... you look real nice honey.
Makes me proud to have your papa see you all dressed up.

HECTOR: Okay. Okay. Don't make a big deal about it. I just don't want him to think--
JUANA: I just feel so happy--
H ECTOR. I just don't want him to think--
JUANA: *¡Hijito!* You love your papa ... don't you?
HECTOR: Mother!
JUANA: I know you a little mad at him ... *pero* when he comes home it's like the sun when it--
HECTOR: Shshshsh! *(Chata, Gallo and Adan come out of the henhouse.)*
GALLO: We have to sharpen and polish those spurs. I want them to flash.
JUANA: *(To Gallo.)* The food's ready ... we fixed what you like ... *mole*, rice, *frijolitos ... tamales.*
GALLO: *Tamales estilo Jalisco!*
CHATA: *(Looking Hector over.) Ay Papi qué rico estas! (Hector quickly sits down.)* Honey! You gonna have to beat all them women off with a stick, when they see you and that rooster tonight.
ADAN: No worry Hector, I be there ... down you *mujeres,* women leave *de* Mr. Hector and me alone ... *Ay Mama! (He has a giggling fit.)*
GALLO: *(Kissing Juana.)* It's wonderful to be in love ... to be touched by the noble fever.
CHATA: Ah, you're better off with a touch of typhoid.
JUANA: I ... *gracias al Señor* qué ... my whole family is here. *(She looks around. She yells.)* Angela! Angie!
HECTOR: Mom!
JUANA: Where is she? Where is your sister?
HECTOR: Talking to the saints! I don't know.

(Juana gets up, goes to the spot where Angela slides under the house, gets down on her hands and knees and yells.)

JUANA: Angela! Angela! You leave them saints alone.
You hear me! *(As everybody looks at Juana, Angela comes
from behind the house and tiptoes toward the henhouse.
Hector is the only one to see her. Using hand signals, she
pleads to him to be quiet. Juana peers under the house.)*
Angie! Honey ... your mama worked for days to fix this
food and now it's getting cold. *(To Gallo.)* You should see
how sweet she looks when she's all dressed up. *(To under
the house.)* You ain't got no manners ... ain't even said
hello to your father. *(To Gallo.)* She prays a lot ... and
she's got real pretty eyes.

CHATA: *(To Gallo.)* She's sorta ... the bashful type ...
you know.

JUANA: *(To Gallo.)* And she ain't spoiled.

CHATA: *(Taking a drink.)* Nah, all them kids smell like
that.

JUANA: *(To under the house.)* Angie!

GALLO: Juana leave her alone.

JUANA: Okay. Angie, I'm gonna ignore you, 'cause you
spoiled my day, this day that I been looking forward to for
years and years and now you making me look like a bad
mama, what's your papa gonna think of us.

GALLO: Juana, she'll come out when she's ready. *(Juana
goes back to the table.)*

CHATA: Maybe was them roosters fighting got her scared.

ADAN: Poor San Juan.

GALLO: Adan, drink up and I'll see you get one of our
famous Champion Morales birds.

HECTOR: What famous Champion Morales birds?

GALLO: The ones I paid for dearly, the ones I came home
to raise ... isn't that right *mi amor*?

JUANA: Yes ... you see honey, your papa's gonna stay
home ... raise birds ... I think *Abuelo* would want that.

GALLO: And after they see our bird tonight ... see, first I
want them to think it's just you and the bird up there. And
the bets are down, I'll take over and they're gonna know we

got roosters. A toast … *(As Gallo stands up, everybody raises a glass, except Hector. Angela tiptoes from the henhouse carrying Zapata. She goes behind and under the house. Only Hector sees her.)* To the finest fighting cocks ever to be seen. *(He slides the bottle to Hector.)*

HECTOR: *(Sliding the bottle back.)* No. *(Pause.)*

GALLO: Too good to drink with your old man.

HECTOR: I only drink with people I trust.

CHATA: Me … I drink with anybody. Maybe that's my problem.

GALLO: I am your father.

CHATA: I like it better when I drink alone. Ya meet a better class of people that way.

HECTOR: But it's my bird. *Abuelo* left it to me.

GALLO: *Abuelo* was my father, and you are my son. I see no problem. Now let's eat.

HECTOR: Mother!

JUANA: Let's eat, honey, and we can talk about it later.

ADAN: *Ay* the *mole muy delicious* ... the *mole muy rico* ... the *mole muy* beautiful *y* Mrs. Juana. Today, you look beautiful, like the *mole*.

GALLO: Hm, *sabroso, exquisto.*

JUANA: I bet you been in plenty of fancy places got better food than this.

GALLO: This is home cooking, I know that your hands made it.... These these are the hands of a beautiful woman....

HECTOR: Ha! Bullshit.

GALLO: We say your mother is beautiful and you call it bullshit? I find that very disrespectful.

JUANA: *Hijo*, you're right ... it's just the way people talk, I know I ain't beautiful.

ADAN: *Sí, muy* beautiful.

GALLO: *¡Ya ves!* ... If your son doesn't have the eyes, the soul, the imagination to see it ... it's his loss.

170

HECTOR: That's right. I just can't seem to stretch my imagination that far.

GALLO: This is an insult to your mother.

HECTOR: It's the truth. That is a plain, tired, worn-out woman.

GALLO: Shut up.

HECTOR: The hands of a beautiful woman! Those aren't hands, they're claws because she has to scratch for her living.

JUANA: Please, Hector, let him say what he wants ... I know I ain't beautiful. It don't go to my head.

HECTOR: But it goes to your heart which is worse. Did he ever really take care of you? Did he ever go out and work to put food on the table, to buy you a dress? All he has is words, and he throws a few cheap words to you and you come to life. Don't you have any pride?

GALLO: Your mother has great courage to trust and believe in me.

HECTOR: Stupidity!

GALLO: You know nothing.

HECTOR: You don't seem to realize that it is my rooster. And that after the fight, depending on the outcome, I will sell him or eat him. I have made a deal with the Filipinos.

JUANA: *Ay* Hector! You've spoiled everything. All this food ... I worked so hard ... for this day.

GALLO: You're not selling anything to anybody. This is nothing to joke about.

HECTOR: I don't want to spend my life training chickens to be better killers. And I don't want to spend my whole life in this valley. Mother, Aunt Chata, excuse me.

CHATA: Ah? ... *O sí hijo pase* ... sometimes Hector can be a real gentleman. *(Hector starts to leave.)*

GALLO: Son! ... You have no courage, no juice ... you are a disgrace to me.

JUANA: *Ay*, Gallo don't say that to him.

HECTOR: Do you think I care what you think ... Father.
JUANA: *Hijo* no ... for me just once for me. I don't wanna be alone no more.
HECTOR: What about me? You have me, you'll always have me, I'll work, I've always worked, I can take care of you. I won't leave you.
JUANA: It ain't the same, honey.
HECTOR: Yeah ... He comes first for you, he will always come first.
GALLO: If you sell that bird, it will be over your dead body.
HECTOR: You can't stop me.

(Exit Hector. Chata takes a plate of food and bowl of peaches to the under-the-house area and tries to tempt Angela out.)

GALLO: He doesn't seem to realize ... coward ... too bad.

(Gallo goes to the henhouse. Juana starts to follow him.)

JUANA: Talk to him ... he's a good boy ... if you just talk ... *(Seeing Adan still eating.)* Is it good? You really like it?
ADAN: Hm! *Sabroso!*
CHATA: Come on Angie ... it's real good.

(Gallo returns running.)

GALLO: He's gone ... the bird is gone ...
ADAN: *Yo no* see *nada, nada.*
JUANA: He'll bring it back, he's a good boy. He's just a little upset ... you know.

GALLO: Nobody fools with my roosters. Not even this over-petted, over-pampered viper you spawned. Go and pray to your Dark Virgin. You know what I'm capable of.

(Exit Gallo. Adan stops eating and tries to comfort Juana as she puts her head down on the table and cries.)

ADAN: No cry, no cry Mrs. Juana. *Di* women cry *y* Adan, he not know what to do. *(Juana cries louder.)* *Ay* Mrs. Juana, for sure *di* flowers will die ... *di* trees will be torn from *di* ground, freshness will leave *di* morning, softness will leave *di* night ... *(Juana's cries increase.)* *Ay Dios!* *(From his pocket, he brings out the letter Angela wrote for him. He crosses himself.)* Mrs. *di* Juana ... *(Reading with great difficulty.)* *Di* ... impulses ... of my ... heart ... are such ... *(Throwing letter aside.)* *A qué la fregada!* Mrs. Juana, Adan have *mucho amor* for you. My heart break to see you cry. I will not a breathe. When you no cry then I will breathe.

(Adan takes a big breath and holds it. Slowly Juana stops crying and lifts her head Adan, suffering some discomfort, continues to hold his breath.)

JUANA: I been dreaming. Nothing's gonna change. I gotta face facts.

(Adan let his breath out in a great whoosh. Angela pops out from under the house and takes a peach from Chata's hand. She stares at the peach with great intensity.)

CHATA: Angie, ain't it nice to have the family all together again?

ANGELA: There is no pit in this peach. It is hollow. Instead of the pit there is a whole little world, a little blue-green crystal-clear ocean, with little schools of tiny darting silver fish. On a tiny rock sits a mermaid with little teenie-weenie kinky yellow hair. A tiny sun is being pulled across a little china-blue sky by teenie-weenie white horses with itty—bitty wings. There is an island with tiny palm trees and a tiny thatched hut. Next to the hut stand a tiny man and woman. She is wearing flowers, and leaves. He is wearing one single leaf. On their heads are little bitty halos. In their arms is a little bitsy baby. He isn't wearing anything.

CHATA: Let me see ... *(Looking at peach.)* I can't see dick!

(Blackout.)

SCENE 2

Later in the afternoon. Chata sits on the porch steps, her legs spread out, fanning herself. Juana sits on a straight-back chair, her hands folded on her lap. She rocks herself softly. She watches Angela, who is sitting on the ground drawings circles in t e dirt, humming softly in time to her circles. The circles get deeper and deeper.

CHATA: It's hot ... I am waiting for a cool breeze ...
ANGELA: Uh ha uh ha uh ha uh haa.
CHATA: *Aire fresco* ... come on cool breeze, come right over here.
JUANA: Uh ha uh ha uh haa.
CHATA: Women! We're always waiting. *(Angela hums for a beat, then there is silence for a beat.)*
JUANA: It's because I'm so plain.

CHATA: Ah, you just work too much.

JUANA: Plainness runs in my family. My mother was plain, my grandmother was plain, my great-grandmother --

CHATA: It was the hard times ... the hard work that did it.

JUANA: My Aunt Chona was the plainest.

CHATA: I don't remember her.

JUANA: The one with the crossed eyes and the little mustache.

CHATA: *Ay,* Juanita, that woman had a beautiful soul, sewing those little tiny outfits for the statues of the saints. That woman was a saint.

JUANA: She's the one that told on you the time you was drinking beer with them sailors at the cockfight.

CHATA: Disgusting old bitch!

(Angela hums for a beat as she continues drawing circles.)

JUANA: I get up at six, I brush my teeth, no creams, no lotions, what they gonna do for me? I work ... that's all. I take care of people and I work. People look at me, they know that's all I do. I ain't got no secrets. No hidden gardens. I keep busy, that's what I do. Don't stop, that's what I say to my self. Don't stop, 'cause you're not pretty enough, exciting enough, smart enough to just stand there.

ANGELA: Mama, I don't wanna be plain.

CHATA: Honey, you're too colorful to be plain.

ANGELA: Yeah, that's what I thought.

CHATA: Your mama forgets ... those years when her heart was filled with wild dreams when she use to weave little white star jasmine vines in her hair and drive all the men crazy.

JUANA: It ain't true ... she was the one always getting me in trouble.

CHATA: I wasn't the one they called Juanita la Morenita

Sabrosita.

JUANA: Oh, Chata. We was young girls together ... in the summer, at Jacinto Park ... cockfights, fistfights, the music. At night we would jump out of our bedroom windows in our party dresses. With our good shoes in one hand, our hearts in the other, we ran barefoot through the wet grass, above us all the stars twinkling go, go, go.

CHATA: Nothing could stop us ... we had such a short time being girls.

JUANA: Now, all I am is an old hag.

CHATA: It ain't true.

JUANA: Sí, it's true enough. I carry burdens, I hang sheets, I scrub. I gather, I pick up, "Here sit down," "I'll wash it," "Here's fifty cents," "Have my chair," "Take my coat," "Here's a piece of my own live flesh!"

CHATA: *Es la menopause*, that's what it is. You getting it early. I knew this woman once, use to pull out her hair.

JUANA: I don't care, I don't want any stories, I don't care what happens to *Fulano* Mangano ... I just wanna stand still, I wanna be interesting, exciting enough to stand still.

CHATA: *Ay, mujer!*

JUANA: And I want to look like I got secrets.

CHATA: Juana!

JUANA: Don't call me Juana. Juana is a mule's name.

CHATA: Ah, you're crazy! That new gray hen, the kids named her Juana. See, they think of you.

JUANA: A gray hen! An old gray hen, that's all I am. An old gray hen in a family of roosters. No more! I want feathers, I wanna strut, too. I wanna crow.

ANGELA: Mama!

JUANA: Don't! Don't call me Mama. I am not Mama ... I am ... I am that movie star, that famous dancer and heartbreaker "Morenita Sabrosita" ... and now if my fans will excuse me I'm gonna take a bath in champagne, eat cherry bonbons and paint my toenails. *(She goes into house.)*

CHATA: *(To Juana.)* We got champagne?

(Chata goes into the house as Angela goes lo the little cemetery and puts up a new tombstone.)

ANGELA: *(Printing on tombstone.)* Here lies Juana Morales. Beloved Wife of *El* Gallo, Blessed Mother to Angela and Horrible Hector. Died of acute identity crisis sustained during *la menopause*.

SCENE 3

Lights go down, as Angela sits on her box/table at the little cemetery. The long shadows of men fall on Angela and the cemetery.

SHADOW #1: There's that spooky kid. You go brother.
SHADOW #2: Ah, it's just a weird kid. Hey! You! Kid!

(Angela does not acknowledge them.)

SHADOW #1: Call her "Angel."
SHADOW #2: Hey, Angel.

(Angela looks up.)

SHADOW #1: See what I mean?
SHADOW #2: Listen kid, tell your old man, we got business to discuss.
SHADOW #1: Yeah, and you make sure he gets the message.

ANGELA: My old man, my Holy Father, my all powerful Father, sees no problems. If there are problems, I am the angel of this yard. I am the comet. I am the whirlwind. I am the shooting stars. Feel my vibrance.

SHADOW #1: I feel it, right behind my ears, like ... like ...

ANGELA: Locust wings.

SHADOW #1: Let's get outta here.

SHADOW #2: Tell Gallo some pals dropped by to settle an old score.

SHADOW #1. Come on!

SHADOW #2: *(Voice trailing off.)* Hey! That kid don't scare me, see.

SHADOW #1: *(Voice trailing off.)* I'm telling ya, my ears hurt.

(Exit shadows. Lights go back up. Angela folds her hands in prayer.)

ANGELA. Holy Father, please help me, I feel the illumination, the fever of grace slipping away. I need to know that you are with me, that you take an interest in my concerns. Send me a little demonstration, a sign. Any sign ... I don't care. Stigmata, visions, voices, send an angel, burn a bush ... I am attracted to levitation ... but you choose ... I'll just lay here and wait.

(Angela lies down on the ground waiting. After a few beats Hector enters. He slowly walks up to Angela and looks down on her for a beat.)

HECTOR: What are you doing?

ANGELA: *(Sitting up.)* Ohhh ... you're no sign.

HECTOR: What is going on?

ANGELA: Weird, shady men came here looking for Gallo. Two of them. They were not polite.

HECTOR: I see.... So your reaction is to lay stretched out on the dirt instead of going into the house.

ANGELA: Hector, please, I am scared ... I wanted a sign

(Hector sits down next to Angela.)

HECTOR: Hey, you're the shooting-star woman, you can't be scared.

ANGELA: I am scared. Really scared. If I grow up will I still be scared? Are grown-ups scared?

HECTOR: Always scared, trembling ... cowering ... this ... this second, now ... this planet that we are sitting on is wobbling precariously on its lightning path around the sun and every second the sun is exploding ... stars are shooting at us from deep distant space, comets zoom around us, meteor rocks are being hurled through distances we measure in light ... This very earth which we call our home, our mother, has catastrophic moods, she keeps moving mountains, receding like an overburdened beast trying to shake off ... Life is violent.

ANGELA: You're scared about the fight ... huh?

HECTOR: No. Whatever happens, *Papi* will still only care about the rooster. That's his son, that's who gets it all.

ANGELA: Maybe if we gave him the rooster he'd stay here and be happy.

HECTOR: He has to stay for us not the rooster ... Angela ... you ... you were great taking the rooster.

ANGELA: He kept killing the little chicks. How could he do that Hector? He's their papa.

HECTOR: Training. Look Angela, you're the angel of this yard. You keep a close guard on that rooster. Don't let anyone near him ... promise me.

ANGELA: Yes.

HECTOR: That's a real promise now. No crossed fingers behind your back.

ANGELA: I promise already. (She spreads her hands out in front of her, then kisses the tip of her thumb.) May God strike me dumb, make me a plain ,whiny person and take away my gift of faith. Forever and ever, throughout my mortal years on earth, and throughout the everlasting fires of hell. Amen. Satisfied?

HECTOR: Yes.

ANGELA: Gee, maybe I should have given myself a little leeway, a little room for error.

(Chata enters from the house with a bottle. and glass.)

HECTOR: Too late now. Can't take it back.

CHATA: Oh, oh, look who's here. Angie, your mama needs some cheering up, a nice hug, an angel's kiss, maybe a little song.

ANGELA: Litany to the Virgin. That's her favorite. *(She exits.)*

CHATA: Men are shit. Pure shit.

HECTOR: And you're still drinking.

CHATA: Stay outta my drinking. You hurt your mama Hector.

HECTOR: Too bad.

CHATA: *Ay Dios,* what a man he is now.

HECTOR: Yeah, well what about you? Didn't you break *Abuelo's* heart when you became a whore?

CHATA: They called me the encyclopedia of love. You want to turn a few pages? Your Aunt Chata could show you a few things.

HECTOR: You're disgusting.

CHATA: Is that what fascinates, you, honey? Is that why I always find you peeping at me, mirrors at the keyhole, your eyeballs in the cracks, spying when I'm sleeping, smelling my kimono.

HECTOR: You're drunk.

CHATA: I ain't drunk, honey.

HECTOR: You drink too much. It's not ... good for you ... it makes you ugly.

CHATA: Ain't none of your business. Don't tell me what to do Hector.

HECTOR: I have to, it's for your own good.

CHATA: You got nothing to say about it, you ain't my man, and you ain't your mama's man. The sooner you learn that the better ... take your bird, leave it, eat or sell it, but get out of here. *(Hector stands alone in the yard, as Chata goes to the door. She turns. They look at each other.)* What are you hanging around here for? Go on! Get out! It ain't your home anymore. *(Chata takes a broom and shoos Hector from the yard.)* Shoo! Shoo! You don't belong here, it ain't your place anymore.

HECTOR: Stop it, stop it, stop it.

(Hector goes to the outside boundary of the yard, where he falls to his knees and buries his face in his hands, as Chata comes slowly up behind him.)

CHATA: I feel like I'm tearing my own flesh from my bones ... He's back. Honey, we got too many roosters in this yard.

HECTOR: Did you sleep with my father? Did he yearn for you as you slept in your little white, chaste, narrow bed? Did he steal you when you were dreaming?

CHATA: *(Embracing him.)* Shshsh ...

HECTOR: I'm not like him.

CHATA: You're just like him, so handsome you make my teeth ache.

HECTOR: Whore, mother, sister, saint-woman, moon-woman, give me the shelter of your darkness. Fold me like a fan and take me into your stillness, submerge me beneath the mysteries, baptize me, bear me up, give me life, breathe on me.

(Chata enfolds him as the lights fade. We hear Angela reciting the litany.)

ANGELA: *(Offstage.)* She is the Gate of Heaven, the Mystical Rose, the Flower of Consolation, the Fire of Transcendence, and the Queen of Love.

SCENE 4

Lights come up to indicate that time has passed Angela is alone in the yard. She sniffs the air.

ANGELA: *Tres Rosas!*

(Angela slides under the house as Gallo enters. He sees a brief flash of Angela from the corner of his eye. He walks slowly into the yard. He stops by the little cemetery and reads the tombstones. He feels the urge for a drink. He goes to the table and has a shot. He sits.)

GALLO: Acute neglect? ... uh-huh ... I thought I felt a little spirit, slight, delicate ... yes I feel it. A little tenderness ... a little greenness … *(Examining the ground.)* What's this? Tracks ... little tiny paws ...there ... *(Following track.)* and there.... (*Gallo pretends to be following tracks to the porch. Then with one great leap he jumps in the opposite direction, surprising the hell out of Angela, and pulls her from under the house by her heels.)* Ah, ha!

ANGELA: Shit! Hey! You're ripping my wings! You shithead! Put me down! Don't touch me! *(Gallo puts Angela down, throws his hands up to indicate he won't touch her. They stand and stare at each other. Angela goes to the little cemetery, never taking her eyes off Gallo. They continue to stare for a beat, then Angela looks up to Heaven, slapping her hands together in prayer.)* There is a person here trying to con me, but I don't con that easy.

GALLO: *(Slapping his hands in prayer.)* There is a person here who swallows saints but defecates devils.

ANGELA: *(To Heaven.)* He comes here smelling of *rosas* using sweet oily words ... it's phony, its obnoxious, it's obscene ... I wanna throw up.

GALLO: I came here to see my baby, my little angel, my little woman of the shooting stars, my light delicate splendorous daughter. But she is as light, as delicate, as splendid as an angel's fart.

ANGELA: Angels do not fart. They do not have a digestive system. That's why they can all scrunch together on the head of a pin.

GALLO: Oh, ... I only come with my love--

ANGELA: *(Interrupting.)* You only came with words ... well, where were these words on my birthday, Christmas, my saint's day? Where's my Easter outfit, my trip to Disneyland, the orthodontist ... You owe me.

GALLO: Sweet Jesus ... What a monster! I owe you ... but Angela! Angela! Angela! How many times have I written that name on prison walls. On bits of paper, on the skin of my arms.

ANGELA: *(To Heaven.)* He's hopeless! You write everybody's name on your arms.

GALLO: Women like to know that they're on your flesh.

ANGELA: I am not a woman. I'm your baby daughter. You said so yourself.

GALLO: I'm afraid ... fathers to daughters ... that's so delicate. I don't know ... what to do ... help me Angela. How do I know what to do?

ANGELA: Instinct! Ain't ya got no instinct? Don't you feel anything?

GALLO: *(Moving closer to Angela.)* When you were a little baby, you were a miracle of tiny fingers and toes and dimples and you had a soft spot on the top of your head.

ANGELA: I still have it, see.

GALLO: I wanted to take you into my arms and crush you against my chest so that I could keep you forever and nobody, and nothing, could ever, ever hurt you because you would be safe ... my little offshoot, my little bud, my little flower growing inside my chest.

ANGELA: *Papi* ...

GALLO: *Sí, sí, hijita.* Your *Papi's* here.

ANGELA: And *Papi* these men come all the--

GALLO: *(Holding Angela.)* Shshsh ... it's nothing, nothing and you thought I forgot about you ... well it just hurt too much, do you understand?

ANGELA: You had to pull down some hard time and the only way to survive was to cut off all feelings and become an animal just like the rest of them.

GALLO: Well, something like that. Honey you know what I wish--

ANGELA: Papa, did the lights really go down when they put the people in the electric chair?

GALLO: Angela, what a ... Honey you know what I wish-

ANGELA: Did they force you to make license plates? Hector and I would look real close at the one that started with a G. We thought you made them. "What craftsmanship!" Hector used to say.

GALLO: Don't you have any normal interests?

ANGELA: Like what?

GALLO: Like swimming ... you know what I wish? That we could take a trip and see the ocean together.

ANGELA: I've never seen the ocean. When?

GALLO: Just you and me. Laying on our bellies, feeding the seagulls, riding the waves.

ANGELA: I can't swim.

GALLO: I will teach you. that's what fathers are for--

ANGELA: *(To Heaven.)* Angels and saints did you hear? My father's going to teach me to swim!

GALLO: Now Angela, I didn't promise.

ANGELA: But you said--

GALLO: I want to but I have to hurry and fix things. I have to find Hector, talk to him and find that rooster fast before Hector sells him. Honey you pray to St. Anthony, your prayers are powerful ... unless ... St. Anthony he listen to you?

ANGELA: *(Crossing her fingers.)* Hey, we're like that.

GALLO: Ask St. Anthony, Angela ... then we can go to the ocean?

ANGELA: Truly *Papi?* Just you and me? And will you stay with us forever and ever?

GALLO: Wild horses couldn't drag me away.

ANGELA: Close your eyes. Tony! Tony! Look around, Zapata's lost and can't be found. *(She goes under the house, gets Zapata, and gives him to Gallo.)* I found him *Papi,* he was--

GALLO: *Ya lindo, ya. (To bird.)* Papa's got you now. Angela you keep quiet now honey, this is our secret.

ANGELA: What about Hector?

GALLO: I'm going to talk to Hector now. You go inside and get all dressed up. So I can be proud of my girl. I'll pick you up after the fight. *(He exits.)*

ANGELA: Your girl! *(Singing.)* We are going to the ocean, we are going to the sea, we are going to the ocean to see what we can see ...

(Angela goes into the house. We hear cha-cha music.)

CHATA: *(Offstage.)* One, two ... not like that ... I'm getting tired ... what time's *Zorro* on?
JUANA: No, no ... Just one more. *(Singing.) Cha, cha, cha, qué rico, ... cha, cha, cha ... Ay,* I could do it all night.

(Enter Gallo running, breathing hard He has Zapata's carrier. He goes to the door and yells.)

GALLO: Juana! Juana! *(Juana and Chata come to the door.)* I need money ... and my stuff. I gotta leave ... something's come up ... Do you hear me? I need money now.
JUANA: I hear ya ... you ain't even been here a day and already you're gone ... nothing's going to change with you ... nothing. I was having fun, dancing, remembering old times, do you know how long--
GALLO: I don't have time for this, just give me the money.
JUANA: I ain't got any!
CHATA: I got some. *(She goes in the house.)*
GALLO: The Filipino, somebody told him about the bird. Oh, ya, ya my little hen, don't you ruffle those pretty feathers, I'll be back.
JUANA: No, you always gonna be running.
GALLO: If it was just me, I'd stay. You know that, Juana? You know I'd stay, but I got the bird to think of, gotta hide him, breed him good, soon as I get some good stags I'll come home ... this is just a little setback. *(Chata returns with suitcase and money.)*
JUANA: You know how long it's been since I went dancing?
CHATA: Here, you're gonna need this. *(Gives him the suitcase.)* And this is all the cash I got.

(Angela enters as Gallo counts the money. She is dressed in a red strapless dress made tight by large visible safety pins, high heels, and a great deal of heavy makeup and jewelry. The effect is one of a young girl dressed like a tart for a costume party. She carries a suitcase, purse and her donation can.)

GALLO: Is this all you got?

ANGELA: *(Shaking the can.)* Don't worry Papa, I got my donation-can money. *(They all stare at her for a beat.)*

JUANA & CHATA: Angela?!!

JUANA: Angie, you got on your mama's old party dress.

CHATA: Yeah, and all my jewelry ... where you going?

ANGELA: Papa, didn't you hear me? I have money. *(She shakes the can.)*

GALLO: Oh honey, don't you look pretty ... now you got a little bit too much lipstick on, let your mama wipe some off.

ANGELA: Are we leaving now?

JUANA: Gallo!

GALLO: Shshsh Juana ... Angela, I gotta talk to your mama for a few minutes. You go in the house and I' II come and get you.

ANGELA: Are you sure?

GALLO: Don't you trust me, Angie?

CHATA: Come on Angie, I'll show you how to draw eyebrows. First you draw a straight line across your forehead and then spit on your finger and rub out the middle. Let's go in and try it.

ANGELA: Really, Aunt Chata, I'm not a child, you don't have to patronize me.

CHATA: Okay, I'll give you the lowdown on blow-jobs. *(Angela and Chata exit into the house.)* Now, don't tell your mama ...

GALLO: Juana, keep her in the house until I leave.

JUANA: You promised to take her with you?

GALLO: I had to get the bird. I said I would take her to the ocean.

JUANA: *Ay bruto!* How could you do it?

GALLO: How was I to know this would happen ... and Juanita, it hurts me to say this but that kid is crazy ...

JUANA: No, no *señor,* she is not crazy and I ain't gonna let you call her crazy. She got the spirit they broke in me. I ain't gonna let it happen to her.

GALLO: Shshsh! Don't get so excited. It isn't important.

JUANA: It's important ... it's her spirit, her soul and you ain't gonna stomp on it ... you hear me. *(Adan enters humming.)*

ADAN: Mr. *El* Gallo ... bad men! Mucho bad, y mucho ugly. Looking for you *y* Zapata. All ober they look for you ... You leave Mr. *El* Gallo. You go far away. I take you. I go for my truck.

GALLO: You are a good friend Adan, and my new partner.

ADAN: Oh, thank you Mr. *El* Gallo. I am proud. But is better I come back here to Mrs. Juana *y* Hector.

JUANA: Thank you, Adan.

GALLO: We better hurry.

ADAN: *Sí, sí,* I come back with truck.

(Adan exits. Juana goes into the house. Hector enters as Gallo starts to pack his suitcase.)

HECTOR.: *(Seeing Zapata.)* You must have really sold her a bill of goods to get Zapata.

GALLO: Look, there's trouble ... the Filipino send you?

HECTOR: No, how could you think I would work for him, but I came to get Zapata.

GALLO: You're the one told him about the bird.

HECTOR: Yes. I made a deal with the Filipino. He'll leave you alone if I give him the rooster.

GALLO: That's a lie and you fell for it.

HECTOR: No, he is an honorable man, we were here unprotected for seven years and he never bothered us. It's his bird, *Papi*.

GALLO: No, I paid seven years of my life for this baby.

HECTOR: And he lost his son. It's the right thing to do.

(A truck horn is heard. Angela comes out of the house with her suitcase, Juana and Chata follow after her.)

ANGELA: Papa? Are we leaving now, Papa?

JUANA: Angie! No!

HECTOR: So that's it ... Angela, get back in the house.

ANGELA: I'm going with him, Hector.

HECTOR: Get back in the house, nobody's going anywhere.

ANGELA: No! I don't have to listen to you anymore. You're not my father.

JUANA: Angie ... he's not going to the ocean ... he can't take you.

(We hear the sound of Adan's truck. The horn is heard as Gallo starts backing away, picking up Zapata's carrier.)

ANGELA: *Papi,* wait for me! Papa, you promised.

GALLO: You're all grown up now, you don't need your old man.

CHATA: Hector!

(Gallo turns, tries to run out. Angela grabs him, knocking Zapata's carrier out of his hand. Hector picks up the carrier.)

ANGELA: No Papa, we need you and Mama needs you, we've been waiting, and waiting, you can't leave, you promised.

JUANA: They'll kill you Gallo.

GALLO: *(Throwing Angela off.)* Stop sucking off me. I got nothing for you.

ANGELA: *(Beating her fists on the ground.)* No, no, Papa! You promised me! ... Oh, Hector ... No, no, I promised Hector. *(Drums begin as punctuation of the pounding of Angela's fists on the ground. Lights change. A special on Angela and another on Gallo and Hector come up, as shadows appear. Angela sees shadows.)* Ah ... Holy Father, *Abuelo.*

GALLO: *(To Hector.)* Give me that bird.

ANGELA: Saints, Angels, Mama.

JUANA: *(Trying to pick up Angela.)* Come on Angie, get up.

GALLO: *(To Hector.)* What do you want?

HECTOR: You, alive, *Papi.*

CHATA: Careful, Hector.

ANGELA: I've lost my faith. I am splintered.

GALLO: *(Imitating Hector.)* You *Papi* ... Give me life ... Make me a man. *(He whips out his stiletto.)* This is how you become a man. *(The drums get louder. We hear howling.)* Come on baby boy, show Daddy whatcha got.

JUANA: Are you crazy! That's your son!

ANGELA: I am cast down! Exiled! *(Gallo stalks Hector as drums follow their movements.)*

JUANA: Oh Gallo, you're killing your own children.

CHATA: Move Hector, don't think, move!

GALLO: Oh yeah, *mi lindo*, you like to fight ... eh?

JUANA: No, stop them! Please, please stop this.

ANGELA: Fallen from the light, condemned to the mud, to the shadows.

GALLO: You gotta learn baby boy.

CHATA: Look at him Hector. He's getting old, his hand is shaking ... take the knife! Stay down old warrior. Stay down.

ANGELA: Alone and diminished. This loneliness is unendurable.

JUANA: Hector!

HECTOR: Do I have it? Is this what you want me to be ...

ANGELA: *(Looking to Heaven.)*
My brains are slammed against the earth's hard crust.
My eyes are clouded
My arteries gush
My lungs collapsed.

HECTOR: *(Letting go of Gallo.)* No! I am your son. *(Drums and cries stop.)*

ANGELA: Holy Father, *Abuelo*, Hector, breathe on me.

(Celestial sound as a white narrow shaft of light falls on Angela. She levitates, her wings spreading. Only Chata and Juana see this.)

HECTOR: *(Taking a deep breath.)* Oh sweet air! *(He gets the rooster and sees Angela.)* Angela!

ADAN: *(Rushing in.)* I am here, I have truck ... *(Seeing Angela, he crosses himself.)* Ay Dios. *(He kneels.)*

JUANA: *(At Gallo's side.)* Gallo look!

GALLO: Did you see the hands on that kid, just like steel, never seen finer hands ... *(Seeing Angela.)* Sweet Jesus, my beautiful monster. *(He crosses himself.)*

CHATA: No, it ain't true.

HECTOR: *(Standing before Angela holding the rooster.)* Oh sweet hummingbird woman, shooting star, my comet, you are launched.

ANGELA: *Abuelo*, Queen of Heaven, All the Saints, All the Angels. It is true, I am back. I am restored. I am ... Hector, take me with you.

HECTOR: Everywhere ... Over the mountains, up to the stars.

ANGELA: To the very edge.

ADAN: Hector! Angelita! You take *Adan (He goes to Angela.)*

CHATA: *(Looking at Angela.)* Shit happens ... been happening all my life, that's all I know.

JUANA*: (Holding Gallo like the Pieta.)* We seen it Gallo, with our own eyes.

ANGELA: *(To Hector and Adan.)* And I want my doorstep heaped with floral offering ... and

(Hector, Adan and Angela freeze. Chata removes the flower from her hair and holds it in her hand, trying to decide what to do. She freezes.)

GALLO: *Ay Juanaita*, I had a vision of a hard-kicking flyer ... *(He yawns.)* the ultimate bird, *noble, fino.*

(Gallo falls asleep. Juana looks at Gallo, smiles, then looks out half smiling.)

END OF PLAY

Evening Star
1989

CHARACTERS in order of appearance:
OLIVIA PEÑA..................................Pretty girl of 14.
JUNIOR RODRIGUES.............................Boy of 16.
VENDOR...................................Wise man around 30.
LILLY RODRIGUES...................Tall, lanky girl of 14.
TINA PEÑA...........................Elegant woman of 58.
JUAN PEÑA.............................Grouchy man of 65.
MRS. RODRIGUES...........Hard working woman of 33.

Late sunset, as sun goes down, the sky is turning a deep blue with orange streaks across the horizon. Very few stars have come out, Venus and the Evening Star are among them It is late spring. On stage we see two houses. One of them, the Peña house, is made of wood. It has a front porch, a neat walk, flowers and grass. It is a modest home, but well cared for. To the side is a small hen house and hen yard fenced in by chicken wire. There area three chickens: Doris, Jacquline and Benito. The second house is made of stucco. It has no garden, just a dirt yard. It is extremely modest, clean but not cared for. This is the Rodrigues house. On the roof of the Rodrigues house we see Junior Rodrigues setting up a telescope. He is 16 years old , wearing jeans, sweatshirt and tennis shoes. Olivia Peña, also on the roof, is a pretty, lively girl of 14. She is wearing a Catholic girl's school uniform, a red sweater tied around her hips. She is busy looking at the sky. We hear offstage *voice of the vendor.*

VENDOR: (*offstage.*) tengo mangos! … Mangos y papayas.
OLIVIA: (*Fingers crossed, eyes closed.*) I wish I may I wish I might, have the wish I wish tonight. I want a hundred beautiful summer nights. I want to eat warm peaches until I'm sick … And string all the pits into a beautiful necklace and I'll wear it all the time to show the world what a greedy girl I am. What did you wish for?
JUNIOR: Nothing,
OLIVIA: Come on!
JUNIOR: It's stupid.
OLIVIA: Come on Junior, you have to wish for something.
JUNIOR: O.K.! … I wish for a summer job at the Dairy Queen.
OLIVIA: That's it? That's all?
JUNIOR: Yup!
OLIVIA: I don't believe you.
VENDOR: (*Off stage.*) From the Shores of Rio Plata I'm proud to bring you nectarines, pineapples. and tangelos... (*Vendor lets out a lecherous wolf whistle.*) Ay mamasita, a dónde vas?

(*Enter Lilly Rodrigues, a tall lanky girl of 15. She wears a short, tight blue-jean shirt, a halter top, and a windbreaker type jacket. Her hair is long and wild. She walks in a provocative manner until she gets close to her house, at which point she drops the walk. As she reaches the front door of her house, she takes a key from under the doormat, opens the door, enters her house and slams the door shut. After a beat she opens the door, puts the key under the mat and goes back into the house, slamming the door shut. This door slamming has disturbed the delicate but cheap Astroscan telescope. Olivia, who is lost in the unfolding wonder of the sky, notices nothing. Junior , trying to set*) *up a tripod for his camera, senses at once that the scanner is off.)*

OLIVIA: We have to be expectant.
JUNIOR: Aw damnit! Damn it! Damn it! Why does she have to slam the door? Huh? I ask her not to slam the ... *(Looking into Astro- scanner.)* I knew it, it's off.
OLIVIA: *(Still focused on the sky.)* We have to be patient and expect miracles.
JUNIOR: *(Fussing with the scanner.)* It has to be just right ...One degree off and ... I'll fix it later.
VENDOR: *(Off stage.)* The sun is sinking. The hour of enchantment, the crack between night and day, the moment of magic is upon us. Are you prepared for the night? *(Tina Peña comes out of her house. She is a delicate, beautiful woman of 58. She is wearing a simple house dress and carries a little coin purse. The Vendor enters on a bicycle pushcart. He wears white pants and shirt, a Panama on his head.)* From the head waters of Rio Negro, I bring you the roots and barks of enchanted trees to guarantee sleep, tranquillity, and sweet dreams. *(Tina looks at a flower in her garden with unusual attention, yet keeping her distance from this flower. The Vendor rides up to Tina, sniffing the air.)* What is it? What is blooming in this garden?
TINA: *Una rosa blanca.*
VENDOR: A white rose ... in your garden? ... With all due respect *Señora* .. This thing has the scent of the white madonna ...
TINA: It must be a joke, Raphael, a cruel joke ... if you know who ...
VENDOR: *(Interrupting.)* No, no *Señora*, don't even think it. Who? Who would do such a thing?
TINA: But I swear to you I did not plant it.
VENDOR: No, of course not.

TINA: It just appeared ... a tight little bud ... like the head of a snake ... yesterday the scent was very strong, a scent so bitter it made me cold ... and nauseous.

VENDOR: Maybe ... you and Don Juan:

TINA: Don't be ridiculous ... I'm too old ... nothing more than an old grey moth.

VENDOR: You? You *Señora*? You are a brilliant Brimstone Butterfly ... but please go on.

TINA: Yes ... yes ... well, this morning ... I saw her.

VENDOR: No!

TINA: Yes! Very early this morning, the white rose became her face, the face of the white madonna ... two leaves became her arms ... and ... and she opened her arms ... I ... I could see it.

VENDOR: No!

TINA: Yes! It was right there, I tell you, growing out of the stem ... a tiny baby with small thorny breasts ... and a green thorny ... penis. It was dripping a sap ... a nectar of roses.

VENDOR: It is very clear, *Señora*, that you must see Dr. Avila at once, if not sooner.

TINA: No. My body has no more seasons, no more cycles.

VENDOR: These things have been known to happen.

TINA: I tell you it's quite impossible ...

VENDOR: What is it, *Señora*? ... You feel ill?

TINA: Nothing ... it's nothing ... only that she was lovely ... radiant ... her delicate skin was like the fleshy white texture of the rose petal, with it's fine mauve veins ... her long chestnut hair, she wore it as I did when I was a girl ... in little waves ...

VENDOR: Ah ... yes ... chestnut hair in little waves. *(He sighs.)*

TINA: Her small velvety nostrils ...

VENDOR: Do go on *Señora* ... please.

TINA: No. *(Beat.)* She looked ...

VENDOR: Yes ...
TINA: Offended.
VENDOR: The madonna looked offended?
TINA: Offended to be in an old woman's garden ... Oh, the whole thing has made me very nervous.
VENDOR: For nerves, hmmm ... Althea tea? Or that weed they call Juan Simon ... I think you should try both.
TINA: Yes ... How much?
VENDOR: $1.33. Everything I sell is $1.33 ... If I can be of further service *Señora*.
TINA: Raphael...
VENDOR: Yes?
TINA: I would prefer ...
VENDOR: I will talk to no one.
TINA: Thank you ... yes, thank you.

(Tina goes into her house, as the Vendor gets on his bicycle. He sits there for a beat.)

VENDOR: If not birth, what could the white rose mean?

(He sits in the "Thinker" position as lights cross fade to roof.)

JUNIOR: Now, is it alright with you if we start? O.K. ... To find Venus ya wanna put two fingers ... not those two ... the other two, O.K. ... two fingers above the southwest horizon ... see? There's Venus ... that's established, right? Now, proceed to the second joint of your first finger.
OLIVIA: Are you sure this is scientific? Just because you say established and proceed, doesn't make it scientific.
JUNIOR: Just do it ... directly above your second joint is the comet.
OLIVIA: It's not there.

JUNIOR: It's there. There's too much light to see. Take my word for it. It's there.

OLIVIA: We're gonna miss it like we missed the meteor shower, like we missed the last lunar eclipse, like we missed the moon shot.

JUNIOR: We're not going to miss it. We're just too early. We have to wait until twilight.

OLIVIA: Sunset . Twilight. What's the difference?

JUNIOR: Twilight is an intermediate state that is not clearly defined.

OLIVIA: When you start talking like that I know we're gonna miss it. *(Junior looks in the scanner, as Olivia stands next to him.)* Let me see.

JUNIOR: I wanna check this ... Olivia!

OLIVIA: What?

JUNIOR: Don't stand so close to me, go over there.

OLIVIA: I wasn't touching you ... I just want ...

(Junior sees something in the sky, but not through telescope.)

JUNIOR: Shooting star, Olivia! Look!

OLIVIA: Where ... Ooooh!

(They both follow star's path.)

JUNIOR: It starts burning as soon as it enters our atmosphere ... so bright.

OLIVIA: Beautiful star burn into our hearts ... burning with love. How far did it come? Just to die at our feet.

JUNIOR: It's called gravity.

OLIVIA: I call it fatal devotion.

(Lights cross fade to Lilly coming out of her house as Vendor cries out.)

VENDOR: From the dark, lapping ponds of Calie, I bring you the roots and bulbs of the languorous night narcissus ... for potency and love.

LILLY: Those things really work?

VENDOR: What things?

LILLY: Those things you were yelling about.

VENDOR: What things?

LILLY: Those roots.

VENDOR: Oh! You want a love potion.

LILLY: Ssh! Do they work? Could they make somebody love you?

VENDOR: Oh no! It's not for them to love you ... it's for you to love them.

LILLY: That's backwards!

VENDOR: *(Offering one.)* Would you like to try it? On the house.

LILLY: No, that's not my problem ... thanks anyway.

(Lilly goes back into the house slamming the door again.)

VENDOR: *(To Lilly.)* Are you sure?

JUNIOR: *(Looking into the telescope.)* Damn it Lilly!

VENDOR: Junior! Junior!

JUNIOR: Yeah?

VENDOR: What's going on?

JUNIOR: Waiting for the comet.

OLIVIA: I saw a shooting star!

JUNIOR: Yeah, and she thinks it committed Hare-Kari for love of her. *(Suddenly, Junior sees something in the astroscanner. He follows it.)*

OLIVIA: What is it? Do you see it? What do you see?

JUNIOR: I see your grandfather turning the corner of Castor Street.

OLIVIA: Oh no! Grandpa's coming!

VENDOR: Coño!

*(Vendor hurries to get on his bicycle cart. Olivia
frantically collects school books and as she starts down the
ladder her shoe gets stuck.)*

OLIVIA: I'm stuck! I'm stuck!
VENDOR: *Coño! (Vendor gets off bicycle cart and goes
to her aid.)*
JUNIOR: He's moving fast. He's going to Arganda's
garage. No, ... wait. He just stopped by to throw a rock at
Johnny Arganda. Johnny's running away ... He's on the
move again. He's taking the short cut between Dog Lady's
and Jessie Luna's house. Oh-oh. He just stepped in some
dog-doo ...
OLIVIA: Hurry! It won't budge.
JUNIOR: He's scraping his shoe on the Luna's lawn. Mrs.
Luna's yelling at him. He's yelling back. Mrs. Luna's
giving him the finger. Now he's going by the Amador's.
He's at the vacant lot. He's passing Big Nick's Bar. He's
yelling BUMS!
OLIVIA: Untie it. l'll go without it. *(Vendor unties
Olivia's shoe. He gathers her books and throws them up to
her.)*
JUNIOR: Big Nick's coming out of the bar ... Oh-oh, he's
throwing a beer bottle after him … he missed … around the
corner he's crossing the alley ... HE'S HERE!

*(Enter Juan, a robust energetic man of 65. He is carrying
a small brown bag of groceries and a copy of "La
Opinion". He sees the Vendor and immediately looks for a
rock.)*

JUAN: Ah ... Ah ... *oyes tú!* Tina! Tina! In front of my
own home. *(Picking up small rock.)* He dares to come to
my own home ... Tina!

VENDOR: Don Juan, don't throw that rock! ... I'm warning you. *(Tina comes out of the house, seeing her, Juan stands still with rock in hand, aimed at the Vendor.)* Forgive me, *Señora*, for causing this excitement but sometimes Don Juan ...

JUAN: *(Keeping rock aimed.)* Mr. Peña, to you.

VENDOR: That man has a very dark nature. Please *Señora*, tell him not to become so excited when he sees me. Not to shout at me and not to run after me in the traffic throwing rocks. He is too old to be doing these things. One day he will hurt himself or, who knows, in this country some person may become offended by his behavior and take it upon themselves to strike back.

JUAN: Too old?!

TINA: *(To Juan.)* That's why nobody comes to see us. Why do you do these things?

JUAN: Too old! Too old!

TINA: Juan don't throw the rock!

JUAN: *(Throwing the rock.)* Too old, am I? I'll show you who's too old. *(Vendor ducks behind his bicycle cart as Juan looks for more rocks.)* He is a thief! Robbing the people ... That's what he does ... *(Shouting.)* Neighbors! Friends!

TINA: We don't have any friends.

JUAN: *(Shouting.)* People on Castro Street! Don't buy from this man. He steals his goods from the back of the central market and then charges you double. You come to my stand, Peña's International Discounts, goods from around the world.

TINA: *(To Vendor.)* Nobody will come. They know him.

JUAN: I can get anything! *(Shouting.)* Anybody from Castro Street gets ten percent off. Next week for my first anniversary sale we got shoes from Brazil

TINA: Juan!

JUAN: What?

TINA: That's enough, give people some peace.

VENDOR: *Vamos Don* Juan! There is room for everybody. We all have a right to make a living.

JUAN: Rights!

TINA: Shhhhhhh!

JUAN: He doesn't even have a license.

VENDOR: *(Getting on his bicycle cart.) Don* Juan, we are now living in a free country. *(Exit Vendor.)*

JUAN: *(Yelling after him.)* Free! Free?! Nobody lives in a free country ... You hear me anarchist?! Nobody! No country is free. You fool, it's all an illusion. Tearing up the world, killing yourselves, all for your stupid illusions.

TINA: Calm down now.

JUAN: *Y la neña?*

TIN A. Typing class.

JUAN: Why she type at night? She took her sweater?

TINA: The red one.

JUAN: What time will she be back? The red one with the little scottie dogs?

TINA: Don't be after her so much. Let her be alone. She needs time for herself.

JUAN: What for? What does she do?

TINA: I don't know. Maybe she needs to think.

JUAN: About what? What is she thinking?

TINA: I don't know! A person needs time to be alone.

JUAN: That's what you said about Sarita. "Let her grow up", you said. "Leave her alone", you said. And look what happened. Her head was filled with illusions. "Make peace not war, hell no we won't go". Stupid illusions. Love, romance ... and the first *babosos* with beads and a flower ... and I lost my daughter.

TINA: Don't ... don't start again.

JUAN: We are the ones that suffer.

TINA: She suffered ... Enough ... fourteen years are enough. If I think about it it's like yesterday ... we should have helped her ...

JUAN: *Vamos Vieja.* Go take your medicine ...

(Juan and Tina go into the house as lights cross fade.
Junior and Olivia look down from the roof.)

JUNIOR: Why's he get so mad?

OLIVIA: He says it's because life is hard.

JUNIOR: Yeah, right.

OLIVIA: Grandma says he does it out of sheer enjoyment.

JUNIOR: Yeah, well, I don't want him getting mad at me,
because you're up here.

OLIVIA: He won't, not really.

JUNIOR: Yeah. Right. That's what you say ... but I'm not
responsible for you too.

OLIVIA: Nobody asked you to be responsible for me.

JUNIOR: That's it, they'll just assume I am. I want to ...
see I gotta ... I have work to do, real work.

OLIVIA: I'm only trying to help ...

JUNIOR: And stop standing so close to me ... I ... I can't
go anywhere without bumping into you … I reach out my
arm ... You brush up behind me ... You're just in my way!

OLIVIA: Fine! I'll just leave. *(She gathers her things and*
goes down the ladder.)

JUNIOR: Fine ... Just be careful on the ladder.

OLIVIA: It's none of your business if I am or not.

(Lights fade on Junior as soft, dim lights come up on the
Rodrigues yard. We see Lilly sitting on the Rodrigues
stoop lost in thought as the Vendor rides his bicycle across
the stage, tipping his hat to Lilly, who does not notice, and
Olivia, who does as she comes down the ladder.)

VENDOR: The sky is indigo blue, the EVENING STAR
has risen, there is a soft breeze, the succulent aromas of
dinners cooking and bubbling. *(He sniffs the air.)*
somebody in this neighborhood is roasting a young. tender

chicken ... Mrs. Amador ... I'll just bring along some wild rosemary.

OLIVIA: Love is a low born thing with a hairy forehead.

LILLY: Huh?

OLIVIA: All he wants out of life is a stupid summer job at the stupid Dairy Queen.

LILLY: Joey used to work at the Dairy Queen ... He used to make black cows.

OLIVIA: Where is his soul?

LILLY: First he would put two scoops of vanilla ice cream into a tall frosty glass ... then he would look into my eyes, as he slowly poured the coke into the glass.

OLIVIA: Well, he says, "I set my goals and I go after them".

LILLY: When he made banana splits, he wrote "I love you," with little chocolate sprinkles right on the top. I ate so many of them ...

OLIVIA: I'm just too good for him.

LILLY. Junior said if I kept eating them I'd look like a land mass with a lobotomy.

OLIVIA: Don't cry, Lilly.

LILLY: Joey was so sweet to me and then he just stopped seeing me. Mama calls him a no good *chinzon* ... and a bum but I still love him and now he won't ...

OLIVIA: *(Interrupting.)* Thats it!

LI LLY: What??

OLIVIA: One of the great mysteries of love ... it makes you love people who aren't good enough for you.

LILLY: Yeah ... that's so beautiful. Olivia, you are the most sensitive person I know.

OLIVIA: It's our job to lift and inspire men.

LILLY: Yesterday you said it was to make them happy.

OLIVIA: Once they're lifted and inspired they'll be happy. O.K. now, where were we yesterday.

LILLY: You slowly see him across the room.

OLIVIA: O.K., so he's across the room, then what?

LILLY: He's not just across the room like some old lamp ... he's across the room. O.K., real slow now ... turn ... look up ... give him the look ... no, don't smile, more like you got a secret ... now look down ... Oh oh oh. (*Lilly clutches her stomach as Olivia comes to her aid.*)
OLIVIA: What's wrong ...
LILLY: Olivia, you gotta promise ...
OLIVIA: What? Promise what?
LILLY: Nothing. just leave me alone, O.K.
OLIVIA: What's wrong?
LILLY: I said leave me alone.

(*Lilly gets up, runs away. Exit Lilly.*)

OLIVIA: Lilly! Lilly!

(*Junior sticks his head out from the edge of the roof.*)

JUNIOR: Hurry up, Olivia, I've got the comet, took two pictures but the tail is so long ...

(*Olivia climbs the ladder, lights fade slowly. We hear the sound of crickets, now and then the bark of a lonely dog. Juan enters from his house. He turns on the porch light, giving the porch, and house the effect of looking like a Japanese lantern. Juan sits down, next to him a small batch of blue envelopes. He reads a letter as Tina enters from the house carrying plates and silverware. She sets a little table.*)

TINA: Don't start.
JUAN. It's all we have left of her.
TINA: You have to give those letters to Olivia someday.

JUAN: *(Reading.)* "I ran all the way back so I could see the reflection of the sunset glowing on all the windows of Paris and to tell you that I am in love. His name is Mario. He has broad shoulders, a black mustache and hard mineral eyes that stab at your heart. He is from Argentina where Mario says people are disappearing". *(There is a moment of silence. Juan takes a few deep breaths.)* I can feel my lungs rattling.
TINA: Rattling? How do you mean rattling? Not wheezing?
JUAN: Rattling! Rattling like an old man before he dies.
TINA: You' re not going to die. Let me feel your forehead. You feel a little warm.

(Juan takes Tina's hand and kisses the palm.)

JUAN: Do my eyes still stab at your heart?

(She turns away from him.)

TINA: Hurry up and water the new corn before you forget.
JUAN: I don't know what's wrong with you.
TINA: I'm like the garden moths. The ants paralyze them with their bite and then suck out their juices ... All my juices are sucked up, just my empty body is here.

(Tina goes into house. Juan steps out into the yard, he kicks the ground. He looks up and down Castro Street. He looks at his watch. He goes back into the house as Vendor enters.)

VENDOR: The black pantheress is on the path ... do you know where your children are?

(The Vendor rides his bike to C. He faces audience as he rides his bike in place as if he was traveling through the neighborhood.)

Out here in the wilderness
the night is a black pantheress
her breath heats the blood
I feel her dark perfection
throbbing and glowering
I am the lone tracker
I follow her path
the imprints of her hands
and feet, her soles and palms ...
Down, down to the very
roots of darkness, to
the very swamp, where
she turns her dark velvet
face and gives birth to
the Day.

(Lights up on Junior and Olivia on the roof. Junior is setting up the camera to the telescope. He removes tripod from camera.)

OLIVIA: I could be an astronaut ... *(As T.V. anchorperson.)* She opened the hatch door and stepped into space, one lone dazzling death defying free fall ... checked by her umbilical cord with Earthship Jupiter II ...
JUNIOR: O.K. Let's be careful, it's very delicate ... Hold this.

(Junior hands her the tripod. Olivia continues her astronaut fantasy using tripod as microphone.)

OLIVIA: *(Into tripod/microphone.)* ... And now back here on Earth, we are talking to the famous astro-physicist Dr. Junior Rodrigues ... tell us, Dr. Rodrigues, who was your inspiration, who or what was it, that first caused you to want to leave this Earth and venture into Deep Distant Space?

MRS. RODRIGUES: *(Off stage.)* Junior! Junior Rodrigues! *(Enter Mrs. Rodrigues, a short, stocky woman of forty. She has a short, curly hair and wears gold hoop earrings. Her pants are rolled up and she has on a white, grease spattered apron.)* Junior? ... Junior, are you up there?

JUNIOR: Yeah, Mom, I am busy with ...

MRS. RODRIGUES: *(Interrupting.)* Did you go to the bank? ...

JUNIOR: Yeah mom.

MRS. RODRIGUES: And did you deposit my check? ...

JUNIOR: Yes mom.

MRS. RODRIGUES: And the phone bill? Did you pay the phone bill? ...

JUNIOR: Yes.

MRS. RODRIGUES: We got a final notice, and if we don't pay by tomorrow they gonna cut us off.

(Mrs. Rodrigues goes into her house.)

JUNIOR: I paid it ... l told you I paid it.

MRS. RODRIGUES: *(Off stage.)* She's gone! Junior she's gone! *(Mrs. Rodrigues comes out of her house.)* Where's your sister?

Junior: She was here ... in and out, slamming doors.

MRS. RODRIGUES: But did you see her? Did you see how she looked?

OLIVIA: I saw her. She was ...

MRS. RODRIGUES: She was what? What was she?

OLIVIA: Sh ... Sh ... She was ... She looked real nice, she was wearing heather grey shadow and musk.

JUNIOR: Musk?

MRS. RODRIGUES: Musk? *Qué es?*

JUNIOR: Something makes her smell weird.

OLIVIA: It's not weird! It's a natural animal scent.

MRS. RODRIGUES: The scent of animals! She is putting on the scent of animals!

JUNIOR: Mom, it's not like that ...

MRS. RODRIGUES: And you, why do I have to tell you, keep an eye on your sister, your duty as a brother is to know where your sister is at all times. I tell you some spirit is trying to steal her.

JUNIOR: Yeah ... right. Who in their right mind ...

MRS. RODRIGUES: Look! Look for yourself. You can see the first signs of captivation in her eyes ... they are not the same. She has been enchanted I tell you.

JUNIOR: Mom, those are moron eyes, she's always had them.

MRS. RODRIGUES: She is being enticed, pulled by a powerful magnet ... she is restless ... can't stay inside the house. At night, when she is asleep she is troubled. She throws the blankets off her bed, her own clothes can not restrain her. Her hair is slippery, it comes loose in my own hands. Some spirit is calling her, stealing her from my side where God in his wisdom put her. We have to go right now and find her.

JUNIOR: I can't leave, I'm in the middle of my project ... it's important.. It's the only time I can do it and it might lead to ...

MRS. RODRIGUES: *(Interrupting.) Ay Virgencita*, help me bear it. My own son won't help me.

JUNIOR: She'll be back, unless she took the refrigerator with her.

MRS. RODRIGUES: There is something wrong ... She's sick or something.

JUNIOR: She's not sick, she eats like a horse ... Ah Mom come on ... don't make me feel ...

MRS. RODRIGUES: *(Interrupting.)* Oh no, I wouldn't dream to make you feel anything. Go back to your magnifying telescopio.

JUNIOR: Astroscanner! ... It's an astroscanner.

MRS. RODRIGUES: Oh, forgive me. Astro-es-scanner. How could I be so stupid.

JUNIOR: I didn't mean you were stupid. I never said that. O.K., o.k.! I'll go ... I just want you to realize ...

MRS. RODRIGUES: *(Interrupting.)* Stay! Stay with your astro-es-scanner. Count the stars, find a cure for cancer, communicate with the aliens, don't concern yourself. Goodbye Olivia.

OLIVIA: *(Waving.)* Bye ... nice to see you.

MRS. RODRIGUES: *Adios* Junior, I hope I haven't disturbed your tranquility with these petty family problems. *(Exit Mrs. Rodrigues.)*

JUNIOR: I AM NOT TRANQUIL! ... Ah Mom ... what's the use ... *(Junior goes to the telescope.)*

OLIVIA: Junior, I didn't want to say anything, but I think Lilly ...

JUNIOR: *(Interrupting.)* Olivia! You moved it! After I told you not to move it. You ... you touched the lens ... How could you? Aw, ya got your fingerprints all over the lens.

OLIVIA: I did not! ... And besides, you didn't say not to.

JUNIOR: I did! ... I said it . .I said it real clear.

OLIVIA: You did not!

JUNIOR: *(Yelling.)* I did too!

(Juan comes out of his house wearing a jacket. He starts down the street when he hears Junior yelling.)

JUAN: Who's out there? Olivia? *(Olivia ducks down.)*

JUNIOR: It's ... me Mr. Peña ... Junior from next door.

JUAN: What the hell you doing up there?

JUNIOR: I'm trying to take a picture of a comet.

JUAN: What for? The Russians already took pictures.

JUNIOR: It's my project for science fair.

JUAN: They pay you for it?

JUNIOR: Well ... no.

JUAN: Then it's stupid. Listen, point that thing down the street, see if my granddaughter's coming ... You see her? She got her little red sweater on ... *Vamos mi hijo si o no.*

JUNIOR: Uh ... I, uh ... I can't see her ... not in the astroscanner ... if you're asking me if I can see her through this astroscanner my answer would have to be no.

JUAN: Astro-es-scanner? Get a Japanese moped instead of that thing ... with a Japanese moped you could be a messenger. Stop all this space nonsense, stay here on earth, run errands, have a good paper route, be of some use.

JUNIOR: I wasn't planning ...

JUAN: *(Interrupting.)* All this hope your Mama's got for you and you gonna be a no good bum ... just like all the men your Mama got mixed up with.

(Exit Juan into his house. Olivia gets back up.)

JUNIOR: That's it. Off the roof.

OLIVIA: Why?

JUNIOR: Because you don't really care about this, because it's gonna take ten minutes to set this up again, because you're always too close, always in my way and because I gotta lie for you all the time.

OLIVIA: Nobody asked you to lie for me.

JUNIOR: What was I supposed to do, say yeah, here she is, she lied to you. She never goes to typing class. She just comes up here and lies and makes up stuff about the stars.

OLIVIA: I do not make up stuff about the stars.

JUNIOR: *(Imitating Olivia.)* Oh, Junior, my eyes are weary from gazing at ancient stars two million light-years away ... Oh, Junior, shooting stars have a fatal attraction to me.

OLIVIA: Not me, us, the Earth.

JUNIOR: You make it sound dumb and crazy. This is science, where you have facts. Real things, things you can count on, things that are solid and firm, things that don't let you down ever. This is serious work. this is expensive equipment I had to borrow, and be responsible for. So I don't have time for you or your crazy ignorant grandfather.

OLIVIA: He is not ignorant, and he is not crazy.

JUNIOR: Everybody in the neighborhood calls him *"Viejo Loco."*

OLIVIA: If you think I'm gonna stay on this shabby roof and keep you company one moment longer ...

JUNIOR: *(Interrupting.)* Your roof is worse.

OLIVIA: While you insult my family ...

JUNIOR: Can't even stand on your roof, did you know that? Or did you think it was a superior roof just because a Cuban family lives under it?

OLIVIA: Yes I did. And it is.

JUNIOR: Well it isn't ... so grow up and face reality.

OLIVIA: I refuse to listen to anyone who uses ethnic slurs.

JUNIOR: I didn't use ethnic slurs, I just said that you think you're superior because ...

OLIVIA: *(Interrupting.)* Besides, all the neighbors call you Junior *"El Nurd"* Rodrigues.

JUNIOR: And you ... *tú es la lier.*

OLIVIA: *Eres*, you shouldn't even speak Spanish if you can't say it properly. It should be *eres "la lier".*

JUNIOR: I don't have to speak Spanish. They don't have Castilian in science.

OLIVIA: You ... you have no culture. Peasant!

JUNIOR: *(Imitating a lisping Spanish.)* *Tú ves qué brillante están las estrallas cómo tus ojos mala guena salerosa.*

OLIVIA: Just shut up. I'm going.

JUNIOR: See how stupid you sound, just grow up. Look at reality, stop making everything so fantastic and phony.

OLIVIA: I see reality, I see too much reality, so don't worry about it, o.k.

JUNIOR: Olivia ... I didn't mean ...

OLIVIA: *(Crying.)* It's all around me hard, ugly reality. I just have to turn it into something else or I'll die ... or stop trying.

JUNIOR: Yeah right. Sometimes I get sick of trying. ... See, I thought if I did this science fair, I would have something to show ... and I would have a chance to work at a lab, ya know ... but nobody's gonna take me seriously.

OLIVIA: I do, I take you seriously.

JUNIOR: Yeah, you're just a weird kid.

OLIVIA: I am not ... I'm a woman in case you haven't noticed, and I say you're perfect just as you are ... you're smart and good and strong and ...

JUNIOR: Yeah?...

OLIVIA: And when you say "yeah, right", you sound like ... like ...

JUNIOR: Yeah? ...

OLIVIA: Like a movie star ... You know, sexy ...

JUNIOR: *(Advancing on Olivia.)* Yeah ... right ...

OLIVIA: I should go ... *(Junior kisses Olivia. It is a long passionate kiss.)*

JUNIOR: Stay. *(Junior tries to kiss Olivia again. Olivia breaks away from him.)*

OLIVIA: No!

JUNIOR: I thought you ...

OLIVIA: No, I mean it's too soon ... I mean I don't know ...

JUNIOR: You don't know what you mean, you're just a baby playing games. Well I don't want no baby, I want a woman. Yeah. Right.

(Olivia runs into her house and slams the door. Silence for a beat as Junior stands motionless on the roof. We hear the offstage voice of the Vendor.)

VENDOR: *(Off stage.)* The stars are out, the air is soft, the night is young. If you want him to be more of a man, be more of a woman. Use lavender, lemon balm, and sandalwood. *(Vendor enters.)* Ssssh! ... do you hear the roots breathing under the cement and asphalt ... did you hear that rumble? They're cracking through stone. *(Exit Vendor.)*

MRS. RODRIGUES: *(Off stage.)* Junior! Junior Rodrigues!

JUNIOR: Yeah Mom, I'm over here. *(Enter Mrs. Rodrigues looking very tired.)*

MRS. RODRIGUES: I couldn't find her. *Virgencita*, I couldn't find her. I looked everywhere, I asked everybody.

JUNIOR: I'll go Mom.

MRS. RODRIGUES: Wait *hijo*, stay with me a minute ... I got this feeling, this bad feeling ... this emptiness ... this empty space inside me where somebody just cut something out and all my insides are gonna cave in.

JUNIOR: Yeah, I know.

MRS. RODRIGUES: Last time I had this feeling was when Emilio left us. Just like that, you was seven years old and I was working over at the tuna factory, Starkist.... What a stupid name. There you were ... sitting by the door holding on to Lilly, both of you crying. Landlord locked us out, and Emilio left us ... we sure as hell weren't kissed by no star.

JUNIOR: I'm nothin' like him.

MRS. RODRIGUES: You were more of a man at seven than that *pinchi pendejo*. Ah, what the hell. Can't be mad at him, times were tough. He just couldn't take it, no job, no prospects. You gonna take it though, no matter what the world throws at you, you can handle it.

JUNIOR: Yeah, right. No summer job, I feel bad about that Mom ... Hey! where have you been? (Enter a reluctant Lilly.)

LILLY: I lost my shoe. *(Mrs. Rodrigues grabs Lilly by the hair and pulls her towards the house.)* Mama, let go of me!

MRS. RODRIGUES: No *Señorita*! I'm gonna fight this curse ... this bewitchment with all my strength.

LILLY: Mama, I don't have a bewitchment ... I have a ... please let go of me ...

MRS. RODRIGUES: No *Señorita*, if I let go of you, you see what happens? *(Lilly takes a step away from her mother when her mother lets go of her.)* Look Junior, look how she backs away ... you see it's like a magnet pulling her away from me. Me, your mother who bore her, who watched her sprout into a young green tree. Now someone, some air or spirit wants her. They want my tender shoot, her greenness, her freshness, her sweetness. But I will fight them ... they will see who they are up against. Tomorrow I will ask the Vendor for beef blood and fresh turkey eggs.

LILLY: Oh, gross! Oh Mama, I'm gonna be sick.

MRS. RODRIGUES: No, you're gonna be strong ... they won't be able to pull you away so easily.

LILLY: Mama please listen ...

MRS. RODRIGUES: *Vas a ve*r, when I was bewitched by that woman ... the one with the red hair and the moles on her neck ... the one they called *"La Pera"* ... Junior, you remember her?... The one tried to give you rotten candy ...

LILLY: *(Interrupting.)* Mama, please, please listen I'm gonna have a baby ... I'm pregnant Mama ... Oh please Mama, don't be mad.

MRS. RODRIGUES: You remember Junior ... you wanted that candy ... Oh you loved your candy.... When you were little you used to hold your hand out and say "crandy". *(Without missing a beat, Mrs. Rodrigues takes her out-stretched hand and slaps Lilly across the face, knocking her back a few feet. Tears are running down her cheeks.)* Oh, how you loved your "crandy".

(Junior rushes to help Lilly.)

JUNIOR: Mom! Take it easy Mom.
MRS. RODRIGUES: *(Looking up to the stars, shaking her fists at the heavens.)* SHIT! PURE SHIT! That's what you send me ... All these years struggling and scraping, bowing and smiling, and you turn my tender, delicate off-shoot into a viper, a common slut, a whore ... Starkist! Starkist! Well kiss my ass!

(Mrs. Rodrigues takes the fist with which she was threatening heaven and turns it on Lilly. Junior comes between them, Lilly breaks away and runs into the night.)

JUNIOR: LILLY! LILLY!

(Mrs. Rodrigues falls to the ground and pounds the dirt with her fists. Junior runs after Lilly. Lights go down.)

VENDOR: *(Off stage.)* Lilly! ... Lilly! ... Come back, come back to your garden little fawn.

(Blackout.)

*(Lights come up on the front porch of the Peña house.
Juan Peña is seated at a little table reading the obituary
column of* "La Opinion". *Seated on the steps of the porch
is Olivia Peña. She has a telephone directory on her lap
and in her right hand a black magic marker.)*

JUAN: Picallo, Lorenzo ... 58 years old ... heart attack.
OLIVIA: *(Looking for name in phone book.)* Picallo ...
Lorenzo ... Got it! *(Finding the name, she crosses it out of
the phone book.)*
JUAN: Another Cuban! Cota, Raule ... 65 years old ...
heart attack.
OLIVIA: *(Looking it up in the phone book.)* Cota ... Cota
... Raule ...
JUAN: Survived by a daughter ... she lives in Alaska.
Poor man his only daughter and she goes off to Alaska!
OLIVIA: *(Still looking for name.)* Cota .. Raule ...
JUAN: On Soto Street.
OLIVIA: *(Finding the name she crosses it out of the phone
book.)* Cota, Raule, on Soto Street .. got it.
JUAN: Plana, Antonio ... 49 years old.
OLIVIA: *(Looking for name.)* Plana .. Antonio ...
JUAN: Columbian, dies of a stroke, no survivors ... got it?
OLIVIA: *(Finding name she crosses it off.)* Plana,
Antonio ... got it!
JUAN: Be careful, don't cross off the wrong name ... Eh?
... You understand? ... Ah! Finally a woman ... María
Elizabeth Martinez ... Ah! A big shot ... head of the Alter
and Rosary Society in Pico Rivera ... born Havana, Cuba ...
82 years old ... killed instantly when her motorcycle
crashed head-on into a six wheel truck on the freeway.
OLIVIA: Way to go!
JUAN: Tina! Tina!
OLIVIA: That's how I wanna go *Abuelo* ... alive to the
very last minute.

JUAN: Stop talking nonsense and cross off her name. Tina! Tina!

OLIVIA: *(Looking for name.)* María Elizabeth Martinez ...

(Enter Tina in faded bath robe. She carries a tray with cookies and coffee.)

JUAN: Listen to this obituary ... this Martinez woman, 82 years old ...

OLIVIA: *(Still looking.)* M. E. Martinez ...

JUAN: Head of the Alter and Rosary Society in Pico Rivera ... guess how she dies?

TINA: I don't want to know.

OLIVIA: *(Still looking.)* María Martinez ...

JUAN: This 82 year old Cuban woman, she dies when her....

TINA: *(Interrupting.)* No! I don't want to hear it.

JUAN: You don't?

TINA: NO! NO! NO! I don't want to know, I don't want to hear it.

JUAN: It's funny ...

TINA: I'm so tired.

JUAN: What's the matter with you? Did you take your medicine?

TINA: Every evening it's the same thing ... death ... more death ... more people dying .. .it's not right ... Why do you have to do this every night in our own home.

OLIVIA: *(Still looking.)* E. Martinez ...

JUAN: What you want me to do, Eh? It costs me money to send the fliers, *y las noticas* through the mail. Every time I send an announcement to tell the people about my sales it costs me money ... How else they gonna know to come and buy, and dead people don't buy anything.

TINA: There must be a better way to do it.

JUAN: Don't mix into business, Tina. You don't know anything about it. All the big companies do it ... Ford, General Motors, they all do it.

TINA: I just don't believe that this Mr. Ford makes his granddaughter cross the names of dead people out of the phone book so he can save money on advertising.

JUAN: She likes it.

TINA: What are you saying?

OLIVIA: I can't find her.

TINA: It's not healthy.

JUAN: Not healthy!? Who's not healthy? Am I the one who locks herself in her room crying all the time? Olivia, tell your grandmother who's healthy around here, go on! *Vamos!* Tell her.

OLIVIA: *(Crying.)* I can't find her!

JUAN: Who! ... Who?

TINA: Leave her alone.

OLIVIA: Mrs. Martinez ... I can't find her.

JUAN: Then forget her! She's not worth it!

OLIVIA: Yes she is! She was 82 years old and she was happy, she had fun.

TINA: *Tranquela hija, tranquela.*

OLIVIA: She was alive!

JUAN: And now she's dead.

OLIVIA: No! No!

JUAN: *Sí, sí, hija.* What can I do?

OLIVIA: *(Continues looking.)* You don't understand, *Abuelo*.

TINA: He never understands, he doesn't listen. That's why were alone.

JUAN: Don't start with that again.

OLIVIA: *(Finding name in phone book.)* Mimi Martinez! That's her! Mimi Martinez, Pico Rivera Boulevard. I found her!

JUAN: Cross her off and we' re finished for today. Now everybody go to bed.

OLIVIA: I can't, *Abuelo*. I can't cross her off. Don't ask me to, please.

JUAN: It's only a name.

OLIVIA: Not to me. She's special ...

JUAN: Goddamnit! It's only a name in the paper.

TINA: Barbarian! She's very sensitive like her mother. You never ...

JUAN: *(Interrupting.)* Stop it! I don't want to hear another word. What next, you want me to drive her to Pico Rivera, to see the old lady's house, talk to the neighbors?

OLIVIA: Could we *Abuelo*? I mean really go to Pico Rivera?

JUAN: Don't be ridiculous!

OLIVIA: I guess it is silly ... kinda stupid, huh?

JUAN: Yes! *Vamos,* at last somebody understands. Now, everybody to bed!

OLIVIA: Night *Abuelo* ... goodnight *Abuela*.

(Olivia kisses her grandparents goodnight and exits into house. Tina looks out from front porch and Juan looks at her.)

JUAN: What's the matter. You gonna get one of your depressions?

TINA: The world is a hard place.

JUAN: That's what I been trying to tell you all the time, competition, back stabbing, hustling just to make a little money. You got nothing if you don't got money in this country.

TINA: It's hard to keep your spirit up.

JUAN: Who's got time to think of spirit? We're no better than animals. That's what I feel like sometimes, Tina.

TINA: All this money, money, money. What happens to people? To our children? Something is very wrong.

(Blackout.)

(Lights come up on Lilly, who is throwing rocks at an upper window of the Peña house.)

LILLY: Psst! Olivia! Olivia! Oh please ... Olivia! *(Tina comes out of the house in her robe and slippers.)*
TINA: Who's out there ... Olivia?

(Lilly tries to run but she is overwhelmed by the pain.)

LILLY: It's only me ... I'm sorry I didn't mean ...

(Tina sees something is wrong and takes hold of Lilly.)

TINA: Lilly ... you shouldn't be out here ... Oh, what is it Lilly? You're trembling ... and perspiring, oh honey you're sick ... Come here ...

(She takes Lilly to the porch.)

LILLY: I'm gonna have a baby ... Mrs. Peña please help me ... Mama's so mad ... I'm scared ... am I gonna die?

(Tina cradles Lilly in her arms and rocks her.)

TINA: Ssh! Now you're not gonna die. I'm here, I'm here to help you.

(Lilly goes into a pain spasm.)

TINA: How long have you been having these pains?

LILLY: Just for the last few hours.
TINA: How often baby, can you remember?
LILLY: Every ... every 20 minutes.

(Tina takes off her robe and puts it around Lilly.)

TINA: Lilly, I want you to stay right here honey. Don't move. I'm gonna call for the doctor and I'll be right back. O.K.?
LILLY: O.K.

(Tina goes into the house as Lilly sits on the porch, we hear the offstage voices of Junior, Mrs. Rodrigues and Vendor calling for Lilly. Lilly hides in the shadow of the porch. Tina comes out wearing Juan's robe. She sits beside Lilly.)

TINA: Your mama isn't home yet but I know she's worried ... Doctor's on his way, so you come into the house, lie down.
LILLY: I don't wanna move yet ...
TINA: Tell me ... tell me about the boy.
LILLY: I haven't seen him much, somebody said he dropped out of school or he moved or something ... I don't know ...
TINA: Did you ... did you have feelings for him?
LILLY: I don't know anymore ... I guess I loved him ... I mean l didn't cry or anything ... I don't know ... I don't feel different ... I still feel the same ... maybe it happens when the baby comes ... I guess everything will change then ... then I'll have somebody ... I'll be a mother, I'll be somebody. I'll get my act together ... I'll study ... work hard after school. I'll get my own place, you know have the furniture, the colors I like. I already thought about the baby's room. It's gonna have little blue and white flowered

wallpaper and white eyelet curtains. and if it's a boy I'm gonna call him Matt and if it's a girl Jessica.

TINA: It isn't a doll! ... I'm sorry ... I'm sorry honey, oh God, how is it we didn't know?

LILLY: Nobody knew. I guess l did a good job hiding it, huh?

TINA: That's because you're so skinny. You haven't been taking care of yourself and you haven't seen a doctor ... something's wrong ... you shouldn't be having these pains now.

LILLY: What do you mean? I'm scared ... am I gonna die? Could I die? ... Like Olivia's Mom?

TINA: No, no, no, you're not going to die ... that was different ... see ... we didn't know ... I wasn't there ... I'm gonna find your mama.

LILLY: No ... she'll just get mad ... *(Lilly runs away.)*

TINA: Lilly, come back.

VENDOR: *(Off stage.)* Lillyl...Lilly!...Come back, come back to your garden little fawn.

(We hear the clucking of chickens, lights go up on Peña house. Juan sticks his head out of his bedroom window.)

JUAN: Who's there?! Tina?! Tina?! Where are you? Where's my rock? Somebody's trying to steal my chickens! *(Juan gets his rock and hurls it out of his bedroom window.)* Get the hell outta my yard! ... *(Juan's rock hits a figure who falls down.)* I got 'em! I got 'em!

VENDOR: Ouch!

(Tina steps out of the porch.)

TINA: Will you stop throwing those rocks!

JUAN: Tina, what's going on? What the hell you doing down there?

VENDOR: I came looking for Lilly, I put two and two together and I came here.

(Tina and Vendor talk to each other in whispers paying no attention to Juan.)

JUAN: Why would you come here? We don't know where anybody is. Because we don't mix in other peoples business ... and that's the way we want it ... That's the way we live. Not like you, putting your nose in everybody's ...
OLIVIA: *(Coming out of house.)* They're on their way!

(Tina and Vendor continue whispering as they go into the house.)

JUAN: Who!?
OLIVIA: Oh, hi *Abuelo* ...
JUAN: Who's on their way?
OLIVIA: The paramedics ... Lilly's having a baby in my room ...

(Olivia runs into the house.)

JUAN: What the hell's wrong with her own house?! Eh? Why can't she have it at her ... Olivia! ... Tina!

(He exits window. Olivia comes out the front door, talking over her shoulder.)

OLIVIA: *Abuela*, please let me stay ... I can help ... it won't affect me, honest! It's my room! *(Olivia sits on porch steps.)* I'm old enough to type. Next year, if I wanted to, I could get a learner's permit and learn how to drive. If we lived in Venezuela I would be old enough to learn how to fly ... If we lived in Missouri and I killed somebody I would be old enough to go to the electric chair ... If we lived with the Masai in Kenya I would be old enough to be exchanged as a bride for a bunch of cows ... So, how old do I have to be around here co be treated like an adult? *(Shouting at the house.)* I know all about these things!... I know all about having babies! ... I saw that Walt Disney movie too, ya know!... You don't know everything!

(Juan comes out of the house, he sits down on the top step of the porch and shakes his head. There is a long beat of silence.)

JUAN: That little girl, that skinny little snot nose, is in our house having a baby.
OLIVIA: In my room ... And I can't even go in.
JUAN: Stop talking nonsense ... you're too young to go in there ... you don't know what this is all about.
OLIVIA: I do too! And I'm the same age she is ... So if she's old enough to be having a baby I'm certainly old enough to ...
JUAN: *(Interrupting.)* WHAT ARE YOU SAYING!? WHAT ARE YOU THINKING OF? WHAT DO YOU MEAN "YOU'RE THE SAME AGE"!? HOW OLD ARE YOU!? ARE YOU DOING THINGS TOO!?
OLIVIA: No! No *Abuela* ... Ah ... Eh ... I just meant we are the same age.... You know.... She's 14, I'm 14 ... Well maybe she is a little older ... see she was born in July, July 12th to be exact. I remember that because I got her an Eddie Van Halen album ... you know the one where he's got that knife stuck in his ear? I thought she would like it but being born in July makes her a Leo and although Leo's are fiercely loyal friends and are full of generosity, creativity, and originality although sometimes they can be

lazy and vain, they don't mind telling you when they don't like something and, well, she didn't like it, which hurt my feelings because I'm a Libra which makes me very sensitive and diplomatic, now Libras, on the other hand,...

JUAN: *(Interrupting.)* YOU'RE CHILDREN! ... DON'T YOU REALIZE WHAT'S HAPPENING HERE!

OLIVIA: I don't know *Abuela* ... I didn't know anything ... She just came over while you were asleep.... She threw rocks at my window because she was sick and she was crying and she said her Mama got really mad and she was scared ... so I got Grandma who was helping her, and I was calling on the telephone for the paramedics, and the man on the phone said I had the wrong number and that I was supposed to call the fire department and how was I supposed to know that and then you yelled something about stealing chickens and I don't know anything about that either.

JUAN: She was your little friend, she didn't say anything to you?

OLIVIA: I didn't know anything.... *(Crying.)* Because I'm so stupid. Junior's right … I'm just a baby ... a stupid, dumb baby ... I'm not sensitive, I'm thick and clumsy and retarded ... Oh, it's all so confusing ... one minute you're up on the roof wishing on stars and the next minute you're grounded, betrayed by your own body, by your own feelings ... and you know it will never be the same again, you know what I mean *Abuelo*? No matter how many falling stars I wish on, I won't ever be as free, I lost something, and I won't ever find it again ... I'm not a little girl any more, but I'm not ready to ...

JUAN: *(Embracing Olivia.)* You'll always be my little girl ... and I got all the things you think you lost up here. *(Pointing to his head.)* So when you get lonesome for all those things and you want to visit, you come to *Abuelo*.

(Tina comes out of the house.)

TINA: *Y los* paramedics?

JUAN: They stopped to have doughnuts ... Who knows where they are ... A person could die waiting for them. And Lilly?

TINA: Olivia, go see if Mrs. Rodrigues or Junior are home yet. *(Exit Olivia.)* Juan, it's too soon for the baby to come ... 6 months, it's too soon. Maybe too small to survive.

JUAN: Maybe it's for the best.

TINA: How can you say that?... You can say that because you're not a woman.... It's the promise ... when I held my daughter ... I felt so ... like part of the earth ...

JUAN: (Interrupting.) And I ... I didn't feel anything? I left the hospital ... as soon as I stepped outside I looked at the stars ... it was pitch black, there was a little wind and all the stars were dancing ... I swear there were angels out there ... I felt proud and humble at the same time and I felt at last at home.

TINA: Why don't you talk to me like this more often? And not always yelling and throwing rocks ... You can be very romantic when you want to ...

JUAN: *(Interrupting.)* What the hell ... Ah, MRS. RODRIGUES! *(Enter Mrs. Rodrigues.)*

MRS. RODRIGUES: Is she alright? Is she alright? My poor Lilly?

TINA: She's in Olivia's room. We're waiting for those *pinchi* paramedics ... I don't know where they could be ... come on ... don't you want to see her?

MRS. RODRIGUES: I ... don't know if I should go ... I said things ... you know I was upset.... Maybe she doesn't want to see me.

JUAN: Of course you were upset, what did she expect? And if I get my hands on that boy he ...

TINA: *(Interrupting.)* Juan! Just be quiet, for once in your life just close your mouth and say nothing. Go out on the street and find those paramedics. *(Exit Juan.)*

MRS. RODRIGUES: *Ay* Tina ... my child ... what will become of her? How will I take care of them? I'm working two shifts now, and I can barely make ends meet ... Maybe if I hadn't taken that second shift I could have been with her more ... Maybe this wouldn't have happened ... But my rent got raised, the utilities, food, clothing, everything goin' sky high ... She's a good girl ... maybe not smart like her brother, but I had hopes ... She always needed so much love ... maybe because her Papa left ... What are we goin' to do? My family is going deeper and deeper into a dark hole ... Will we ever climb out?

TINA: Hush now, don't think about that now.

LILLY: *(Off stage.)* Mama! Mama! Are you there Mama?

TINA: Go, give her strength.

MRS. RODRIGUES: I'm coming baby, your Mama's here, your Mama's here.

(Exit Mrs. Rodrigues into the house as Juan enters.)

TINA: Well?

JUAN: I found Junior. I told him to stand on the corner and wait for them.

TINA: That's all?

JUAN: Oh yeah, I told him he wasn't a bum and not to think he wasn't a good boy.

TINA: What about the paramedics? Didn't you call them again?

JUAN: How can I call them? The phone's in the house and you don't want me to go in the house.

TINA: You're impossible.

JUAN: What do you want me to do?

TINA: Nothing. I'll do it myself. Just stand there. Stay out of the way. Just stand there and ... and eh ... and pray.

(Exit Tina into the house. Juan stands there and looks up to the heavens. He folds his hands in prayer, feels uncomfortable, gets down on his knees, tries folding his hands again, feels uncomfortable, gets up, puts his hands in his pockets and continues to look at the heavens.)

JUAN: What the hell's going on?! You playing a joke?! A person works hard ... we ain't got no angels to help us down here ... it's hard down here ... what's right? What's wrong? Sometimes I can't tell....What are we doing wrong? How can we help ourselves? How can we have hope? And if we don't have hope, what is left to give our children? And what will they give their children? Are we dying? Sometimes I feel dead and grey, then I look at my granddaughter stepping out like a young butterfly from a split chrysalis ... Oh God, let me have the joy of seeing her fly, of spreading her wings and gaining her color.... Don't shoot her down in mid-flight.

(Lights go down as we hear the sound of a siren. Pin spot on Olivia and Junior on the roof looking at the stars. As the sun begins its slow ascent on the horizon, we hear the offstage voice of the Vendor.)

VENDOR: *(Off stage.)* The sun is rising ... Another day of life, try not to abuse it ... Anyway as little as human frailty will allow.

(Lights slowly fade to black.)

END OF PLAY

PROPERTY LIST

Door key
Astroscan telescope
Coin purse
Pushcart bicycle
Herbs in packets
School books
Ladder
Rocks
Brown bag of groceries
Copy of *"La Opinion"*
Small batch of blue envelopes with letters inside
Plates and silverware
Camera with tripod
Telephone book
Black Magic Marker
Tray with cookies and coffee

SCENE DESIGN

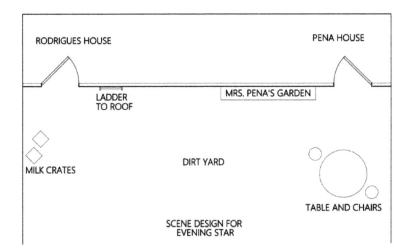

RODRIGUES HOUSE

PENA HOUSE

LADDER
TO ROOF

MRS. PENA'S GARDEN

MILK CRATES

DIRT YARD

TABLE AND CHAIRS

SCENE DESIGN FOR
EVENING STAR

The Old Matador
1991

CHARACTERS in order of appearance:
COOKIE (Raphael) Peña, a young 15 year old boy
ENRIQUE Peña, father of Cookie and Jessie, in his 50's
MARGARITA Peña, mother of Cookie and Jessie, around 40
Voice of NEWS ANNOUNCER
Voice of FRENCH SPORTS ANNOUNCER
1ST BOY
2ND BOY
JESSE Peña, a young 19-20 year old girl
PACO, dancer
MANUEL, guitarist
EVELINA, dancer, bartender
FATHER STEVEN, Jesuit priest in his 40's, clumsy, funny
EL BONITO, chicano, vampire poet of the night on the radio
ANGEL, angel who falls to earth, ageless.
NEIGHBORHOOD KIDS
VOICEOVERS

TIME: The present

PLACE: Somewhere in the Southwest

ACT ONE

SCENE ONE

(Stage and house are dark. Slowly lights come up. It is a large summer sunset. The sky is a deep Matisse blue with orange and pink wisps across the horizon. There is a wood frame house with a porch. To one side of the house there is a small chicken pen. On the other side a tree. Everything is neat and well-tended. The feeling is that the sky overwhelms the house and its inhabitants. Sound of rap music comes up and continues over as Cookie, a short, pudgy boy of 15 enters. He wears a dirty white t-shirt, baggy black pants that have been cut off just below his knees, black high-top sneakers, long white socks and a red baseball cap. He is pushing a beat-up bike with a twisted front wheel. The bike has a saddle pack filled with the evening newspapers, on the handlebars a horn, a transistor radio, radio antenna, and a fox-tail. The bike makes a sound from the twisted front wheel as Cookie pushes it along. He kicks on the standing brake as he parks it in the middle of the yard. He looks to the house then quickly takes all the undelivered newspapers out of the saddle pack and throws them under the house. He looks around. He turns the radio off. He sits on the porch steps and looks at his broken bike. Sound of offstage voice gets louder and louder.)

MARGARITA: *(Offstage)* I don't believe it! I'm not going! *No, señor,* I'm not.
ENRIQUE: *(Offstage)* Ah you, you know nothing! You believe in nothing!

234

MARGARITA: *(Offstage)* And where's the money coming from… *Dios mio!!* You took our money outta the bank. Ahh! Come back here I'm talking to you.

(Cookie goes to his bike and turns on the radio. As he turns the dials, we hear scraps of music and commercials. Suddenly, the voice of News Announcer pops out.)

NEWS ANNOUNCER: After scouring the rocky slopes of the San Jacinto Mountains for three days, searchers are still hopeful of finding a 12-year old Boy Scout, who is still at this moment, lost in the wilderness.

(Rap music returns. Cookie hops on his bike. With his kick brake still on he begins to peddle his bike faster and faster. Music turns to cheering crowd, as he pretends to be racing in the Gran Prix of Monaco. Lowering his head and turning his baseball cap backwards, he peddles frantically. We hear the voice of French Sports Announcer.)

FRENCH SPORTS ANNOUNCER: And there he goes past the British team, past the Canadians and now past the Italians, who gave him a very rough time. The handsome young American, Cookie Peña, is leading the pack.

(Cookie holds both arms up in victory. As sound of a crowd cheering comes up, a suitcase is shown flying out the door. We hear a woman scream. Cookie turns off his bike's radio and jumps off his bike and stands in front of it as if to hide it. Another suitcase is thrown out through the door followed by Enrique, a portly man is his fifties who is dressed as a bullfighter. His hands are full as he tries to balance articles of clothing and a shaving kit while trying

*to dodge his wife, Margarita, who is dressed in a simple
housedress and apron.)*

MARGARITA: *¡Sinvergüenza! ¡Desgraciado!*
ENRIQUE: Stop this! I have to get to work.
MARGARITA: *(Holding a savings bond passbook.)* You
took everything! Everything! All the money we had...
what about our little *ranchito*? And what about your
daughter's wedding, eh? We're gonna need money for her
wedding.
ENRIQUE: I'm gonna give her money for the wedding.
I'm the father. I know how these things are done.
MARGARITA: Ha! You know, you know, I see how you
know... And what about me Enrique, eh? What about me?
And what about the little avocado ranch we were going to
buy... I was going to have a little garden with cucumbers,
string beans, radishes...
ENRIQUE: Well, it's my money and now it's my turn to
do what I want
MARGARITA: It's our money. Our little *ranchito* money.
You're wasting it on a foolish dream.
ENRIQUE: It's my money! I'm the one who works for it.
MARGARITA: Yes, you and that woman.
ENRIQUE: Not that again. *Mira, mi amor...*
MARGARITA: Get out! Get out!

*(She kicks the suitcase down the stairs and goes into the
house. Enrique brushes himself off. He sees Cookie.)*

ENRIQUE: Hello, son.
COOKIE: Hi, Papa.
ENRIQUE: *Tu ves...* you see how the women are? *El
amor es un desastre.*

(Margarita comes out to the porch and throws out two large framed portraits of bullfighters.)

MARGARITA: You… you are the disaster.

(Margarita goes back into the house. As Enrique picks up the pictures and gently dusts them off.)

ENRIQUE: Modeno… Manolete, the woman has no respect… these were the two greatest bullfighters in the world. Look at them, son. *(holding up the picture of Modeno)* Look, look into his eyes… grave and gentle like a priest.

(Cookie stares hard at the picture.)

ENRIQUE: Hemingway described him as a tall, grave boy who fought the bull as if he were serving mass… You could see in his eyes a mystical glow… Do you see it?

(Cookie keeps looking at the picture unsure of what he sees.)

ENRIQUE: Well, do you see it? Come on son.
COOKIE: Yeah… sorta.
ENRIQUE: He knew there was to be a sacrifice and he was ready for it.

(Margarita comes back onto the porch. Cookie runs back to his bike as if shielding it. Enrique picks up the picture of Modeno and holds it over his head for protection. Margarita throws a cape and two swords off the porch.)

MARGARITA: Look at him, Cookie! Comparing a blood sport to the holy Mass. Stop talking nonsense to the boy.

(Margarita goes back into the house.)

ENRIQUE: *(Yelling toward the house.)* His name isn't Cookie, so stop calling him Cookie. *(To Cookie.)* And you stand up straight and don't answer to the name Cookie... your name is Raphael, like the angel... *(Yelling toward the house.)* And it's not nonsense I'm teaching him, it's his heritage. *(To Cookie.)* Modeno had only one fight, son, and he gave this one fight over and over. Year by year he polished it. At Pamplona in '62, he gave two such fights on the same day. The first near perfect, but spoiled by the kill. Ay, Modeno hated to kill.

(Margarita comes out and throws a set of bull horns off the porch and stands looking at Enrique, who picks up the cape, dusts it off, and strikes a bullfighter's proud stance with his cape. With great defiance, Enrique acts out the fight, challenging Margarita as if she were the bull.)

ENRIQUE: Moreno moves toward the bull with his usual exaggerated slowness, stalking it... when the bull charges him, he does not move except to lift the cloth... calmly, slowly... letting the bull pass by performing these passes with the right hand and with the left hand, teaching the beast to concentrate on the cloth.
MARGARITA: *(Running down from the porch.)* I want the money back in the bank today.
ENRIQUE: It's not your money. It is my retirement money and if I want to go to Spain, then we go to Spain.

(With Margarita at him. Enrique puts Cookie and bike between him and Margarita. As Cookie moves to keep his mother from seeing his damages bike)

ENRIQUE: This... this is not the time for confrontations, *mi amor*... think of the boy.
MARGARITA: *(Advancing toward Enrique.)* You... you think about him.

(Enrique walks backward trying to get away from Margarita. He points to a spot offstage and starts waving.)

ENRIQUE: Look! Look! It's Mrs. Amador, standing at the window... Good. Morning... good morning, dear, Mrs. Amador. Good morning. *(To Margarita.)* I am late. I am very late for work.
MARGARITA: Go, go to your woman, *Desgraciado!*
ENRIQUE: *Mi amor,* you...
MARGARITA: *(Interrupting).* The money, Enrique, today. In my hands.

(Exit Enrique. Margarita goes back to the porch. She stands there for a beat. She takes a pack of cigarettes from her apron pocket, pulls out a Zippo lighter, lights the cigarette and takes a long drag. Cookie and Margarita look at each other for a beat. Cookie becomes uncomfortable and moves closer to his bike, still hiding the damaged bike from his mother. Margarita looks away and takes another drag off her cigarette.)

MARGARITA: I ain't making anymore *paellas*, no more *arroz con pollo a la Valencia*, no more little *tapas*, and no more *sangrias* for his majesty... *El Maestro... El Matador*.

When your sister comes home with the car, we're gong to *la* Burger Queen, have us some French fries, triple bacon burgers, onion rings. We're gonna eat like real human beings.

(Margarita starts to go into the house. Cookie turns away from his bike and lets out a sigh of relief. Margarita turns back to Cookie)

MARGARITA: And another thing. I ain't paying to fix that bike.

(Margarita goes back into the house. Cookie slumps to the ground and looks at his bike. He turns on the bike radio. We hear the voice of News Announcer.)

NEWS ANNOUNCER: Still no new signs of the little Boy Scout who was separated from fellow scouts on a hike to the San Jacinto Summit. Dispirited searchers have used helicopters, tracking dogs, and sophisticated heat seeking equipment. The end of Day Four and no sign of the little scout.

(Cookie turns off the radio. Lights get dimmer. Sunset falls into twilight. Cookie sits on the porch steps and lowers his head. Margarita comes out on the porch.)

MARGARITA: Fourth day and they ain't found him yet. Stupid Boy Scouts… why can't they stay home… clean up the yards, help the old people, but no! They gotta go out to the wilderness… breaking their mommas' hearts. That's what them Boy Scouts are doing.

(She sits on the steps behind Cookie. She holds him and strokes his hair.)

MARGARITA: You hungry, *mi hijo*?

COOKIE: Yeah, I guess.

MARGARITA: Now we got your sister to worry about.

COOKIE: Mama... the scout. They say he's got plenty of water up there on the mountain.

MARGARITA: She's late... I don't like her closing up that place all by herself.

COOKIE: One guy made it. He ate moss and ants for 39 days.

MARGARITA: I told her to call if she's gonna be late.

COOKIE: Maybe he's hiding. Maybe he thinks he's gonna get punished.

MARGARITA: Anything could happen to her... people could be waiting for her to lockup... close out the register... take the money... hit her over the head.

COOKIE: Maybe he fell down a ravine.

MARGARITA: She could be lying in a pool of blood... no, no. I bet she's talking to her fiancé... that's it.

COOKIE: Maybe he fell down and can't get up.

MARGARITA: That's it! They're making up. You know what I think, Cookie, I think we're gonna have a wedding after all.

(Margarita holds Cookie. Sound of a car and rap music. Offstage sound of boys letting out cat calls.)

1ST BOY: *(O.S)* *Hola mamasita.* Little mermaid, I love you.

2ND BOY: *(O.S)* Yo, little mermaid, come over here, baby.

(Enter JESSE. She is dressed in a mermaid's costume with a crown on top of her head.)

1ST BOY: *(O.S.)* Hey, little mermaid, I'd like to...
JESSE: *(Interrupting.)* Eat shit and die!

(Exit Cookie running in the same direction Jesse entered.)

MARGARITA: Jesse! And now you talk like that.
JESSE: I'm sorry, Ma... I had to walk two blocks with those fools following me.
MARGARITA: What happened to the car?
JESSE: It broke.
MARGARITA: Again?
JESSE: Again and again and again.
MARGARITA: I told your father not to buy that old Nova, anybody that speaks Spanish can see, it says *no va*.
JESSE: I left it at the Texaco station. The mechanic looked at the engine and I saw Hawaiian vacation written in his eyes. *(She looks round the yard.)* What's going on here?
MARGARITA: Your father.
JESSE: Spain, huh?
MARGARITA: This time he bought the tickets... took all the money outta the bank.

(Enter Cookie)

COOKIE: It was them Arganda boys...
MARGARITA: Aha! Your *fiancé's* cousins.
JESSE: Ex! Ex! Ex! Ex! Ex-*fiancé*. When will you understand, ex-*fiancé*. *Fiancé* no longer. Ex means you're not going to go through with it. You X-ed it out.

MARGARITA: Stop yelling. I understand. He is X-ed…
so you didn't talk to him.
JESSE: Right! I'm starting a brand new life… I have
started and am well into my brand new life.
MARGARITA: As a mermaid.
JESSE: Okay.
MARGARITA: Frying fish.

*(Cookie proceeds to remove the tire from his bike. It is a
slow task which he does during the rest of the scene.)*

JESSE: It's temporary.
MARGARITA: Temporary insanity.
JESSE: You promised me you wouldn't.
MARGARITA: He's a good boy, Jesse, good family,
steady worker.
JESSE: Mama! He dumped me.
MARGARITA: I don't know what your father's gonna
say.

*(Long beat as Jesse takes off her crown, takes off her shoes
and gets money out of her handbag.)*

JESSE: Here's the refund from the caterer's and the VFW
hall.
MARGARITA: And the dress?
JESSE: They'll take it back.
MARGARITA: You've got one hundred and twelve
presents to send back.
JESSE: I know.
MARGARITA: The limo?
JESSE: Canceled.
MARGARITA: Flowers?
JESSE: Canceled.

MARGARITA: You called everybody on the invitation list?

JESSE: No, Mama... I'll... I'll do it tomorrow.

MARGARITA: Well... so that's that.

JESSE: Except the eh... eh...

MARGARITA: Except what?

JESSE: The cake.

MARGARITA: The cake?

JESSE: They already made it.

MARGARITA: They already made it?

JESSE: Mama, stop echoing everything I say.

MARGARITA: The cake.

JESSE: They sort of froze it. They make the layers then they freeze them and frost'em and freeze them... I don't know.

MARGARITA: The little doves and angel?

JESSE: They freeze'em.

MARGARITA: And the little tiny bells?

JESSE: Yes... yes... I guess so... I don't know it's in the car.

MARGARITA: It's in the car?

JESSE: Stop it Mama. You're doing it again.

MARGARITA: Sitting in the car? That big wedding cake? You left it in the car. What are we supposed to do with it?

JESSE: I don't know, Mama, I don't know. That's why I left it there.

MARGARITA: Since when?

JESSE: Yesterday.

MARGARITA: *(Tossing Cookie the car keys.)* Get your sister's wedding cake out of the car.

JESSE: He can't, Mama. It's too heavy for him.

MARGARITA: Cookie, go next door and get Mrs. Amador's wheelbarrow, then tell that mechanic at the Texaco station to help you load up the cake.

COOKIE: Me Mama?

MARGARITA: Yes, you.

COOKIE: But Mama, I…
MARGARITA: Just do it. *(Looking at the broken bike and then at Cookie.)* O.K.?
COOKIE: *(Sighing.)* Yeah. Right.

(Exit Cookie.)

MARGARITA: We spent over one hundred dollars for that cake plus twenty-five dollars extra for the little bride and groom. *(Beat.)* Did they freeze the little bride and groom?
JESSE: I don't know, Mama… I didn't know what to do with it. Little white doves, angels, and cupids, the world isn't like that. It isn't all sugar clouds and silvery bells… *(She starts to cry.)* I'm sorry, Mama. I didn't know what to do with it. I don't know what to do.
MARGARITA: Maybe your father will eat it because I ain't cooking for that man anymore… *los hombres son perros.*

SCENE TWO

A starry night at the El Cid, a local Spanish bar where Enrique works as a waiter/bartender. Sounds of upbeat flamenco music, rhythmic clapping and stomping. Hanging from the rafters is a pink neon sign reading "El Cid." Beneath the sign, a flamenco dancer, Paco, is dancing with great passion. Manuel, the young guitarist, with his fingers on fire, is having a good night on his guitar. Evelina, the bartender, is eating pistachio nuts and making eyes at Father Stephen, a Jesuit priest with a limp, who after a long afternoon of confessions is relaxing with a glass of sherry and trying to clap with the music - he is off. Paco's dance goes on several minutes. At the end, we hear loud applause, whistling and "Ole's." Enrique enters, wearing a matador's outfit and a small white apron. He is carrying a tray of glasses.

ENRIQUE: ¡Si! ¡Si! ¡Ole! ¡Vamos! ¡Psst Paco! ¡Paquito!

(Enrique puts the tray of glasses down as Paco goes to the bar.)

ENRIQUE: Paco… Mira, Hombre, lo que…

(Paco raises his hand to stop Enrique from talking and taps out a message on the bar with his knuckles.)

ENRIQUE: Si, hombre, si. Evelina, vino tinto.

(Evelina pours a glass of red wine for Paco. Enrique can barely contain himself as Paco drinks the wine down and then raises his arms as if to say "what happened?" Enrique pulls out tickets and brochure from his pockets.)

ENRIQUE: Mira, Paco… Paquito. I… I bought the ticket… I'm going.

(Paco claps and taps his feet. Evelina looks at the tickets.)

EVELINA: ¡Vamos! Look at this… he's going. He's really going this time.

(They all cluster around Enrique.)

EVELINA: I don't believe it! This man, as I have always said, has big *cojones*. He's going. He's really going.
ENRIQUE: *Si, si*, I'm really going.

(All cheer, except Father Stephen.)

FATHER STEPHEN: *(Confused.)* Drawers, Enrique has big drawers?
EVELINA: Father?

(She whispers into his ear.)

FATHER STEPHEN: *(Embarrassed.)* Oh my!

(Group laughs.)

EVELINA: Enrique... Enriquito, send me back a shawl... a silky white shawl with red roses and little blue butterflies... won't that look good on me, Father?
FATHER STEPHEN: Uh... yes... I'm... where are you going, Enrique?
ENRIQUE: Father, I'm going home...

(Group claps, Manuel, strums his guitar, Paco taps his feet. They cheer and stomp during Enrique's speech like a chorus.)

ENRIQUE: I'm going to Toledo.
GROUP: *¡Ole!*
ENRIQUE: Zaragossa.
GROUP: *¡Ole!*
ENRIQUE; Granada.
GROUP: *¡Ole!*

ENRIQUE: Barcelona.
GROUP: *¡Ole!*
ENRIQUE: *Y* Madrid.
GROUP: *¡Ole!*

(Group continues rhythmic clapping and foot stomping.)

FATHER STEPHEN: *(Thinking aloud.)* Let's see.
Toledo, Zaragossa, Granada, Barcelona *y* Madrid... Spain!
Enrique's going to Spain.
GROUP: *¡Ole!*
FATHER STEPHEN: *(Reading aloud from brochure.)*
"The Whitmore Tour, twenty-one days and nights in
Spain."
EVELINA: *(To Father.)* Twenty-one sunny days and
long, hot nights.
GROUP: *¡Ole!*
ENRIQUE: I am going to dump the tour after Madrid...
it's just a cheap way to get there, Father.
FATHER STEPHEN: You mean, you're... going there to
stay.
ENRIQUE: Yes.. to stay.
GROUP: To stay?

(Long beat.)

EVELINA: *(In a deep, firm voice.)* *¡Ole!* *(beat.)* Drinks
are on the house.
FATHER STEPHEN: What about Cookie and...
ENRIQUE: *(Interrupting.)* Stop calling him Cookie! His
name is not Cookie... He's not gonna be known as Cookie
anymore. He's real name is Raphael, and from now on he
will be called Raphael.
GROUP: *(Holding up their drinks.)* Raphael!

ENRIQUE: A toast to Saturday. My daughter's wedding day.

GROUP: *(Toasting.)* To the wedding! *(GROUP drinks.)*

ENRIQUE: And… and after the reception at the El Monte VFW hall to which you are all invited …

GROUP: *(Interrupting.)* ¡Ole!

ENRIQUE: The bride and groom are going on their honeymoon …

EVELINA: *(Interrupting.)* *Viva la luna de miel.*

GROUP: ¡Ole!

ENRIQUE: And me and my son, Raphael, are going to Spain.

(GROUP cheers and they start a rhythmic clapping and foot stomping.)

FATHER STEPHEN: … what about Margarita?

ENRIQUE: Let that mule of a wife stay home!

GROUP: ¡Ole!

ENRIQUE: Let her stay grazing, fenced in her little corral.

GROUP: ¡Ole!

FATHER STEPHEN: But, Enrique, you can't just…

ENRIQUE: *(Interrupting.)* *Miren me… eh!* Gaze at me… at my nose, at my forehead… look at my eyes. Is this the face of a man who would spend his last remaining years retired to a little *ranchito*, basking in the sun like a fat, old iguana? No *muchachos*, no!

GROUP: No!

FATHER STEPHEN: But Enrique, you're a family man, you can't just …

ENRIQUE: *(Interrupting.)* Yes, yes I can, and do you want to know why? Eh? Do you? Do you want to know why?

FATHER STEPHEN: Yes … yes, I do.

ENRIQUE: Because Father, I have asked her to come with me. I have begged her to come with me. I have gotten down on my knees … on my knees, Father, and I have asked in the gentlest, the sweetest tone … *"mi Reina," "mi precious" … "me cielo" … mi …*
FATHER STEPHEN: What you just said *"cielo"* means sky… *"mi cielo"* means sky. Right?
ENRIQUE: Yes, Father.

(Beat. Everybody glares at Father Stephen.)

FATHER STEPHEN: I… I am sorry Enrique. Please… please go on… please.
ENRIQUE: I forgot now… where was I?
GROUP: *"Mi cielo."*
ENRIQUE: *Si, si, si, "mi cielo," (to Father)* my sky! *"Mi amor"* please, please come with me to Spain, come with to the land of my youth, come, see me in my glory.
GROUP: *¡Ole!*
ENRIQUE: See me in my passion.
GROUP: *¡Ole!*
FATHER STEPHEN: *(Off a beat.) ¡Ole! (GROUP stares at him.)* ah, sorry.
ENRIQUE: And do you want to know what that mule of a wife said? Do you? Do you? Do you really want to know what she said?
GROUP: No!
FATHER STEPHEN: Yes!

(GROUP shakes their head and roll their eyes at Father Stephen.)

FATHER STEPHEN: *(To GROUP.)* What?
ENRIQUE: Well, the first time I asked her, she laughed and called me an old fool. The second time, she wanted to

send me to a doctor, she said I had the … the old-timer's disease.

GROUP: *Que?*

FATHER STEPHEN: Alzheimer's … you mean Alzheimer's.

GROUP: Ahhh!

ENRIQUE: *¡Si esso!* So, the third time I asked her, she said "shut up! Can't you see I'm busy."

EVELINA: Madonna!

ENRIQUE: And just this afternoon I asked her to come with me again and she said "never… never!"

GROUP: *(Disappointed.)* Ohhh!

FATHER STEPHEN: Give her time Enrique.

ENRIQUE: I'm running out of time Father. We leave after my daughter's wedding.

FATHER STEPHEN: Be patient Enrique… after all Margarita, being from Mexico, does not really share your… your enthusiasm for Spain.

EVELINA: If you ask me, that's the trouble. She brought nothing but order to his life… you should have seen him, Father, when he first came here, he was wild, crazy like a beast. What a man! He was wonderful. She tamed him… but nobody's gonna tame me, not even this baby blue Marine of a priest.

GROUP: *¡Ole!*

ENRIQUE: Is it true that she tamed me and that I have been her beast? I have never missed a day of work.

GROUP: *¡Ole!*

ENRIQUE: I have been a devoted, a doting father.

GROUP: *¡Ole!*

ENRIQUE: We are not rich. I could not give them everything but I have worked day and night for my family and now it's my turn.

(GROUP claps and whistles except for Father Stephen.)

FATHER STEPHEN: I don't understand why you and Margarita …

ENRIQUE: *(Interrupting.)* No! What you don't understand and what she don't understand, is that I must go back. I must! I must! I left part of my life… a piece of my soul… a young piece, the piece where your dreams are born, even if they got broken… I must go back. I must go back… back to the savage African wind, back to the foot of the Pyrenees, amid the fragrant roses where I left him standing… broken… disillusioned.

FATHER STEPHEN: Who?

ENRIQUE: Me! Me! Me! Me, the boy… me, the boy dreamer… me, the hungry boy… me, the boy *matador de torros.*

FATHER STEPHEN: Mat-a-door?

GROUP: *Si, matador!*

ENRIQUE: I won't rest until he is in me *(pointing to his chest)* here, inside me, where I won't ever abandon him … where I can be whole … where I can pass him on to my son.

FATHER STEPHEN: You left Spain a long time ago, Enrique.

ENRIQUE: She will recognize me, the roses, the mountains, the little stones, the waves will rush to the shore in greeting … they will smell this old Spaniard. Yes… yes, this one is ours… Old Enrique… Old Enrique.

(GROUP clapping as the music stops.)

ENRIQUE: Old Enrique, *como estas* … It was a long time ago. Will you remember me Spain? Maybe Father is right… I was too poor and of too little consequence.

FATHER STEPHEN: I didn't say that.

EVELINA: Ah, what does he know. *(To Father Stephen.)* Excuse me, Father, nothing personal. *(In a sexy voice.)*

Truly, *muchachos* … this *Padre*, what does he really know about life, eh?

FATHER STEPHEN: I was in Vietnam… I lost my leg in Vietnam.

EVELINA: Ha! Nothing else?

GROUP: Ooh ooh! Ooh ooh!

EVELINA: Come on Enrique. Cheer up… dance, Enrique. Dance with me.

(Music. Enrique and Evelina dance. Paco joins in and the two men dance.)

EVELINA: Have pity on him, Father. This is a man whose life was broken in half. He dreamt of being a *matador* but he was too poor and of too little consequence. He couldn't afford bulls to practice on. He snuck onto the ranges of Andalusia at night and caped bulls by moonlight. *Veronicas y Medio Veronicas, Chicuelinas*, spinning slowly as the bull goes by… right hand passes, chest passes, left hand passes. All the time ears open for the sound of the hoofs of another bull or the trucks of ranchers riding him down. If they caught him, they would beat him and throw him in jail. Sometimes he would escape with horn wounds which no doctor ever saw… and always the hunger, the pain in the gut from days without food. He had gone hungry so often that he began to go insane… his spirit cracked.

(Enrique staggers in his dancing. He is panting, clutching his chest.)

EVELINA: The pain was so great, he had to leave Spain. He had to admit defeat, had to admit he would never be a *matador*.

(Music stops. Enrique falls down, Paco and others run to his side. They prop him up. People say to give him air. Paco listens to his chest.)

ENRIQUE: Ya, ya, Paco, it's just age… my trembling heart remembering, longing, trembling and longing and trembling.
FATHER STEPHEN: Rest, Enrique, rest.
ENRIQUE: I can't Father. I hear the voices of my dead beneath the earth. They speak of a life I left suspended, unlived, broken, beseeching me to take it up again and something mounts me and rides me like a horse, whispering, "Espania! Espania! Espania!"
FATHER STEPHEN: Rest, Enrique, rest.

SCENE THREE

Front yard of the Peña house, same beautiful summer night. A huge starry sky with a full moon overwhelms the scene. Night sounds - crickets, sirens, and dog barks. Jesse and Margarita are sitting on the porch steps. Jesse's head is against her shoulders.

MARGARITA: You're gonna have to tell your father and everybody else.
JESSE: I know.
MARGARITA: You got a fever.
JESSE: No.
MARGARITA: I know when somebody's got a fever. I can see it… look at you, pale and trembling. *Que tienes?*
JESSE: The stars are too bright, they pierce my skin.
MARGARITA: Well, I can't do anything about the stars… don't look at them.

JESSE: If I close my eyes, they're inside me. Mocking me.

MARGARITA: Ay, Jesse.

JESSE: Mama, press your hands on my forehead... press it hard, Mama... press it out... please, press it out.

MARGARITA: Press what out?

JESSE: This... this... I don't know.

MARGARITA: Tell me what he said.

JESSE: He said I was immature. He said I was self-indulgent. He said I was irresponsible, neurotic, anti-social, anti-love, anti-life. He said I was death on a soda cracker.

MARGARITA: He didn't say that. You made it up.

JESSE: He said everything except for the part about the soda cracker.

MARGARITA: And then?

JESSE: And then nothing. I just got depressed.

MARGARITA: *Por Dios,* Jesse, you should smile more, eh. You got a beautiful smile, baby. When I was your age I used to smile all the time, smiling, smiling, smiling, all teeth and hair.

JESSE: Yeah, right.

MARGARITA: *(Through clenched teeth.)* I smile all the time, Jesse. I am the one who brings this family forward.

JESSE: I know, Mama.

MARGARITA: Now tomorrow you go to him, you smile, you talk...

JESSE: I'm just too tired to smile. I'm too tired to talk. I'm too tired to get married.

MARGARITA: I'm tired, too!

JESSE: You're never tired. You never stop... it has no meaning.

MARGARITA: What are you, a philosopher now? One year at Los Gatos Junior College, she's a philosopher. Life has no meaning ... stop thinking about life. Keep moving, that's what I say. Every morning it's an effort but I keep

moving. You wanna know why? Why? *(Beat.)* You
wanna know why?
JESSE: Why, Mama?
MARGARITA: Because I'm a serious person… I got
responsibilities.
JESSE: That's it? That's all there is to it for you?
MARGARITA: Well, what more do you want?
JESSE: Something… something more, Mama…
something.

*(Enter a dirty, disheveled, Cookie, with a giant, damaged,
melting wedding cake in a wheelbarrow. Jesse starts to
cry.)*

MARGARITA: What took you so long? Look at this
cake… what happened to this cake? What happened to
you?
COOKIE: It wasn't my fault, Mama. Everybody was
stopping me, wanting a piece of cake. I tried to stop them.
JESSE: Everybody!
COOKIE: It wasn't my fault, Mama. The Arganda boys
were painting *placas* on the side of the garage.
JESSE: The Arganda boys!
COOKIE: And Nicky Arganda sprayed "*La* Jesse got
dumped" right next to the men's room, so I threw a little,
tiny piece of cake at him.
JESSE: Everybody knows!
COOKIE: And then Mrs. Ruiz was getting gas in her
Toyota and she got mad cause she bought a new dress and
everything for the wedding.
JESSE: Everybody knows.
COOKIE: But, I said that you thought there was still gonna
be a wedding.
JESSE: Oh, no, no, no.

COOKIE: You said that, Mama. You said so. And then all these people came across the street from Tio Taco saying they were invited and...
JESSE: Oh, no...

(Jesse falls to the ground and crumbles into a fetal position.)

MARGARITA: That's enough, Cookie.
COOKIE: It wasn't my fault I didn't get...
MARGARITA: *(Interrupting.)* Shut up, Cookie. Jesse, get up... come on, Jesse, get up... sit in a chair like a person.
JESSE: I just want to curl up here and die.
MARGARITA: Get up. Sit in a chair please.
JESSE: I just want the earth to open up and swallow me.
MARGARITA: Cookie, go get your sister some aspirin, some water.
JESSE: I don't want an aspirin!
MARGARITA: Move it, Cookie.
COOKIE: She said she don't want an aspirin.
MARGARITA: Do as I say. Can't you see your sister's got cramps?
JESSE: I don't have cramps. I don't have a fever. I don't have love. I don't have a future.
MARGARITA: Cookie!
COOKIE: Okay, okay, *Papi*'s right, *las mujeres son...*
MARGARITA: *(Interrupting.)* Cookie!

(Cookie goes into the. house. Jesse sniffs the earth.)

MARGARITA: Stop it, Jesse, you're not a dog to be sniffing the earth.
JESSE: It stinks... the earth stinks.
MARGARITA: Then stop smelling it.

JESSE: It stinks of chicken shit and…
MARGARITA: It's the fertilizer I put in…
JESSE: *(Interrupting.)* and wounds.
MARGARITA: Wounds?
JESSE: My wounds, your wounds, the cat's wounds, everybody's wounds… and these weeds stink. *(pulling up herbs.)*
MARGARITA: Those are my herbs… cilantro… basil, now stop it.

(Jesse is furiously pulling up herbs and clumps of dirt.)

JESSE: I hate them, Mama. I hate them. *(She stands up.)* Oh, how I wish something would happen to me.

(Cookie comes out of the house with water and aspirin.)

MARGARITA: I wish something would happen to you too. Look at my herbs. Cookie, give your sister the aspirin.
JESSE: Anything! Anything! Come on, let a car hit me, let the moon blind me. *(She looks up at the sky.)* Come on, touch me lightning, make me bio-luminescent, make me a firefly… give me spontaneous combustion.
MARGARITA: Don't speak to God that way. You speak to Him that way, you're gonna get it.
JESSE: Oh, give it to me, God!
MARGARITA: This is why you got no boyfriend. This is why you go to future.
JESSE: Come on God… give it to me, come on, smite me, burn me… I dare you.
MARGARITA: *(Crossing herself.)* ¡Porqué miseria! She dares God!
COOKIE: Wow!
JESSE: Ahhh! Come on life, show me something.

(Jesse runs off.)

MARGARITA: *(Yelling after Jesse.)* Come back here! You still gotta tell your father! Look at her! Just look at her standing in the middle of the street like a crazy person.
COOKIE: Wow!
MARGARITA: Let her scream like a mad woman... we're not paying attention, we're going inside.

(Margarita and Cookie go towards the front door and linger. Cookie looks back at Jesse.)

MARGARITA: What's she doing? Is she gonna scream again?
COOKIE: Uh, uh. She's sitting on the white line... oh, oh.
MARGARITA: Oh, oh... what?
COOKIE: Now she's stretched out on the white line, flat on her back.
MARGARITA: No!
COOKIE: Yes! Oh, oh...
MARGARITA: Again, oh, oh...
COOKIE: All the neighbors are coming out of their houses.
MARGARITA: *(Looking out at the street.)* *Aye Dios,* look even Mrs. Amador is sticking her nose into our business... oh, this is terrible. Go in... call your father, tell him it's an emergency, tell him to come home immediately, if not at once.

(Cookie starts to leave. Margarita pulls him back.)

MARGARITA: Come back, come back... don't tell him I'm upset... tell him I'm very cool.
COOKIE: Why don't you talk to him.

(Margarita and Cookie exit through the front door. Lights fade and change to indicate passage of time. Margarita comes out, sits on the porch steps and stares dead ahead. After a few beats, Cookie comes out of the house.)

MARGARITA: Well, anything?

COOKIE: I let it ring for three minutes and nobody answered.

MARGARITA: We've been trying to reach that man for two hours.

COOKIE: Maybe he doesn't have the money.

MARGARITA: What money?

COOKIE: You said, "the money, Enrique, today. In my hands."

MARGARITA: I know what I said, son, but your father knows I didn't mean it.

COOKIE: It sure sounded like you meant it.

MARGARITA: That's just the way grown-ups talk.

COOKIE: And you threw all his stuff out.

MARGARITA: That's just the way grown-ups do things, your father knows.

COOKIE: Then why don't they answer?

MARGARITA: How should I know? They're out there in the night, drinking, charlando, having fun. *(Stares out at the street.)* It's a miracle that truck didn't flatten her… everybody just drives around her.

COOKIE: Mrs. Amador put out the wooden horse and the detour sign.

MARGARITA: Look at the neighbors… all looking. *(She starts to cry.)* I can't bear this family anymore.

(Enter Paco and Father Stephen, between them they hold up Enrique.)

COOKIE: *Papi*!

MARGARITA: Enrique! Enrique, you're drunk.

ENRIQUE: You see how she is Father? You see how she accuses me?

FATHER STEPHEN: No, no Margarita, he... he's not... no, not at all.

MARGARITA: Enrique! *¿Que te pasa?*

ENRIQUE: Don't make a fuss!

FATHER STEPHEN: He's alright. He just fainted.

MARGARITA: Fainted!

ENRIQUE: Woman, are you going to let me go to sleep?

FATHER STEPHEN: Well, not really fainted. He just got extremely tired, couldn't catch his breath.

MARGARITA: Couldn't catch his breath!

ENRIQUE: I'm breathing, can't you see that. Look, Father, she won't even let me go to my bed and sleep. Tormentor!

MARGARITA: This is no time to be joking around Enrique. *Dios mio*, I've had my hands full all day.

ENRIQUE: *Aye mi amor,* don't get so excited. You see, Father... you see how she gets... tell her Father, tell her I'm alright.

FATHER STEPHEN: Nothing to get excited about, everything will be alright, right as rain.

MARGARITA: *Mira,* Father, I don't know about the rain but he's not alright. *(Pointing to the street.)* She's not alright, nobody around here is alright. There's been far too much excitement in this family.

FATHER STEPHEN: I... I only meant... he just needs to rest Margarita.

MARGARITA: *Aye,* I can only deal with them one at a time. Cookie! Cookie!

COOKIE: What!

MARGARITA: *(Pointing to the street.)* You keep a close eye on your sister out there.

(Margarita and Paco exit as they help Enrique into the house.)

Father Stephen: He's just tired Cookie... er... Raphael. Don't worry... where's your sister?

(Cookie points toward the tree, Father Stephen looks towards the tree. He tilts his head in several directions in order to get a better view of Jesse..)

FATHER STEPHEN: Is that Jesse? Is she alright?
COOKIE: Uh-huh... she's been there for two hours.
FATHER STEPHEN: Two hours! What is it exactly that she's doing out there?
COOKIE: Yelling and stuff... she got dumped.
FATHER STEPHEN: Ah huh.

(Father Stephen sees the wedding cake and then looks at Cookie..)

COOKIE: Don't look at me Father. It wasn't my fault. She's the one got dumped.
FATHER STEPHEN: Uh... huh, I see.
COOKIE: You do?
FATHER STEPHEN: Sort of...
COOKIE: Look, shooting stars.
FATHER STEPHEN: *(Paying no attention.)* You see, the soul is very delicate thing Cookie... when a woman gets rejected...
COOKIE: *(Watching the stars.)* That's two... three... wow!... four.
FATHER STEPHEN: ...they become vulnerable, delicate, fragile.

(Enter Jesse running in from the street with her hands over her head.)

JESSE: *(Screaming.)* Holy blazing shit! Somebody's shooting at me! Out there!

COOKIE: It's a meteor shower stupid!

JESSE: *(Noticing Father Stephen.)* Oh.

COOKIE: Yeah, shooting stars.

JESSE: I know what they are.

COOKIE: They burn up before they hit the earth, don't they Father?

FATHER STEPHEN: *(Looking up at the stars.)* Yes, they are attracted to us but they burn up when they enter the earth's atmosphere.

COOKIE: *(Counting stars.)* Seven... eight... nine, ten.

JESSE: Father, I'm sorry Mama made you come over here... I'm really alright.

COOKIE: She didn't call him. *Papi* fainted.

FATHER STEPHEN: Don't worry, Jesse, he's alright, just tired. Everything is going to be just fine... *(looking up at the stars.)* There's another one! Look at them... spectacular!

COOKIE: Father, you think that lost boy, the boy scout, you think he can see the stars falling?

FATHER STEPHEN: I hope so... *(Singing.)* The stars at night are big and bright...

COOKIE: *(Interrupting.)* Yo! Look at that one.

COOKIE and FATHER STEPHEN: Wow!

FATHER STEPHEN: It's coming straight down.

JESSE: It was riding high, in its prime, in its glory and somebody just shot it right out of the sky.

COOKIE: Look, it's falling straight down... over there. It's going to land by the Texaco station or the taco place.

(Cookie starts to run towards the falling star.)

MARGARITA: *(Offstage.)* Cookie!

(Cookie stops in his tracks.)

MARGARITA: *(Offstage.)* Cookie, Jesse, get in here.
JESSE: Coming!
FATHER STEPHEN: 'Night you two.

(Cookie and Jesse exit running into the house. Father Stephen exits offstage. There is a large "Boom" and a large flash of light. Cookie runs out on the porch followed by Margarita.)

JESSE: *(Offstage.)* What is it, Mama?
MARGARITA: Goddamn gang bangers shooting up the neighborhood! Get inside Cookie, close your window, Jesse.

(Cookie and Margarita exit into the house. Lights change. Special light comes on. An old man enters, dressed in what was once a white shift. His clothes are torn and dirty as though he has survived an explosion. He is injured. He is wearing feather wings and one of them appears to be broken. He seems confused. He walks in front of the house. He trips over the wedding cake and falls down. Lights out.)

ACT TWO

SCENE ONE

Stage and house are dark. Slowly house lights come up. It is dawn at the Pena house. The roosters are crowing. The little wood frame Pena house is dark, overwhelmed by the freshness and colors of a dawning sky. In the middle of the yard, the sugary wedding cake is hardening into something quite grotesque. Next to the wedding cake, the elderly angel is blissfully sleeping, dreaming perhaps. We hear the sound of an alarm going off in the house. A small light comes up in the dark house, then the sound of a radio playing a low rhythmic guitar. After a few beats, the voice of El Bonito, the vampire poet, comes up and, with the low rhythmic guitar as a background, continues over as Cookie enters from the house carrying his transistor radio. He is wearing pajamas, a plaid bathrobe, black high top sneakers, long white socks, and a red baseball cap backwards. He looks around and then goes down the porch steps and retrieves the undelivered newspapers from under the house, dusts them off and arranges them on the saddle pack of his bike. He sits on the porch steps and looks at his bike.

EL BONITA: *(V.O.) (Low, sultry voice with a cholo accent.)*… for those of you who have ridden out the night with me and those of you who have just tuned in, it's past the five a.m. hour here at KCKT, 727 on your radio dial, and this is El Bonito, the vampire poet, the midnight *caballero,* here to pass on a few new items. Item one… the end of the world has been postponed for yet another day.

We have successfully navigated through another long, lonely night. We have had no aberrant stars suddenly changing orbit, the oceans have not, I repeat, have not dried up or run wild, and no major earthquakes to report. Many of us have passed the night in a trance, others in dreams, visions, exhilaration and illusions or maybe some of us have sat face to face with that caged thing within us. Fret no more, we are experiencing some light out there... little pink fingers of lights... and you know what that means, indifferent to all catastrophes, the sun, Mr. Consistency, Mr. I Haven't Missed in Four Billion Years, is once again knocking at the eastern horizon. Item two... still no signs of the little boy scout lost in the San Jacinto Mountains... lost in the wilderness.

(Song comes up on the radio, Cookie is still staring at his bike. The music wakes the Angel, who yawns, stretches, yawns again. He gets up and stretches his wings full out. As he does this, a special light comes on and he appears to glow. Cookie catches this out of the corner of his eye. He turns and gets the full impact of the Angel. It is a terrorizingly magical moment. The two look at each other for a long beat. Cookie screams, the Angel screams back. Special light goes out and the Angel falls back in a dead faint. House lights snap on and Margarita throws open the door and sticks her head out.)

MARGARITA: Cookie! Cookie! Is that you?
COOKIE: Y... Yes.
MARGARITA: What's going on down there? Your papa's sick. He needs his sleep.
COOKIE: Ma... Mama... there... there's an angel down here.
MARGARITA: *Qué angel y qué nada*, it's only a Mormon. They come every Saturday morning... waking

up decent hardworking people, talking about missions to China. Tell him to go away.

COOKIE: He's alive, Mama. I didn't kill him. The angel's alive.

(Margarita looks at the Angel very, very carefully, narrowed eyes penetrating every aspect of the Angel, until the Angel himself starts to shake and whimper.)

MARGARITA: That ain't no angel... that's a wino.

COOKIE: A wino?

MARGARITA: One of them wino's from Soto Street.

COOKIE: He's got wings and everything.

MARGARITA: I know a wino when I see one. Look, see them runny eyes... wearing an angel's costume, probably came from a wino's costume party.

COOKIE: Wino's have costume parties?

MARGARITA: Well, he's not staying here on my front yard. Vamos, you wino.

(Margarita takes the broom from Cookie and swats the Angel, trying to drive him out of the yard as the Angel lets out eerie birdlike yelps.)

MARGARITA: *(Swatting Angel.)* *Desgraciado,* wino, *salte de aqui.*

(The racket wakes Jesse up. She comes out of the house in her pajamas with sleep shades pushed up on her head.)

JESSE: Who's making so much noise... *(Looking at the* ANGEL: Who is that?

COOKIE: It's an angel, Jesse, a real angel.

JESSE: Yeah, right. Can't a person even sleep in this house? Sleep is my only refuge.

MARGARITA: It's a stinking wino! And I want him outta here.

(Margarita swats the Angel causing him to faint once again.)

COOKIE: You killed him! You killed him!

JESSE: For God's sake, Mama, it's too early for this.

MARGARITA: *(Standing over the Angel.)* He ain't dead... I see him breathing.

(Cookie rushes over to the Angel.)

COOKIE: You hurt him, Mama. You hurt the angel!

MARGARITA: It's not an angel I tell you.

COOKIE: Yes, he is. You didn't see him. He had a light and everything.

(Cookie starts to help the Angel up.)

MARGARITA: Don't touch him! He's got lice on his wings right there... see!

(Angel scratches himself.)

JESSE: Ugh!

MARGARITA: Jesse, call 911. Tell them we got a sick wino here...

JESSE: I'm gonna be sick.

MARGARITA: Not before you call 911. Tell them we got a sick...

JESSE: *(Interrupting.)* Yeah, yeah, yeah.

(Jesse goes into the house..)

MARGARITA: I'm gonna get this wino off my lawn. Look at this mess out here... pictures of bullfighters, your broken bicycle, Jesse's wedding cake. All I need out here is a stupid wino with wings. Go on shoo, shoo!

(Margarita starts for the Angel with her broom. The Angel rears up bearing his teeth at Margarita, emitting an eerie birdlike call. He backs away from Margarita as she herds him toward the chicken pen.)

MARGARITA: Look! Look! How vicious he is, *condenado*, open the gate, Cookie.
COOKIE: No!
MARGARITA: I'll do it myself... just like I do everything else around here.

(Jesse enters from the house and sits on the porch steps watching Margarita as she gets the chicken pen gate open and herds the Angel into the pen.)

MARGARITA: Now the ambulance can pick him up and take him to the hospital! Right, *mi hija?*
JESSE: Wrong! 911 said it's not in their jurisdiction. They said to call Human Services.
MARGARITA: Well, call them, *mi hija*... and you *(to Cookie.)*, eat your breakfast and deliver those newspapers.
COOKIE: But listen, Mama...
MARGARITA: *(Interrupting.)* That's your responsibility, Cookie. People are out there waiting for their newspapers.

(Beat.) Your papa came home sick last night… things are getting out of control and it's gonna stop.

(Margarita goes into the house. Cookie takes off his bathrobe and pajamas. Underneath he is wearing the same dirty white tee-shirt and black baggy cut-off pants. He sits down and looks at his bike for a beat, he gets up and kicks his bike.)

COOKIE: My responsibility!

(Cookie looks at the Angel. The Angel looks at Cookie. Cookie hangs his head down.)

JESSE: *(Reading from a slip of paper.)* Human Services… 464-5945… hmmm.
COOKIE: What?
JESSE: Hello, Human Services? You don't know me, but I am molten and aching. Will you come over and rescue me … will you wake me from my state… will you treat me like an amnesiac and teach me the alphabet again … will you treat me like a car crash victim, separating me from the glass, the tangled metal and twisted strands of my life … do I turn to you Human Services, when I feel fevered like a starving coyote, when I feel like dyeing my hair red and letting it blow like a flame in the wind, when I want to fill my life with tattooed sailors and lie in a gutter with winos and lepers. Do I turn to you Human Services … do I have the right number?

(Margarita comes out of the house wearing rubber gloves, carrying a tray with bowls of breakfast cereal, milk, orange juice, and a bag of Oreos.)

270

MARGARITA: *Andale mi hijo,* eat your Fruit Loops.

(Jesse exits into the house as Margarita takes a bowl of Fruit Loops and a spoon to the Angel. She carefully opens the chicken pen gate and sets the bowl down. The Angel falls on the bowl with a great hunger and makes loud smacking sounds as he eats.)

Margarita: *Aye,* animal! *(calling to Jesse in the house.)* *Andale,* Jesse, call the number. *(She then takes chicken feed from her pockets and throws it at the chickens while calling them.)* Here chick, chick, here, chick.

(Cookie takes an Oreo out of the bag. He splits it in half, licks the white icing off one half and crumbles it into his cereal. He does the same with the other half as he keeps a close eye on Margarita and the Angel. Margarita looks at Cookie and then exits into the house. Cookie looks at the house making sure the coast is clear, then he takes the bag of Oreos and goes to the Angel.)

COOKIE: I can't touch you, you got lice.

(Cookie puts Oreos on the flat part of the broom and gingerly offers it to the Angel over the chicken wire fence as though they were communion wafers. Angel grabs the Oreos and eats them with great relish. Angel's rapid movements scare Cookie and he jumps back dropping the broom. Angel seeing he has scared Cookie looks at him gently and extends his hand toward him. Cookie looks at Angel, Angel looks at Cookie. Angel glows. Cookie picks up the Oreo package, digs out some Oreos and goes up to the chicken wire fence offering the Oreos directly from his

hand. Angel takes the Oreo, splits it in half and licks icing off. Angel points to Oreo package and Cookie shows him the package.)

COOKIE: *(Clearly drawing out the word.)* Oreos.
ANGEL: *(In pig Latin.) Soreo.*
COOKIE: *Soreo?*
ANGEL: *Soreo's reay* Oreos.
COOKIE: Pig Latin! You talk in pig Latin.
ANGEL: Esay, esay.
COOKIE: I *ancay eakspay igpay atinlay.*
ANGEL: *Esay, ookiecay, esay.*

(Cookie gets closer. Angel and Cookie whisper in pig Latin as lights dim to indicate passage of time. Lights change as Margarita comes out of the house and stands on the porch watching Cookie and Angel for a beat.)

MARGARITA: Jesse. Jesse.

(Jesse comes out of the house.)

JESSE: What?
MARGARITA: Did you call those people to pick up the wino?
COOKIE: He's not a wino.
JESSE: They said to call the police.
MARGARITA: Then call the police
COOKIE: *(Running out of the chicken pen screaming.)* No! No! You can't call the police. He hasn't done anything. He's an angel, a real angel. He speaks pig Latin.

(In fear, the Angel curls into a fetal position hiding his face and wings and gets as close to the ground as possible.)

MARGARITA: Stop screaming. You'll wake your father.
COOKIE: You can't call the police! Jesse… you can't.
MARGARITA: Jesse, call the police … *mi hija*. How many times do I have to tell you?
COOKIE: *(Interrupting.)* No! No! I'll run away, I swear I will.
MARGARITA: Jesse…
COOKIE: No! No! Jesse.
JESSE: Okay! Okay! I'll call Father Stephen. Maybe he'll know what to do, okay?

(Jesse goes into the house.)

MARGARITA: *Mi hijo*, what's wrong with you, eh? You're supposed to be the sensible one. Even your sister knows it's not an angel.

(Enrique comes out of the house in his bathrobe.)

MARGARITA: Get back into bed. Do you want to get sicker?
ENRIQUE: I'm not sick. I'm fine.
MARGARITA: You fainted last night. Your friends had to bring you home. Manuel said you were sweating.
ENRIQUE: So, can't a man faint in peace? Can't a man sweat without all this fuss? I don't care what Manuel said, I'm fine.
MARGARITA: That's right. You know everything.
ENRIQUE: I know what the hell I'm feeling.
MARGARITA: You know better than everybody … me, Manuel, the priest.

ENRIQUE: You're not me. Manuel is not me. I alone am me. I alone can feel what I feel, and I feel fine.
MARGARITA: Get back in bed.
ENRIQUE: Leave me alone, tormentor. I am still going to Spain.
MARGARITA: You want to get sicker? You wan to die now?
ENRIQUE: Yes... yes, I want to die. Maybe then you'll leave me alone. Or will you follow me to the graveyard? Yes, yes you will. You won't leave me in peace, fooling with my gravestone, weeding, planting flowers, lighting candles, coming to my grave three times a day, saying your prayers over me, never leaving me in peace.
MARGARITA: Because you are my husband and I...
ENRIQUE: *(Interrupting.). Ya Basta!* Leave me alone. Let me enjoy life.
MARGARITA: Go... go to Spain, go enjoy your life.
ENRIQUE: *¡Aye!* You mule of a woman. You have a stone for a heart and cactus for skin. That's it! That's it! Raphael and I are going to Spain.

(Enrique turns to Cookie and gives him a big hug, then seeing Cookie's troubled face, holds his face in his hands.)

ENRIQUE: *¿Mi hijo,* Raphael, *que te pasa?*
MARGARITA: Don't tell him Cookie... don't tell him what's wrong... don't tell him you might not want to go to Spain.

(Enrique backs up and is about to stumble into the wedding cake.)

MARGARITA: And watch out you don't stumble on your daughter's wedding cake because I'm gonna have to tell

you that she's not gonna have a wedding… that the boy left
her *plantada*!
JESSE: He did not!

*(Enrique looks sadly at the wedding cake, then at Jesse.
Jesse runs to her father and hugs him.)*

ENRIQUE: *Aye mi hijita…* love… love is a torment
(Looking at Margarita.) love is a tormentor.
MARGARITA: Love is responsibility.
ENRIQUE: Why are you so hard?
MARGARITA: Life is hard. She can't have everything
her way.
JESSE: It was me *Papi*, I couldn't do it.
MARGARITA: Of course she couldn't, the boy was too
normal.
ENRIQUE: It's all right, Jesse, your mother is not so hard.
She is remembering how she never fell in love with a
normal person either. *(Looking at Margarita.)* Oh yes, she
had flashing eyes with flecks of amber, her hair like
sunning silk, her perfumed flesh, like the skin of a sun
ripened peach. She had the pale white feet of a Saintess
and eyelids like the petals of a white rose.

*(The Angel responding to the love and poetry in Enrique's
voice has unfurled himself from the fetal position and is
now standing full upright with his wings out and trembling.
Enrique stops mid-speech and stares at the Angel. The
Angel stares back and then moves his feet like a bull to
charge. Enrique turns quickly away and spaces out.)*

MARGARITA: It's just a wino.
COOKIE: It's an angel… you can feel it, Papa, when he
looks at you, he glows.

MARGARITA: He's got lice!

JESSE: Papa, I need to talk to you.

MARGARITA: And Enrique, don't think that all this talk about love has made me forget the money you took outta the bank.

COOKIE: *(Taking his father's hand.)* Come on, *Papi*... look at him. Don't be afraid. He is translucent, on fire with love.

ENRIQUE: *(Shaking off Cookie's hand.)* No! Leave me alone all of you. I have to get to work.

(Enrique runs into the house.)

MARGARITA: *(Looking at Cookie.)* Translucent? On fire with love?

(Jesse turns toward the house and yells after Enrique.)

JESSE: *Papi*, please talk to me... talk to me about love.

(Margarita turns toward the house and yells after Enrique.)

MARGARITA: I want that money, Enrique. Today. In my hands.

(Cookie turns towards the house and yells after Enrique.)

COOKIE: Can we keep him, *Papi*? Can we keep the angel?

SCENE TWO

*(Late morning at the El Cid. Father Stephen sits at the bar
drinking coffee. All the chairs are turned over on top of the
tables. Manuel, the young guitarist, Paco, the dancer, and
Evelina are rehearsing a number. The music is a slow
rhythmic flamenco/fado guitar. Paco claps, snaps his
fingers and yells "Ole" and "Esso," as Evelina dressed in
a simple black street dress, with a cigarette in her mouth,
works on small, intricate dance steps. She takes the
cigarette out of her mouth and sings/talks a song of destiny
and love. Paco , clapping, Manuel on guitar as they join
Evelina on chorus. Evelina speaks/sings with guitar.)*

EVELINA: *Aye la lie, la lie, la lie. A la lie, la lie, la lie. A
la lie, la lie la lie. Aye la vida, la vida, la vida es, la vida,
la vida, la vida...*
Winds cut and the bruised heart howls
Life fills your lungs
With the scent of broken dreams
You see the face of the man you love in a rain drop
And you make of this face an altar
Where you cry *"ay mi vida" "ay mi amor"*
and you crawl to your shrine
on your knees
and raise your arms and beckon the sky to help you
So tell me, tell me, tell me, *di me, di me, di me,*
What is the salt that keeps your wounds alive and burning
*Es la vida, la vida, la vida, si la vida, la vida
La vida, solamente la vida*

*(THEY all clap at the end of Evelina's song and
congratulate her on the beauty of her voice. Enrique
rushes in wearing his bullfighters outfit. He is sweating
and out of breath.)*

EVELINA: Enrique! *Hombre,* what are you doing here? I told you to take the day off. You should be in bed, drinking milk.

(Paco leans his head on folded hands to indicate he should be sleeping.)

FATHER STEPHEN: Does Margarita know you're here?
ENRIQUE: *¡Dame una copa!*

(Evelina pours a whiskey into a shot glass. As Enrique gulps the drink down, THEY all shake their heads in disapproval. Enrique slams his empty glass down on the bar and asks for another.)

ENRIQUE: *¡Da me otra!*
EVELINA: *¿Como, hombre?* Do you want to kill yourself? It's very bad for you.

(Paco shakes his head "no.")

FATHER STEPHEN: A man in your condition, Enrique…
EVELINA: *(Interrupting.)* Should not be drinking whiskey.

(Paco continues to shake his head "no.")

ENRIQUE: You would not deny me if you had seen what I just saw.
FATHER STEPHEN: Now he's seeing things.
EVELINA: *(To Father Stephen.)* Shshshshhhh *(to Enrique.)* What? What was it?
MANUEL: *Que paso?*

(Paco gestures with his hands, "what? what?" Enrique looks at them and then grabs for the bottle of whiskey. Evelina pulls the bottle away. THEY all shake their heads no to the whiskey. Enrique pulls an invisible zipper across his mouth, meaning no whiskey, no telling what he saw. His lips are sealed. THEY all look at each other weighing the decision. THEY nod their heads yes and Evelina reluctantly pours whiskey into the shot glass. Enrique gulps it down, slams the glass down on the bar.)

ENRIQUE: A strange man has come to my house.
FATHER STEPHEN: Who?
EVELINA: Who?
MANUEL: Who?

(Paco signals, "who?".)

ENRIQUE: I don't know who! My wife says he's a wino; my son thinks he's an angel... but when I looked into his eyes... something opened like a fan, a door into something familiar, like a sea wind scented with salt and sage... and then, I saw them beckoning to me.
FATHE STEPHEN: Who?
EVELINA: Who?
MANUEL: Who?
ENRIQUE: Manolete standing in the sand with his suit of lights...
MANUEL: *(With a flourish of his guitar.)* ¡Ole!
THE OTHERS: Shshsh!
ENRIQUE: Next to him, Modeno, with his grave priest's face... standing together beckoning me... and then...
FATHER STEPHEN: And then?
EVELINA: Yes?
MANUEL: Go on!

ENRIQUE: And then they separated and from behind them passed the biggest blackest train of a bull .. hooking to the left … or was it to the right? I get mixed up, it happened so fast … but the important thing is that without saying a word they told me that this bull was mine … the honor of this bull was mine.

(Paco makes the sign of the cross.)

FATHER STEPHEN: You were hallucinating.

(THEY all look down for a long beat, except Evelina.)

EVELINA: What does this mean? Eh? Are you going to kill this wino/angel man?
FATHER STEPHEN: It was a dream, he had a fever, he's hallucinating. It happens to me all the time when I have my allergies.
EVELINA: Eh? And what is it he really saw in the man's eye?
ENRIQUE: The big black bull.
EVELINA: And what does a big black bull mean?
(THEY all stand around for a beat scratching their heads.)
FATHER STEPHEN: Let's see… hmmm… big black bull… hmmm… manhood, I would imagine.
ENRIQUE: Honor!
EVELINA: Power!
MANUEL: Sex!

(THEY all look at Paco, who does a short dance of a bull, full of manhood, honor, power, and sex. At the end of the caricature, he puts his hands on his head to indicate horns.)

ALL: Horns!?

EVELINA: Just as I suspected?

FATHER STEPHEN: What?

ENRIQUE: What?

MANUEL: Huh?

EVELINA: This wino… angel. I suspect treason with your wife, Margarita?

FATHER STEPHEN: No! Angels don't go in for that sort of thing. No.

ENRIQUE: Never!

MANUEL: Naaa

EVELINA: Think about it carefully, Enrique… he put the bullfighters in his eye to beckon you to Spain… Go! Go to Spain he says, but standing behind the *matadors* is his true intent, the bull… your manhood, your honor… sex and the horns.

ENRIQUE: But I must go to Spain.

(Evelina slinking around Enrique like a snake.)

EVELINA: To your wife, he appears as a wino, in need of mothering and reform.

FATHER STEPHEN: That's… that's quite irresistible to women!

EVELINA: To your son, he appears as an angel, ready to offer tender companionship.

ENRIQUE: The boy loves me!

FATHER STEPHEN: The boy is lonely, he appears lost, Enrique. A very dangerous thing these days.

EVELINA: You're lucky, Enrique, that your daughter will be married and out of the house. He could really cause trouble there.

ENRIQUE: But… but the wedding is off.

FATHER STEPHEN: She got dumped.

MANUEL: *¿Si?*

(Paco does a brief dance of anger and frustration.)

EVELINA: Something evil is brewing.
FATHER STEPHEN: But this is nonsense!
EVELINA: You must act now, Enrique, quickly, swiftly.
MANUEL: *¡Ole!*

(Paco does a pass with an imaginary cape.)

FATHER STEPHEN: But... Margarita loves him.
EVELINA: Women can be treacherous... deceptive.
MANUEL: *(With a fast flurry from his guitar.)* *¡Esso!*

(Paco does a pass with an imaginary cape.)

EVELINA: She can't help it. She's under a spell.

(THEY all gasp, except Paco, who taps his feet furiously.)

FATHER STEPHEN: This is ridiculous, you're behaving like...
EVELINA: *(Interrupting.)* Has she been acting unreasonable?
ENRIQUE: Yes!
EVELINA: Fits of anger... screaming and yelling for no good reason?
ENRIQUE: Yes!
EVELINA: Enrique, you must think about this next question very, very carefully...

(THEY all lean in to hear Evelina.)

EVELINA: Have circular things been broken? Or objects that depend on circular movements like maybe a clock?

(THEY all look at Enrique as he thinks and then suddenly flashes.)

ENRIQUE: *¡Dios mio!* My son's bicycle! The car!

(THEY all gasp in unison.)

FATHER STEPHEN: Coincidence.
EVELINA: Worse than I expected!
ENRIQUE: No!
EVELINA: *¡Si!* Your family is in grave danger.

(THEY all gasp again.)

ENRIQUE: But I must go to Spain!
EVELINA: No, you can't go now Enrique... think *hombre!* Your family is in grave danger.
ENRIQUE: ...but my dreams... my dreams... my poor dreams!
FATHER STEPHEN: This is all nonsense.
EVELINA: Ah! So you call it nonsense.
FATHER STEPHEN: Yes... yes, I do.

(Evelina twists around Father Stephen in a threatening manner as Father Stephen backs away.)

EVELINA: So you think this is nonsense. You think I'm a lazy, stupid gypsy woman.
FATHER STEPHEN: Oh, no, never...
EVELINA: Only you are allowed visions.

FATHER STEPHEN: No, no that was just my allergies.

EVELINA: You find us little, cute, quaint.

FATHER STEPHEN: No… never, well, maybe cute.

EVELINA: *(Menacing.)* Get out of my bar!

FATHER STEPHEN: I'm being kicked out of a bar!

EVELINA: Out!

(Father Stephen runs out of the bar.)

ENRIQUE: *¡Desgraciado! ¡Sinverguenzo!* Animal! Wino angel trying to steal my wife…

EVELINA: And family! Quickly, swiftly, you must dispatch this stranger.

ENRIQUE: I'll teach him to play with my family.

MANUAL: *¡Desgraciado!*

(Paco lifts his arms in the international gesture of up yours.)

ENRIQUE: Hold me back! For I swear on God's forehead that I'm ready to kill this… this…

(Enrique breaks out into a coughing fit as the others help him to a chair. Evelina gives him water as Paco fans him with a newspaper.)

EVELINA: This is grave business, Enrique. You can't just go off in the moment of anger and passion. One must think about these things carefully. One must be in control.. one must be prepared.

ENRIQUE: Prepare… yes, I must prepare.

EVELINA: You must stand straight… proud like a man of stature and substance… without rancor, without resentment, and with the deepest sincerity you must ask

forgiveness for what you have to do and you must seek the help and intervention of the *Virgin de la Macarena*.
ENRIQUE: Then I will fight!!
PACO AND MANUAL: *¡Ole!*
EVELINA: Fight? Fight for what?
ENRIQUE: I'll fight despair, for my children. I'll fight for hope. I'll show them what it means to be an old *matador*. I'll show them how to fight for their dreams.

(Lights change as Paco starts a rhythmic tapping of his feet, then Manuel plays La Virgin de La Macarena on his guitar. Evelina brings the statue of the Virgin down from the shelf over the bar and gathers the table candles around the statue and lights them. She creates an altar and feeling of ritual as she kneels down to silently pray the rosary. In the meantime, Paco aids Enrique in the cleaning and grooming ritual. Paco brings out a long, long, long thin red cummerbund, symbolizing a string of blood. As he wraps it around Enrique's waist, Manuel changes the tune on his guitar. Evelina speaks/sings the Cuchillo song. Paco then dresses Enrique in his suit of lights. After which Enrique kneels in front of the altar. Evelina continues singing and Paco begins a dance. Music continues up and over to scene three.)

EVELINA: *Aye la lie, la lie, la lie! A la lie, la lie, la lie! A la lie, la lie, la lie! Aye la vida, la vida, la vida, es la vida, la vida, la vida.*
> The boy-men with their *cuchillos*
> Their finger nails like claws
> Do they feel black wings
> Beating within,
> Beating, beating, beating

Within their suit of lights
Beating within,
Their mouths filled with wild roses
Beating and waiting
Beating and waiting a century, a millennium
Waiting the boy-groom
To marry the night in black silk
Waiting to be newly-born
Waiting to blossom, like the evening star
Radiant, hypnotic, waiting
For blood to turn to Flame
(Repeat Chorus.)

SCENE THREE

Music continues over and then goes under. It is mid-afternoon at the Peña yard. The music changes to street sounds and the voices of mothers calling their children home. Jailed in the chicken coop, the Angel, sits munching on some M&M's. This is a new experience for him, he spits some out and then puts them back in his mouth, he sucks his fingers which are sticking with chocolate. Cookie has made a shrine out of the chicken coop with flowers and candles. As HE and a small group of neighborhood kids stand around the shrine and watch the Angel in great fascination. The sound of rap music comes up from transistor radio on Cookie's bike.

1ST KID: He likes them M&M's.
2ND KID: *(Offering a corn dog.)* Hey *esse…* see if he likes corn dogs.
1ST KID: Nay, he's spitting it out man.
2ND KID: *Orale esse!* That's disgusting.
COOKIE: He's got a delicate stomach.

286

(Margarita enters from the house.)

MARGARITA: Cookie! Put them candles out! You gonna set fire to the place… and you kids stop feeding that wino… time to go home… go on now… go on.

(Kids, afraid of Margarita, leave in a hurry.)

2ND KID: *(To Angel.)* Later Homie.

(Sound of rap music fades out as News Announcer comes up.)

NEWS ANNOUNCER: Here's a news update… coming to the end of day five… teams of searchers using sophisticated heat seeking equipment have found no signs of the little Boy Scout lost in the San Jacinto mountains. The little Scout was separated …

(Margarita snaps off the radio on Cookie's bike. Cookie looks dejected.)

MARGARITA: Did he drink the coffee?… Cookie! Cookie!
COOKIE: What?
MARGARITA: I'm talking to you. Did he drink the coffee?
COOKIE: No, he don't like coffee. It makes him nervous.
MARGARITA: I'll make him nervous. *(To Angel.)* Father Stephen's coming. He's gonna put an end to this charade… and then things will get back to normal.

(Jesse enters from the house wearing a lovely soft summer dress and gloomy expression.)

JESSE: When has anything been normal around here?
MARGARITA: Jesse, I'm sick of your sarcastic remarks. Cookie stop this nonsense. Go inside and clean up… Father Stephen is coming to talk to you.
COOKIE: Father Stephen will know, he'll tell you that's a real genuine Angel.
MARGARITA: Yeah, yeah, yeah, now get inside. Jesse get rid of that wedding cake before Father gets here.

(Margarita and Cookie go inside the house, as Jesse gets a plastic garbage bag and a dust pan from the porch. She picks up chunks of the wedding cake and throws them into the plastic bag. She picks up the little bride and groom, she starts to throw it away but finds she can't. She looks at it carefully and softly begins to cry, she falls to her knees, holding the little bride and groom to her chest, she cries softly and rocks herself, as the Angel watches her with great intensity. He seems to glow. Enter Margarita from the house, she looks at her daughter then turns as if to go back in the house, the Angel looks at Margarita's back, Margarita stops and turns to look at Jesse crying. Margarita wrings her hands in frustration, she turns back to the house, feels the Angel's eyes on her back, turns to the Angel and glares at him and shoots him a dirty look. She looks at her daughter, her face softens, she gently goes over to Jesse and gathers her in her arms and then rocks her. The Angel watches intently.)

JESSE: Oh mama… the little sugar bells… the little bride… the little groom… so silent. Is there no one to say that my mouth tastes like Hawaiian flowers? No one to say that I am radiant, hypnotic, beautiful? No one to say that my eyes are as tender as the Virgin de Guadalupe, my teeth whiter than the clouds on which angels sit? These are the hieroglyphics of love... who will say them to me mama? Who?

MARGARITA: *(Looking at the Angel and then to Jesse.)* I will baby, I will.

(They hold each other for a beat. They both look at the wedding cake.)

JESSE: What did I expect to create here?

MARGARITA: Dreams...

JESSE: Rosy mornings with the smell of strong coffee and sliced melons... long nights on crisp white sheets, beneath a quilt... soft, as the petals of flowers... speaking in whispers and incantations, each syllable a secret illumination... I expected the sweet breath of babies, kissing their feet and their bellies and making them laugh... I expected sweet herbs in terra-cotta pots on the window sill... and polishing worn linoleum.

MARGARITA: Small dreams and the pain of tiny needles.

JESSE: In exchange for these dreams, I would allow him the pleasure of cataloging my inadequacies... in exchange I would spend my life on my knees... in exchange I would be smiling and subservient.

MARGARITA: *¡Los Hombres son perros!*

JESSE: No mama, can't you see, it's me. I'm the one who will never be able to say to any man, I am yours, yours, yours, take me, mold me, own me, you're my God.

MARGARITA: *(Laughing.)* Ha! *Aye mi hija*, did you really expect any daughter of mine to say to a man, take me, own me, you are my God?

(Jesse and Margarita laugh together and hold each other.)

JESSE: *(Looking at the Angel.)* It was a dream, mama … just a dream.

(Jesse leans her head on her mother's shoulders. Lights begin to change.)

MARGARITA: Did you know, my Jesse, that you are radiant, hypnotic, beautiful? That your teeth are whiter than the clouds on which Angels sit … that your eyes …

(Margarita's voice drifts off, as lights change to indicate the passage of time. It is a large summer sunset. The sky is a deep Matisse blue with orange and pink wisps. Enter Cookie bursting out of the house.)

COOKIE: He's here, he's here. Father Stephen's here.

(Jesse continues looking at the Angel, Angel gazing back at her, seems to have locked her in a spell. Cookie runs to the side of the house to meet Father Stephen.)

MARGARITA: Cookie, *por favor*, stop yelling.
COOKIE: *(Offstage.)* He's over here Father, over here… hurry up, Father!

(Cookie returns leading Father Stephen by the hand.)

FATHER STEPHEN: Hello… hello… hello *(singing.)* "hello everybody hello."
MARGARITA: *Si, si*… hello, hello. Listen, Father, the boy has gone crazy with this wino and he…

COOKIE: *(Interrupting.)* Here he is Father, I found him this morning... and he's a real angel, with real wings and everything and...

FATHER STEPHEN: *(Interrupting.)* Ah ha!

(Margarita, Jesse and Cookie are standing in front of the Angel, blocking Father Stephen's view, as Angel tries to look at Father Stephen and Father Stephen tries to look at Angel, it becomes a game of peek-a-boo.)

MARGARITA: And he's got real lice on them fake wings!

JESSE: *(Still gazing at the Angel.)* Maybe they're not fake, Mama, I mean, doesn't he seem to glow.

COOKIE: I told you... and he's got a light and everything.

MARGARITA: *(To Jesse.)* So now you're seeing things too ...

JESSE: Look Mama, the wings come right out of his back.

MARGARITA: Wires, it's done by wires.

JESSE: Mama, don't you feel warm and sort of light and dreamy around him?

MARGARITA: No! No I don't!

COOKIE: That's because he's a Seraph... they're the angels that are aflame with love.

FATHER STEPHEN: Seraphs are the highest order of angels, Margarita. They have six wings.

MARGARITA: There, you see... you see, this wino is a liar. He's only got two wings, Father.

COOKIE: They got burned up when he hit the earth's atmosphere.

MARGARITA: Yeah, yeah, yeah... Father, I want you to look at this mess! Candy wrappers, pop cans, popsicle sticks! All he does is eat and eat and eat some more!

COOKIE: So far he likes M&M's, Fruit Loops, Ding-Dongs, Yo Hos, Twinkies, Eskimo Pies and pizza!

FATHER STEPHEN: Angels don't have a digestive system, Cookie. No sir, that's why so many of them can fit on a head of a pin.

MARGARITA: There, you see, Cookie! You see! That wino can't fit on the head of no pin.

COOKIE: He's just tasting stuff. He ain't digesting . He's been here a whole day and nothing's come out… you know, the other end.

MARGARITA: *Aye* Cookie! *¡Por favor!* In front of Father you say that!

FATHER STEPHEN: That's all right, Margarita, that's all right… the boy really believes. That means we'll have to administer the language test.

COOKIE: Will it hurt?

FATHER STEPHEN: No, no, Cookie. You see, angels speak all tongues. That's the ultimate truth.

JESSE: I don't care what he speaks. I could stand here and gaze at him all day.

MARGARITA: *(Urgently.)* Hurry up, Father, hurry up. Give him the test.

FATHER STEPHEN: *(Trying to get to the Angel.)* If you'll permit me.

(Margarita pushes Cookie and Jesse to one side.)

MARGARITA: Let Father see him!

(Father Stephen confronts the Angel.)

FATHE STEPHEN: *(Speaking slowly and carefully.)* ¡Ola! ¿Como esta usted?… ¿Viene del ceilo?

(The Angel smiles at Father Stephen. Father Stephen smiles at the Angel. They become lost in each other's

smile. Cookie and Jesse also become lost in the Angel's smile.)

MARGARITA: See! He doesn't answer… he don't speak Spanish. He's no angel! Right, Father? Father, tell him he's a wino … Father? Father! *(pulling on his jacket.)* Father!
FATHER STEPHEN: Uh! What?
MARGARITA: Is he a wino?
FATHER STEPHEN: *(Turning back to the Angel.)* Fascinating …
MARGARITA: ¿¡*Que fascinating y que nada. Es un* wino, *si o no?!*
FATHER STEPHEN: I don't know, Margarita, but clearly he has a beautiful soul … the most beautiful soul…

(Father Stephen, unable to talk, turns back to gaze at the Angel. As Jesse, Cookie, and Father Stephen gaze at the Angel, Margarita is beside herself with frustration.)

MARGARITA: Fools! Is everybody going crazy around here? *(To Angel.)* I'll show you… you… you wino!!

(Margarita runs into the house.)

COOKIE: He doesn't like coffee and he speaks pig Latin.
FATHER STEPHEN: Remarkable.
JESSE: *(Sighing.)* Wonderful.
COOKIE: And music… he loves music.

(Cookie gets his transistor radio off his bike and turns it on. Music comes on and the Angel sways to it, as Jesse, Father Stephen, and Cookie also sway and gaze at the

Angel. They all seem lost in a spell, after a few beats, Margarita enters bursting out of the house with a pair of wire clippers and heads for the Angel.)

MARGARITA: Faker! Wino! I'll teach you to try and pull the wool over...
FATHER STEPHEN: *(Interrupting.)* Margarita! That's one of God's creatures.
JESSE: Mama!
COOKIE: Angel killer!

(As Margarita goes after the Angel, he escapes the chicken coop and turns and jumps around the yard with Margarita chasing him, as the others try to protect him.)

MARGARITA: I'm not gonna kill him, I'm just going to show you his fake wings.
FATHER STEPHEN: Leave him alone Margarita...
JESSE: Fly Angel! Fly Angel!
COOKIE: Don't let her catch him , Father.
FATHER STEPHEN: In the name of the Holy Spirit, I order you to stop this Margarita!

(As Margarita continues to pursue the Angel, she slips on a piece of wedding cake and falls into the arms of the Angel. They both go to the ground. As the Angel cradles Margarita in his arms, she looks up and gazes at the Angel's face and the Angel looks down at her and locks her in a spell.)

MARGARITA: *Ah... aye que lindo... que guapo... que bonito.*

(Enter Enrique, in his suit of lights, running and out of breath, followed by Evelina, Paco, and Manuel.)

ENRIQUE: Margarita!
EVELINA: Too late, he has her Enrique.

(Paco and Manuel cross themselves.)

ENRIQUE: *Mi amor...* come here, *mi amor...* you are in grave danger.

(Margarita rushes to Enrique's side and they embrace.)

MARGARITA: *¿Enrique, mi amor, que te pasa?* You're trembling.
ENRIQUE: You... my Madonna, with the flashing eyes, with the hair like running silk.

(Enrique turns his eyes on the Angel. The Angel confronts Enrique like a bull. He paws at the ground.)

ENRIQUE: *(Grabs his chest in pain.)* Aye! Look, look how he taunts me.
MARGARITA: *(Holding on to Enrique.)* No, Enrique! No! Somebody help me!

(Father Stephen, Jesse, and Cookie come to Margarita's aid.)

ENRIQUE: Look Margarita, look how big he is. The honor of this bull is mine... for me and my children.

MARGARITA: Here… here are your children who love you because you have always been there for them and for me.

(Father Stephen, Jesse, Cookie, and Margarita try to hold on to Enrique. We hear the music that opens the bullfight. Enrique turns away from the Angel and looks at Margarita.)

ENRIQUE: *(Touching her face.) Mi amor…*
MARGARITA: *Vaya con Dios, mi matador.*

(Enrique slips out of their grasp.)

MARGARITA: *(Falls to her knees.)* No!

(Music comes up. Father Stephen, Jesse, and Cookie crouch down and surround Margarita in a semi-circle. Lights change and focus on Enrique, as he enters an imaginary Plaza de Torros. Paco, acting as his second, gives him his cape and sword. Enrique steps in to the center of the arena, wearing his matador's hat, carrying his cape and sword. He takes off his hat and addresses the audience.)

ENRIQUE: *Al amor y la vida.*

(He throws his hat in the air, turns and confronts the Angel, who in turn has become the BULL.)

ENRIQUE: *¡Eh-he! ¡Torrito! ¡Eh-he torro!*

(The BULL makes a pass as Enrique executes a long, slow, beautiful veronica. He does a series of long, slow, beautiful passes in silence and white light. At the final pass, the Angel and Enrique become entwisted in the swirling cape. As the others surround them, the Angel disappears. A small series of lights, like fireflies, go up, up toward the heavens. Father Stephen makes the sign of the cross. We see Enrique's body across Margarita's lap like the "Pieta," Margarita cries softly.)

FATHER STEPHEN: In the name of the Father, and of the Son, and of the Holy Ghost.

(Cookie steps out and looks at the lights.)

EL BONITO: (V.O.) Damas y caballeros… it's seven p.m. here at KCKT and here is a special news flash. The little Boy Scout, our little homie who was lost in the San Jacinto Mountains, lost in the wilderness, has been found. Look out there, look out at the beautiful summer night and count the stars with me. One… two… three…

(Fade out.)

THE END